Stephen Louis Simeon, Antonio Fogazzaro

Daniele Cortis

A Novel Translated From the Italian of Antonio Fogazzaro

Stephen Louis Simeon, Antonio Fogazzaro

Daniele Cortis

A Novel Translated From the Italian of Antonio Fogazzaro

ISBN/EAN: 9783337029777

Printed in Europe, USA, Canada, Australia, Japan

Cover: Foto ©Thomas Meinert / pixelio.de

More available books at **www.hansebooks.com**

Daniele Cortis

A Novel

TRANSLATED FROM THE ITALIAN

OF

ANTONIO FOGAZZARO

BY

STEPHEN LOUIS SIMEON

London
REMINGTON & CO., PUBLISHERS
HENRIETTA STREET, COVENT GARDEN, W.C.
1890.

CONTENTS.

CHAPTER I.

AGE

WIND, RAIN, AND CHATTER, ... 1

CHAPTER II.

A GRAVE MATTER, ... 14

CHAPTER III.

THE IDEAS OF DANIELE CORTIS, ... 32

CHAPTER IV.

AMONGST THE ROSES, ... 44

C APTER V.

FOR HIM! FOR HIM! 56

CHAPTER VI.

SIGNORA FIAMMA, ... 82

CHAPTER VII.

READY! 97

CHAPTER VIII.

IN THE FIELD, ... 108

CHAPTER IX.

VOICES IN THE DARK, ... 129

CHAPTER X.

THE BARON'S AFFAIRS, ... 143

CHAPTER XI.

PAGE

FROM CEFALÙ TO ROME, ... 161

CHAPTER XII.

DIFFICULT WALKING, ... 186

CHAPTER XIII.

VERTIGO, ... 199

CHAPTER XIV.

THEY WERE WORTHY OF THIS, ... 208

CHAPTER XV.

THE SIGNORA'S SECRET, ... 221

CHAPTER XVI.

IN THE CHAMBER OF DEPUTIES, ... 236

CHAPTER XVII.

AN INTERVENTION, ... 250

CHAPTER XVIII.

NOCTURNAL STRUGGLES, ... 270

CHAPTER XIX.

"OUGHT I TO GO?". 290

CHAPTER XX.

A HIDDEN DRAMA, ... 299

CHAPTER XXI.

THE POEM OF SHADOW AND OF LIFE, ... 329

CHAPTER XXII.

AS THE STARS AND THE PALM-TREES, ... 348

CHAPTER XXIII.

HYEME ET ÆSTATE, ... 367

DANIELE CORTIS.

CHAPTER I.

WIND, RAIN, AND CHATTER.

THE balls knocked together sharply, twice over.

"Tac, tac," said Count Perlotti, watching them attentively, with the chalk in his right hand, and his cue in his left.

"Bless my soul!" exclaimed the senator, "what cues you have, Countess Tarquinia. This one has no top to it. It is impossible to play."

"That is the twelfth," said the countess, in a low voice, to a group of ladies. "My dear son-in-law," she added, stretching her arms, "I keep on writing for some to be sent to me."

He turned to Countess Perlotti, who smiled quietly, as she stood watching the weather through the glass door.

"All very well," he grumbled. "This is the twentieth time I am told that. Does she want me to make the cues myself?"

"What weather," answered the lady prudently. "It is enough to frighten one."

In front of the glass door the great dead cypress, enveloped in wisteria to its top, raised the bright green of its burden to the sombre sky; an occasional drop of rain splashed on the gravel.

"Yes, indeed, signora. It is enough to frighten one. That is the right word."

These remarks came as a chorus from four or five men and some ladies, in all their finery, who seemed very stiff and ill at ease at the great honour of being received in the house of Countess Tarquinia Carrè.

"Six to me!" shouted the senator.

"How many?" inquired an invisible person.

"Six, six, six; are you deaf?"

"No, but those priests! Listen to them."

"Yes, indeed, they must be having an orgie. Do send and keep them quiet, Countess Tarquinia."

The priests, who were playing at cards in a room overhead, were screaming and shouting.

"My dear Grigioli," said the countess to a young man who was seated on a sofa, talking to the Baroness Elena Carrè di Santa Giulia, "be so good as to go and ask those reverend gentleman, very nicely, not to make such a noise."

The latter bowed.

"By-the-bye," said the countess to him quietly, "you know I expect great things of you!"

"In what, countess?"

"Where is your head? Cortis."

"Oh, he will be all right, countess. Fifty votes certain; here. I was just saying so to Baroness Elena."

"Please, my dear friend, do not talk of these things to my daughter, who does not know which is right and which left. Go up to those priests now— Where is Cortis?" she said to her daughter, when the young man had left her.

"Go, go, young man, and silence those priests," said the senator to Grigiolo, as he passed through the billiard-room. "Tell them to take a lesson from these other gentlemen. Silence, Don Bartolo!'

At the far end of the large room, near another glass

door, a group of men were discussing some apparently mysterious and important question. One of them called out: "Doctor Grigiolo!"

"What is it?" answered the young man. "I am coming in a minute," and he went on.

"Is that boy a doctor of medicine?" asked the senator of his companion.

"No, signore, a doctor of law," replied the other respectfully.

The priests had finished their game. The chaplain, Don Bartolo, was reciting some verses from a paper which he had in his hand, amid the shouts of laughter of his colleagues.

"Excuse me, Don Bartolo," said the ambassador.

"Come in, doctor," replied Don Bartolo. "Come in, pray, and listen to this:

"'The syndic replied he was quite in the right.'"

"No, excuse me."

"But you must listen to this."

Doctor Grigiolo decided, with a shudder, to listen to another verse, which ended thus:

"'And the syndic replied that again he was right.'"

"Very good; but permit me."

"Forgive me, why won't you listen? I am just coming to the best part."

Don Bartolo, excited by several glasses, continued to recite his anonymous satire, of which the subject was a wrangle between some common councilmen and a syndic, who said that they were each right in turn.

"The syndic remained with his head in the air,
And at last he replied that none was wrong there."

At these lines the audience was convulsed with laughter.

"Good, very good, excellent," exclaimed Doctor Grigiolo in spite of himself; "but, my very dear chaplain, I don't see any necessity for breaking the drums of your neighbours' ears. You see there are a good many ladies downstairs, and the countess begs you—"

"Women?" answered Don Bartolo. "But women can make noise enough too!"

"Be quiet; let us go away; do be quiet, chaplain," said his friends.

"Thank you, now I must go downstairs again. Besides, for the sake of Count Lao, who is not well."

Doctor Grigiolo looked at the oldest priest in the room with a face which was half laughing and half serious.

"Come here," shouted the incorrigible Don Bartolo, "come here, doctor, and don't be off after those women again. Stay and have a glass with us. Why did you mention Count Lao? You know perfectly well that his rooms are on the other side of the house. Don't you know, too, that he is in better health than you or I? Don't you know that he is mad?"

"Do silence Don Bartolo," shouted the senator from downstairs.

"Can they have heard what you said?" asked Doctor Grigiolo in terror. "That man will be after us with his cue."

"Heavens!" ejaculated the chaplain.

His disappearance, and his comic anguish, raised such unbridled hilarity amongst the others that Grigiolo fled with his hands to his head, while Don Bartolo, who had recovered himself, began to read the end of the poem, a speech to the electors:—

"Choose you the man who seems to you least evil,
And banish all the others to the devil."

"So you failed, Grigioli!" cried Countess Tarquinia in the distance. Another voice from among the conspirators said,—

"Come here, Doctor Grigiolo."

The latter answered: "In a minute," and was going on, when Baron Di Santa Giulia stopped him with a heavy hand, and exclaimed in his voice of thunder,—

"Answer! Are you Grigioli or Grigiolo?"

The pleasant-looking, slender youth jumped, took one step backward, and gazed at the senator as he might have gazed at Attila.

"In reality it is Grigioli," he replied, "but the people—"

"Ah, the people! I understand," said the baron. "So you failed to silence Bartolo."

"Impossible, senator. Quite impossible, countess. Your white wine is too strong. It would take a pump and plenty of water to quiet him. We are just going to have a deluge."

"Do you think so?"

"Yes, countess."

"Don't you think the clouds are lifting?"

"I don't see it, countess."

"Have you really looked?"

"Yes, I really have, countess."

"And you cannot see it?"

"No, I really cannot, countess."

"How many more times 'countess?'" muttered the senator, leaning over the billiard-table and practising a stroke, his eyes fixed on his adversary's ball.

"It is the custom, baron," answered Perlotti humbly, standing opposite him.

"Now do be off; the electors are expecting you," said the countess to Grigiolo, giving him a slight push. He was bored with the election, and would much rather have stayed where he was. Then the countess turned to her guests and said: "I wager that this storm will come to nothing."

And immediately there rose a chorus of obsequious voices.

"I quite think so, too. I am sure you are right. It will not be anything."

At the same moment a peal of thunder made every window rattle.

"Hulloa!" exclaimed the senator, throwing down his cue on to the billiard-table.

"Good heavens!" ejaculated the countess. "The windows upstairs!" and she rushed to the bell.

A young lady, who now opened her lips for the first time, began to groan.

"What darkness!" shouted Grigiolo. "It is coming from here, countess, if you wish to see it."

A tremendous gust of wind rushed through an open door, blowing the curtains about and scattering papers and letters as it tore round the billiard-room. As Perlotti went to shut the door, the parish priest rushed out into the storm.

"Is the priest mad?" exclaimed Perlotti, through the half-closed door.

"They will want me to bless the storm," answered the priest, holding on his hat, while the tails of his coat fluttered in the wind.

The storm, coming from behind the mountains on the west, had gone round to the south. The black clouds which had collected on the summit of grey Rumano, threatened to overwhelm the wooded base of the mountain; and the poor, scattered cottages, the newly-mown fields in front of the Villa Carrè were touched by a sinister light.

Countess Tarquinia, the Perlottis, and the rest of the party were huddled together at the end of the room, which looked south.

"Nasty weather," said old Picuti the lawyer.

"I am thinking of my corn," exclaimed Signor Zirisòla, one of the chief proprietors of the district.

"And the grapes," added his wife.

The priests had not stirred from the room, where they were making more noise than ever, as if to deaden the thunder and the wind which raged round the house, and scattered branches and leaves about the garden.

Baroness Elena alone did not seem to be disturbed by the storm. Leaning against the back of the sofa, she stood, with her head inclined forward on to her breast, and her arms tightly crossed, as though she were cold. Her large black eyes watched the branches of the young fir-trees in the garden, unceasingly shaken by the wind. From her grave and statuesque immobility, one might have thought that in those waving branches she saw some phantom, and that some voice, inaudible to the others, was speaking to her from them. Suddenly a downpour of rain beat with fury against the windows and the walls, hiding from view the sky, the mountains and the fir-trees, and appearing to lighten up all the doors and windows of the dark room.

She heard Countess Tarquinia say in a loud voice: "Daniele has taken root up there. I must go and see what is happening."

She stopped near her daughter, and said to her, in a low and complaining tone,—

"You leave me entirely alone, Elena; you do not help me in the least. I suppose your husband does not wish you to?"

The baroness scarcely raised her head, and, without looking at her mother, replied,—

"My husband does not trouble himself about me."

Her voice was somewhat grave, but very melodious, and she spoke in a tone of careless indifference, as of one who is buried in his own thoughts, and who, on being distracted from them for a moment, merely gives an answer with his lips, so as not to disturb their current, and then turns to rest in them once more.

"That is true," answered the countess.

"Oh, how tiresome, Elena! Here is your mother," exclaimed the always amiable Perlotti, suddenly appearing at her side. "And just as I was coming to make love to you, too!"

She raised her eyes.

"Do join the rest of the party, Elena; do go and look after them," insisted her mother.

"Poor thing, she is so bored with them; small blame to her!" observed Perlotti caressingly, and in a melancholy voice.

"It is all right, Sofia is there," said the baroness.

"My wife? Yes; but she is not the hostess."

"No more am I."

With this answer, given somewhat disdainfully, Elena rose and joined the guests.

"I am afraid, my dear Tarquinia, that you will have to house all these people for the night," said Perlotti in the ear of the countess, gently leaning his hand upon her arm.

She was still a handsome woman, and very well dressed.

"Heaven forbid! I have a feeling of Christian charity for all of them, and they come to my house twice a year; but I hope to have done with them this evening!"

"I hope you will put me with that pretty little fair woman, Ziriseta, Zirisèla—what is her name?"

"You wretch!" said the countess, turning away laughing. "I am going up to Lao," and she moved away, followed by a laugh from Perlotti.

She stopped at the far end of the room, near a door leading to the staircase.

"At last!" she said; "how did you find him?"

"Sad," answered a masculine voice.

"That is nothing new! He is only ill because he eats and sleeps, and passes hour after hour in reading and playing. I do not say that he may not suffer sometimes, but he pays a great deal too much attention to himself. The doctor says that he must be kept amused. Well, we must do our best. But if you knew, dear, how hard it is to keep others amused! If you knew how disgusted I feel sometimes, and how I struggle to hide it!"

"Disgusted, aunt?"

The countess was silent, bit her lips, and swallowed a sob.

"Nothing, nothing," she answered nervously, closing her eyes, in which the tears were shining. "You will not go away in this storm? Bravo, then do go and look after some of these people for me."

She went upstairs, and he to whom she had been talking entered the room just as all the ladies were turning away from watching the storm, and were settling themselves on the sofa and the row of chairs between the billiard-table and the west door. Elena came round outside the chairs, in order to pass near him, and she whispered to him,—

"Thank you, Daniele, for having stayed so long with my uncle."

Cortis pressed her hand without speaking. Elena looked at him closely, and started.

"Is anything wrong?" she asked.

"A grave matter," he answered.

"Here is our candidate," shouted the baron. "These gentlemen all want to know if you will bark at Tunis, and bite the ministry."

The baron looked like an old Norman brigand, with his big person, his long yellow beard, and his loud voice.

"What have we to do with Tunis? We don't care about Tunis," said Checco Zirisèla, a patriot who was afraid of nobody. "We are not in Sicily."

"Long live Italy!" answered the senator. "Think of that, all of you." And he turned away.

"Let him go, that trombone," muttered Doctor Grigiolo. "Signor Cortis," said he to the new-comer, "our friends here, who belong to this division, would be glad to say a few words to you."

Daniele Cortis turned towards his friends who, leaning against the door in an attitude which, although respectful, scarcely concealed the consciousness of their power, were watching the man as he came forward into the watery light. He was tall and slim, his well-cut features were remarkable for their dignity and soldierly resolution, and his blue eyes were open and intelligent.

"It is nothing," said Doctor Picuti, who always began his gravest speeches with these words; "it is nothing. Here we are all of one mind, you know, but it sometimes happens that we talk to our friends from other divisions. I, for example, or my friend Zirisèla."

"Quite true," said the latter, encouraging his friend to continue.

"Well, then, I say that we two and some others are often frequently obliged to go amongst people belonging to other divisions, and there we hear it said that you are but little known (they are ignorant people, and one cannot help that), and that they have no idea as to your opinions on certain questions; so that we think it would be well that you should, either by means of a speech, or by means of the press, I don't know if I make myself clear—"

"They want a programme," said the baron, in a somewhat modulated tone, from the end of the room. "They are quite right. Who ever heard of a candidate without a programme? It is like a house without a front to it."

"That is better than having so many fronts without houses, or programmes without men behind them," said his wife hastily.

"Is it true, Elena, that your cousin is called Daniele Volveno?" asked Countess Sofia Perlotti suddenly.

"Yes," answered Elena drily.

"What ridiculous names you people have here!" exclaimed the baron.

"It is not a name of our Veneto country, baron," answered Signora Perlotti. "It is a name of Friuli. Signor Cortis comes from Friuli."

"Of course, I know that! And, pray, where is Friuli, if not in the Veneto? Pretty geography you are teaching me."

The lady bit her lips.

"I am sorry," she said, "but—"

Here her husband thought it advisable to go and flatten his nose against the window, exclaiming,—

"Oh, do look here! Look here! Is not this Malcanton coming?"

They saw an umbrella slowly advancing under the dripping fir-trees. Every one rushed to the window except the baron and his wife.

"Yes, it is certainly he! Countess, here comes Malcanton!"

"Bless my heart," exclaimed the countess, re-entering at that moment, "I had forgotten all about him."

She had sent this Malcanton a few hours previously to do some commissions.

"I had entirely forgotten him. But what an object he is. He looks like a drowned rat."

She opened the door, put on her most amiable voice, and putting out her head, cried to him: "Quick, quick! Do come in!"

Signor Malcanton came in, and shook himself like a spaniel, holding the umbrella with outstretched arm, while the countess groaned.

"Oh, dear! oh, dear! I have been in such distress about you all this time. How drenched you are! I am so sorry! Quick, somebody, go and order some hot brandy-and-water."

"I have done everything!" answered the poor spaniel. "I have seen Signor Momi and Signora Catina. I have engaged the band, and telegraphed for the fireworks."

"And taken in plenty of water into the bargain," roared the baron, who was seated behind the others, on the billiard-table, with his legs dangling. Every one laughed, except Malcanton, who stared at him open-mouthed.

"Thank you, thank you a thousand times; but, now, do go upstairs," said the countess, suppressing her laughter. "Elena, go to your uncle, and, on your way, see about that brandy-and-water."

"By-the-bye," continued Malcanton, "I have written for that book about the *laven-tennis*, and I have asked how it should be pronounced."

"Laan-tennis," said Countess Perlotti.

"Loon, loon!" bellowed the baron.

"Whether it be *laan*, or *loon*, I still say *laven*," maintained Malcanton. "But we shall soon hear."

Countess Tarquinia had ordered a set of lawn-tennis, the first which had been seen in the neighbourhood. Nobody knew how to play, and every one pronounced it differently; but all the same, there was the lawn-tennis at Villa Carrè. Even at the Italia, the *café* in the town, they had discussed at great length whether it should be *laan* or *loon*.

"Now, if you will allow me," concluded Malcanton, and he disappeared behind the baroness, while the senator said in a marked voice,—

"So you are going to have great doings here, Countess Tarquinia?"

"Too great," muttered the wretched Malcanton to his companion, to whom he ostentatiously talked as though she were still a child. "Do you not think, Elena, that such a washing—"

But she did not wait to listen to him; she flew up the stairs, forgetting all about the brandy, and entered the large empty room on the second floor. She heard the confused voices of the priests, the senator and the rest of the company rise indistinctly, and the rain seemed to repeat to her, in a deep bass voice: "A grave matter." She crossed the room slowly, with her eyes fixed on the door of the room in which Daniele had spent so much time.

A grave matter!

She knocked twice gently at the door; a loud voice answered, "Come in."

CHAPTER II.

A GRAVE MATTER.

"COME in," said Count Lao, "and shut the door quickly, for there is an infernal draught. So you've come at last! And what a damnable row those priests are making: to think that I can't get at them with a stick! What in the world does your mother mean by asking priests here? They are all drunk already! What wine did she give them, the goose?'

Elena, very seriously, made him a deep curtsey, and said,—

"I will go and enquire, count."

"Ah, you naughty child," he exclaimed, recovering his temper, "come here. She came up to me ten minutes ago, as fresh as a rose, to ask me if I wanted anything. She must have lost her senses. As if I wanted anything, with this hurly-burly resounding all through the house. I told her I wished she would send them all to the deuce. But I don't believe you are listening to me. They seem not to think I have troubles enough as it is, and they want to deafen me into the bargain. Will you come in? What are you standing at the door for? Why are you staring at me? Am I pale? Am I green or yellow? Do I look like a dead man?"

"No, no, uncle; you look like a bear in a rage."

"A white bear?"

"No, a grey bear, uncle."

Instead of replying, Count Ladislao drew a looking-glass from his pocket, and approached the window.

"Oh, no," he said, "I am not pale, or only very little."

But he was pale, and his pallor was heightened by two large black eyes and a black beard, which, though short, was very thick, by a high yellowish forehead, scarcely covered by bristly hair. He turned his back to his niece, and looked at his tongue.

"You are looking very well, uncle," said she, "you are really, so you may be quite happy."

Her uncle turned round sharply, and drew himself up.

"If only I were not ill," he said.

He was tall and well-made; a large, shapely nose did not spoil his face, which was partly sentimental and partly comic.

"If only you did not think you were ill," said Elena.

"So, I think, do I! This life amuses me, does it? I enjoy being unable to digest anything by day, or to sleep by night, do I? I enjoy being in pain from January to December, I suppose! Do you hear those abominable priests? Perhaps I enjoy that, too! Hold your tongue; come and play me that symphony of Corelli's."

He seated himself in an arm-chair behind a table, in the darkest corner of the room, the farthest from the door and from the three windows. Close beside him the upright piano, which stood against the wall, was open.

"I can't see, uncle."

"Never mind; you know it by heart."

She began to hum the melody in a sweet, resonant voice, full of feeling.

"I don't feel in the humour to play to-night."

"Why not?"

Elena made no answer. Seated between the window and the writing-table, she watched him fidgeting with an open book that lay aslant on the very edge of the table. Count Lao evidently interpreted her silence in his own fashion, for he did not insist, but lighted a cigarette.

"The fault is not with me, certainly," said he, throwing the match into the ash-tray.

"What fault, uncle?"

Count Lao leaned his arm on the table, and watched the match as it burned itself out.

"That we have come to this," he said.

Elena did not understand.

"This English poet is not worth much!" exclaimed Count Lao, as though to break the thread of disagreeable thoughts. "He is worth very little! He is full of nonsensical ideas. I expected as much. The idea of Heaven being rendered seven times more divine by the assumption of Mazzini! Rubbish!"

"To what have we come, uncle?" asked Elena, rising. She came and sat down on the music-stool near him.

"Where is your head?" answered Lao. "Tell me, were they playing at billiards a short time ago before the storm?"

"Yes."

"Was your husband playing?"

"Yes, he and Perlotti."

"He is a philosopher!"

He remained in thought for a moment, then suddenly jumping up, he threw away his cigarette, and went and laid his hands on either side of Elena's head; she, with a movement of involuntary pride, tried to free herself.

"Look here," said he, pulling her head forward till it rested on his chest, "you have a great scoundrel for a husband." He placed his lips on her hair, and whispered: "I will be even with him!"

Elena contemptuously shook herself free from his embrace, and looked at him with glittering eyes.

"Do you know that you pain me by saying such things?" she said. "Do you know that they offend me? I knew about my husband before I married him. I allowed him to be engaged to me before I married him. Think what you please, but say nothing. He has never deceived me; he has always been the same. It would be dishonourable in me to allow you to say such things to me."

She turned her back upon him, and looked out of the window, while her uncle continued angrily,—

"All very fine! very fine! But nobody knows that you were little better than a child! Nobody knows how you were forced into it!"

"No, I was not forced!" answered Elena, turning sharply round. "Mamma pressed me a little at first, perhaps, but poor, dear papa always repeated up to the last moment: 'Remember that you are free; remember that there is still time!' But he need not have said that, because I was not a child. I was nineteen years old, and I quite understood what I was about."

"Well, then, why in the world did you consent? I vow that, if I had been in your place, I would not have done it."

"Oh, uncle!" she said proudly.

She disdained to speak, to admit that she had accepted the first husband offered to her, because certain intrigues carried on by her mother had been distasteful to her.

"And now," she exclaimed, "of what new monstrosity has my husband been guilty? I know he has asked you for a little of your money. Is it on that account that mamma has a fit of the blues, and you are in convulsions?"

"Body of Bacchus!" exclaimed Lao, turning round and slowly bowing his head towards some imaginary beings, some invisible judges of appeal, "I leave it in your hands."

He raised his hands, and let them fall heavily again by his sides.

"Let us say no more about it," he remarked, and seating himself at the piano, as if he had nothing more to do with the matter, he began to strum a noisy polka, muttering to himself as he played: "You have been well brought up, indeed! Upon my word, you have! A little of your money! What would be the use of that? A little money, alas! Well brought up! By Diana! a fine education!"

"Calm yourself, calm yourself uncle," said Elena; "how foolish you are this evening. I have never seen you like this before."

"Dance, my child, dance!" said the count sarcastically. "Don't you see that I am playing for you? Dance, my treasure! What do you need to worry about money for! Dance, and be happy."

"What nonsense, uncle. Do you wish me to torture myself for the sake of this money? Do be quiet. Your music is tiresome, you know."

The count seized with both hands the music-stool upon which he had been sitting, and swung himself completely round.

"Oh, I know all about it," said he, "you want me to stop, so that you may give me your views. It does not matter to you that your husband, after having gambled away your money as well as his own, wants ours to gamble with, too! It does not matter to you that he comes swaggering here, pretending to claim money that he has no right to, saying that you scatter money right and left—'

"Perhaps I do," said Elena, coldly.

"Threatening to shut you up for ever at Cefalù, like an unfaithful wife, unless this money is given to him."

The baroness started, and asked abruptly,—

"Has he said that to you?"

The count tapped his chest with his forefinger, raising his eyebrows.

"To me?" he said. "I would very quickly have given him his money, and then would have thrown him out of the window—him and the money together in one heap. But he said it, or what was equivalent to it, to your mother."

"When?"

"This morning. I thought that, of course, you knew."

"I knew nothing about it."

"Very good; then know nothing about it when your senator says it to you; don't let him know I told you."

"No."

"I have let him know that he had better not repeat those things to me. Your mother will have already given him my message Your mother is always trying to serve both God and Mammon. She is always whimpering. Is it true that you knew nothing about all this?"

"I knew that my husband was in want of money. Before coming here, he begged me, as is his wont, to ask you for some. I told him that he was perfectly at liberty to do as he liked about it, but that, for my part, I would not mention the subject to you?"

"Who knows how he may have bullied you?"

"Bullied me! He has not said a word about it since. He does not bully me."

"Never?" asked Lao incredulously.

"No, he never does," answered his niece, apparently surprised at having to affirm a thing twice over. "If he did, I should soon put him in his place."

The other was silent.

So this, thought Elena, is the grave matter. Is it really so grave? The doings of her husband troubled her but little. Clearly her uncle would never hear of her being imprisoned at Cefalù. She tortured herself thus because of what Daniele had said to her. And still the rain fell outside, when her sonorous and sad voice began again,—

"Uncle, what induced you to tell this to Daniele?"

"I? What? I have told nothing to Daniele."

"Nothing? Yet I saw him just now as he came away from you, and he told me that something serious had happened."

"Something serious? I don't know!"

Elena noticed a change in her uncle's voice, an exaggerated indifference.

"Does my being banished to Cefalù not seem serious to you?" she asked, smiling.

"Oh, yes, certainly. Can it have been that?"

"But, uncle—"

"You are worrying me, do you know!" exclaimed the count. "We did not talk of your husband, or of yourself, or of myself. If you want confidences, go to Daniele for them."

Elena made no answer.

"Forgive me," continued her uncle. "It is a matter which concerns him alone. I cannot tell you about it."

She regretted having revealed those two words of her cousin's which might testify to a very intimate and confidential friendship. All of a sudden she jumped up as though she heard something, went to the window and opened it. A noise of running water filled the room.

"Are you mad?" cried Count Lao, jumping up, and seizing the cape of his overcoat from a hook on the door. "Shut the window, for Heaven's sake! What the devil are you doing?"

It had stopped raining; only a few large drops fell from the eaves of the house on to the gravel path.

"It is not raining, uncle! There is not a breath of wind stirring."

"Oh, indeed, is there not a breath! Good God, no air! Shut the window at once, I say. With this dampness! The Rovese torrent seems to be rushing through the room, and you tell me there's not a breath! Quick, now, shut it, and have done with it!"

Elena paid no attention to him.

"Forgive me, uncle, I have just heard the billiard-room door open, and I want to see who is going out," she said hastily, and in a low voice.

The priests appeared with a great trampling of feet, and a great demonstration of low bows. The senator was with them. He took the parish priest of Caodemuro by the arm, and whispered something to him. All the others crowded round them. He, a fat, rubicund priest, with gold spectacles, answered in a loud voice,—

"Yes, but you know that we must stand by the Pope; we cannot openly do anything else. *Non expedit.* If I had a hundred votes to give, this gentleman here should not have one of them; and I shall be delighted if he gets well beaten. But I am afraid that won't happen, because, about here, every one will vote for him. The most that we can do is to persuade one or two people to stay at home. But even these—"

"Let us go on; let us go farther away," said the senator, who did not care to have these things said in a loud voice so near the house. But at that moment Elena called him from the window.

"Carmine!"

The baron looked up. The priests turned round too, and saluted with a sort of dismayed humility, bowing their heads, and raising their eyes. The baroness scarcely acknowledged them with a movement of the head, and asked her husband whether Cortis were still in the billiard-room.

"Yes," he returned; "why?"

"Because I want to speak to him," replied Elena quietly, as she shut the window.

"And mamma?" she said, turning to her uncle, "what does she say about it?"

"Have you shut it properly?" asked the count, taking off his cape. "She is making herself miserable about it: she weeps, she storms at me because I will not undertake offhand to do what her son-in-law wishes. She will never persuade me. If she likes to sacrifice her own possessions to him, well and good; but I think she will turn a deaf ear to such proposals."

"Poor mamma," said Elena, smiling. "Tears are cheaper. Good-bye, uncle."

She offered him her hand. Count Lao held it firmly for a minute, and kept her thus without speaking.

"Look here," he said in a choking voice, "you know me, don't you?"

She put out her left hand also, and, with an affectionate impulsiveness, seized both of his, and held them tightly.

"Good," he said.

Elena knew that she could rely upon that honest, manly heart, so warm under the covering of laziness, which had become almost a craze, which had its origin in some secret defect of the mind, and had been encouraged by family tradition, increased by habit, fostered by suffering really existing either in his body or in his imagination, strengthened by a bitter scepticism, apparently the natural position of the man towards the world.

A servant entered to see whether Signor Daniele had left his gloves there.

The baroness broke loose hastily from her uncle, hurried from the room, and went down to the verandah by a dark back staircase. At the foot she met somebody coming up.

"Who is there?" she asked.

"Your fisherman, contessina, Pitantoi."

"I am glad to see you. You will vote for Signor Daniele?"

"I? When all the poor people, and all the fishing folk have votes, then I will vote too. But they tell me that the law has not yet been made."

"Are you not an elector?"

"No, indeed, I am not, contessina. What would you have? We have a lot of electors here that I don't think much of; look at them; and besides—"

The baroness passed him quickly, and disappeared.

Cortis had just come on to the verandah, and was walking there with Grigiolo, when Elena joined them from the back staircase.

"Are you going?" she asked.

He stretched out his hand towards her.

"Yes," he answered; "I am going home."

"Because I should like to speak to you," continued Elena.

Doctor Grigiolo dropped a few paces behind them discreetly.

"Will you do me the favour, Grigiolo, of telling mamma that I have gone out for a moment with Daniele?"

Elena spoke with a smile, and with the frankest indifference.

"I fly, baroness, I fly," replied the zealous youth. "And so, Signor Cortis, I may come to you to-morrow morning to discuss this programme."

"No," replied the other; "to-morrow I am going away."

"You are going away? But you will be back soon?"

"I don't know."

"But before the election, at any rate?"

"I don't know."

"But what shall we do? Excuse me for interrupting you, baroness."

"Of course," exclaimed Elena, "I am very deeply interested in all this! I feel like a political agent myself, you know."

Meanwhile Cortis reflected.

"Come this evening," he said. Grigiolo was in rather a fix. Countess Tarquinia counted upon him to keep her party amused. How could he manage? "Come when they are all gone to bed," said Cortis, "at eleven, or midnight, or when you like."

The other, at the end of his excuses, grumbled out a dissatisfied "All right," full of laziness and of anticipated sleep. But Cortis, partly from inability to understand this weakness, partly because his head was full of other things, considered the matter settled, and having dismissed the young man, turned towards the large eyes, which were full of questionings.

He answered by a long and solemn gaze. Neither spoke.

After a pause, which seemed to each of them an eternity, they moved slowly towards the portico, by silent consent, neither knowing which had made the first step. They reached in silence an open space, whence one path ran to the right, across the fields, towards Villascura and Cortis's house; another sloped away to the left towards the torrent of Rovese, opposite to the naked, overhanging boulders of Monte Barco; and a third ran straight to three tall firs, which overlooked the valley, from the edge of a steep declivity. Elena trembled, fearing lest her cousin should take the path to the left, which led to his own house. Could she, in such a case, follow him, and so to say compel him to speak? However, he went straight on towards the fir-trees. Her heart beat high, and her cheeks flushed.

"Dear Elena," said Cortis.

His masculine and sonorous voice sounded as though it were muffled by a mortal pain.

"A grave matter," he said, stopping and looking at his cousin. He read apparently in her face her great trouble, for he added hurriedly, "No, dear, it is not too much for me."

"I believe that," she said, gazing straight in front of her with fixed eyes.

She did not seem to be the same Elena, either in voice or look, who had spoken two minutes previously to Doctor Grigiolo.

"You ought to know it," continued Cortis; "but it is not easy to say."

"Then tell me nothing. I was wrong to come and impose myself upon you in this manner," answered Elena, in a low voice, still gazing into space.

She thought that perhaps her cousin did not consider her presence an imposition, and she stretched her hand to him, with a forced smile.

"I wish you a pleasant journey," she said.

He made a gesture of impatience, and only answered, "Oh!"

Elena blushed, as if by that "Oh" she had been reminded with a gentle reproof, of so many intimate matters, of so many signs of a friendship that was rather felt than expressed. She withdrew her hand, and said timidly,—

"Forgive me!"

"Of course," answered Cortis. "Let us walk on, and see whether, with your cleverness, you can guess anything

They walked a few steps in silence, Elena keeping her eyes firmly fixed on the ground.

All at once she raised her head.

"My husband?" she said.

She had scarcely uttered the words when Cortis answered, "No, no." She repented bitterly of having spoken, and was angry with herself. Her husband was never mentioned in her talks with Cortis. No act, no word, passed between the cousins of which he could complain.

At length they reached the firs, which were groaning overhead, blown about by the wind, and which showered down large drops of rain. On the left, the oldest of the three bent his long arms over the little level space on which they were planted, and over the steep declivities, which descended on one side towards the meadows, on the other towards the river. On the right, the road wound downwards under wooded banks.

"Where are we going?" asked Cortis.

In their carelessness, they had walked straight on, and had come into the long grass, wet through with the rain. They turned back, and neither spoke again until they had descended into the quiet winding path, which sheltered them from behind.

Then he stopped.

"You know," he said, "all the sad things that happened years ago at home?"

She was reassured, and, forgetting her previous giddy question, answered quickly, "I do."

She had not expected this. She knew that Cortis's mother, having been proved unfaithful to her husband, had been driven from his house a few years after the birth of Daniele, and had since died in neglect.

She considered.

"Perhaps," she exclaimed, leaving much unexpressed, —"perhaps she has left—"

Cortis interrupted her by shaking his head.

"No," he said, after a moment.

Elena remembered having heard that the name of the seducer had never been known for certain, and hazarded another guess.

"Perhaps you have discovered who—"

Cortis again shook his head.

"Imagine the most incredible thing," he said, and he looked at his cousin in such a manner that the truth suddenly became clear to her.

"Ah!" she said, seizing his arm.

He nodded his head.

They continued looking at one another in silence, amazement written upon one face, and horror on the other.

"And you had never suspected it?" asked Elena gently.

"Never," he answered, raising his arm, and sighing. "My father had always made me believe that she was dead. But now I remember on one occasion (it only came back to me to-day), when I was asking him about a great many things, I might have understood, had I not been a mere boy, that he was hiding the truth from me."

She dared not go further, or put any other questions; she feared to learn something terrible.

"I know nothing about it yet," continued Cortis. "So far, I have only received a letter."

"From her?"

"No; from a person who lives with her."

"Where?"

"At Lugano. A letter which would drive me mad if I had not a brain of steel. This person writes to me that my mother is still living, that she is ill, and wishes to see me," he added, answering Elena's anxious glance. "It might be a great happiness, but you must put together my mother's story, and the high-flown futilities, as well as the scented writing-paper of her friend, in order to understand it all properly."

He stopped, choked by a sob.

"You know, Elena," he continued, in a scarcely audible voice, "I used to think sometimes: If she were still living, if she were buried in some quiet place where by her work she could gain bread and respect, and if I could find her there, I would straightway forget all that my father had suffered. You don't know what a heart my poor father had, and with what tears he used to make me say every night—do you follow me?—every night a prayer for the eternal rest of my mother's soul. But I thought that I would forget all that, and—"

Cortis broke off suddenly. Words were inadequate to express the feelings of tempestuous love with which he would have flung himself into the arms of his mother. He abruptly moved away from Elena, who remained motionless.

"But you will go?" she said, with unexpected force.

Cortis turned back.

"You know very well," he answered sharply, "that I would go if it should cost me my life."

"Yes, go!" exclaimed Elena, coming close to him. "Think of what she has suffered. I would go if I could."

"You? But suppose she has suffered nothing?"

Elena started in surprise.

"Oh, that is impossible," she said.

The man of steel had no strength to reply; he was

choked with tears. With all his leonine strength, he still often had, both in joy and in grief, attacks of infantile weeping that passed away like clouds heavily charged with electricity. To Elena, those tears came as a revelation of what he dreaded; she regretted that she was so ignorant, and so slow to understand certain forms of depravity of which she had heard, but in which she had never quite believed; she regretted having suggested to Cortis involuntarily a bitter comparison between herself who could not understand evil, and a mother who, it might be, could not understand remorse. Conquered by his emotion, she spoke to him breathlessly, with a strange, new voice, which she strove to render calm.

"But she wants you," she said; "and that expresses so many things."

"Enough, dear," he returned, appeased. "It is folly to be so overcome, and in this place, too. One can only do one's best, can one, Elena? See what a beautiful sky."

They were looking towards the lowlands on the east, and there, between the mountains, the sky and the open plains of Veneto were bathed in transparent serenity; but a thick veil of clouds still overhung the valley, throwing a blue-black shadow on the peaks of the mountains; and the stiff, sombre fir-trees, which rose up to heaven from a neighbouring height, seemed to be on the look-out for a second storm.

Elena kept her eyes fixed for a moment on the brilliant distance, and then said,—

"You start to-morrow?"

"Yes, dearest. How all the poor little flowers in the grass are quivering, and how boldly those old fir-trees up there stand!"

Elena looked at the green plain, carpeted with marguerite daisies, and which stretched to the very foot of the old trees.

"At what time?" she enquired.

"Early, at dawn. I am sorry to be absent from your birthday party. You must make my excuses to your mother, won't you? I have already told her that I am obliged to go away on important business, but you must tell her again. Before saying anything more, I wish to make quite sure that it is not an imposture; everything is possible! In any case, you will tell her how sorry I am to miss her party."

Elena made no sign of having heard, and said,—

"Write to me."

"Yes," answered Cortis; "but—"

She blushed slightly.

"No, no," she said, "you may be quite certain."

"And how much longer do you stop here?"

"I don't know. Mamma wishes to go away about the middle of July, if that suits my uncle, but we might have to start at any moment if we were recalled on account of the Senate."

"And then shall you remain in Rome, or shall you go to Sicily?"

"We did talk of going to Aix-les-Bains once, but now I know nothing about it."

They both remained silent and motionless, as if the words, "*I know nothing about it,*" had answered, in their own mind, a grave suggestion. Neither Elena nor Daniele knew anything of the road in life which they were to follow; they could foresee no probable future, nor any prospect of meeting again at present. Sicily, Aix; how dead these names sounded! The overcast sky, the foaming Rovese, with its thundering noise, seemed conscious of coming troubles. Great gusts of wind passed high above the heads of Cortis and his cousin, who could not tear themselves away from their quiet asylum, where the wind was so hushed that they could almost hear the noise made by the gravel as it sucked in the grateful moisture after the long drought.

"Think of me sometimes," said Cortis, in a low voice.

Elena made no answer. They retraced their steps slowly towards the house, she with her face turned away, and her lips set; he talking continually, feverishly.

"I know," he said, "that you are a good friend. It was stupid and unkind of me to tell you not to forget me. I feel so much in my heart that I cannot say to you. Perhaps you would do well to forget me. How can I say good-bye to you, Elena? But perhaps at another time I might not have strength to say it. My life is becoming a severe struggle. I don't yet know when the great battle is coming, but it will not be long now. I must not waste time, for my post is in front, far in front, and I must fight day and night to reach it. You know my ideas; you can judge whether I shall leave my blood on the track or not! No, no; do not think of attaching yourself to me, there is only suffering to be gained there. It is better to leave me alone, Elena."

"Is it?" she asked, raising her face.

The baroness, as soon as she was with Daniele Cortis, became timid and humble as no one had ever seen her before, since she was a little child; but at this moment all her natural haughtiness shone in her eyes. Cortis had spoken with the full consciousness of his superior energy, and suddenly he found himself face to face with an equal whom he had hitherto ignored. His proud eyes opened widely.

"Then—" he began with violence.

She turned very pale, and placed her finger on his lips. Cortis was silent, and regarded her in astonishment and sadness.

"You ought not to face your life alone," continued Elena quietly, but with a somewhat trembling voice. "You want a family round you. I know that mamma has some plans for you, good plans too."

Indeed, Countess Tarquinia had imagined that it would

be a good thing to marry him to a certain Signorina V., who was rich, clever, and good-looking.

"Dreams," he said coldly. "I shall not marry."

They spoke no more till they reached the cross-roads, at which they were to part. Elena stopped first.

"Good-bye," she said; "go." And as Cortis's eyes began to blaze, and his body to tremble with passion, as it had a short time previously, she quieted him again with a sign, and gave him her hand, which he took in both of his. Her pale lips worked for a moment before they could articulate the words, "comfort her."

Daniele made no answer. She freed herself from the strong hands that held her, and moved towards the porch. Thence she turned round once, as though to throw after him all the soul that was in her eyes; and then she vanished.

CHAPTER III.

THE IDEAS OF DANIELE CORTIS.

SHORTLY before midnight, Doctor Grigiolo rang the bell at the garden railings of the Villa Cortis. A sleepy servant opened the gate, and led him round outside the right wing of the house to the large flight of stone steps which cuts in half the long frontage.

"Will you wait here, sir?" he said. "I will go and call my master."

"What do you mean?" answered Grigiolo in surprise. "Is your master not in the house?"

"No, sir."

"Bless me! Where is he, then?"

"In the garden."

"At this hour! There's no accounting for taste! And I suppose it will take you half an hour to find him, won't it?"

"No, sir," answered the servant, moving away at no great speed.

"Gently, my friend, not too fast, you might hurt yourself," grumbled Grigiolo, out of patience.

He looked up at the sky.

"And with these drops of rain that keep on falling!"

Sky and mountain, all was black, from the Passo Grande, which carries on its lowest ledge the Villa Cortis, with its woods and fields, away to Monte Barco, and to the high, narrow gully, whence issues the Rovese torrent. At the top of the steps, against the whitish background of the house, a lighted door shone in the darkness. Grigiolo decided to go up to it, shaking his head, unable to make up his mind at that hour in such weather, with no moon, to go and play at hide-and-seek with his host in the garden, and run the risk of breaking his head against a tree.

He entered the house. An enormous lamp, placed upon a table, was burning in front of the door, and illuminated the hall from its pavement to its huge black beams, throwing into relief the four doors in the walls, the disorder of papers and books, heaped up anyhow on the table, and on the sofa and chairs, and the two stuffed eagles, with outspread wings, in the corners facing the entrance. Between these two corners was a large door, leading into the French garden, and this was open. Grigiolo went and looked out. In front of him was Passo Grande, looking very black: on his right, rising above him, were the branches of the dense wood which grows over the mountain and valley, and which covers peaks and ridges, streams and pools, with the terrors of its black shadows.

The wonderful fountain in the garden made its voice heard, though it was invisible in the night.

"Good heavens!" exclaimed Grigiolo, turning back into the room, and throwing himself upon an uncomfortable sofa. "Unless they are mad, they have no chance! This fellow is sure to be elected!"

He watched the big lamp in the middle of the room, with the unpleasant recollection that he must wait there, no one knew how long, to say no one knew what, and finally to walk a mile before reaching his luxurious bed at the Villa Carrè.

The bright, steady glare of the lamp made him furious. A huge dog trotted in through the open door facing him, with his tail in the air.

"Here I am," said Cortis, in his ringing voice. "Saturn, lie down."

The dog curled himself up near his feet, and his master, turning and speaking to some one outside, said,—

"Bring the coffee."

"How are you?" he asked, extending his hand to Grigiolo. "You are as punctual as the stars."

The young man bowed, smiling. He expected some apologies, and was quite ready to say, pray don't mention it, but Cortis gave him no opportunity, and plunged straight into his business.

"Now you want," said he, "to talk over this election. Sit down, I beg you. You must not mind if I stand, as I am excited and must walk about; but please sit down yourself. You see I never can talk in the bosom of the Constitutional Association, but here amongst the woods, in an empty room, I will speak willingly and clearly."

He was excited evidently. Followed by his dog, he walked up and down with his hands in his pockets in front of Grigiolo, who, seated in a most respectful attitude, watched him open-eyed. When he stopped, the tense muscles in his arms and legs quivered.

"I hope you understand," he said, "that I am very grateful to you and your friends for your assistance. You support me because my personal opinions are moderate, and also because my share in public affairs has been too slight to authorise any one to believe me a friend of the ministry with which it has pleased Providence to afflict Italy."

He stopped for a moment, looking at Grigiolo with an amused and sarcastic twinkle in his eyes.

"But I am not a moderate," he said.

"Not even that?" exclaimed Grigiolo, candidly.

"How, *not even that?*"

Grigiolo bit his lips. He had thought to himself: "What can I do with a lunatic like this, who is not even a moderate?"

"Nothing," he answered, "I was going to say—" but

Cortis interrupted him, indifferent as to what he was going to say.

"But nevertheless I find myself quite in a position to be able to accept honestly the support of the Association," he said.

"That's lucky," thought Grigiolo.

"I want you to understand," continued Cortis, "that, as I wish to succeed in politics, and as I do not possess the hypocritical vanity which is called modesty, I must work for myself as every honest citizen may legitimately do; and the support of a few gentlemen at a distance, while it cheers my heart, is of very little practical utility to my cause."

Doctor Grigiolo rose somewhat piqued.

"Oh," he said, "if you fancy—"

"No, no," broke in Cortis; "sit down again, please. Now, let us have some coffee."

The servant entered at this moment with a tray, on which were two large cups.

"Thank you," said Grigiolo, frightened at the size. "I never drink it at night. I should not sleep."

"What is the matter with you to keep you from sleeping?"

"Indeed I should not. No, really not, thank you."

Cortis sent away the servant, poured himself out a jorum of coffee, and began talking again, holding his cup in the right hand and his saucer in the left.

"In saying this I am doing you no injury. I think it is a great humiliation, that in order to get into public life, one has to sneak through such low doors as the patriotism and political wisdom of the electorate. I praise you for not being able or willing to speak the only language that these electors understand. As for me, who have had to wade through the mud of political economy in order to please my constituents, *omnia præcepi atque animo mecum ante peregi.*"

Cortis lifted his cup to his lips, keeping his burning eyes on Grigiolo.

"It is not necessary to commit any acts of dishonesty or baseness. One need not spend money, or distribute cockades, like my opponent, but it is necessary to have an intimate knowledge of the local requirements of the constituency. I know them all, in all the communes, and the chief electors know that I know them, just as they know that to-day I have some powerful supporters, and they guess, because they are shrewd, that to-morrow I shall myself be of importance. Besides, there is—" (Cortis here named an important person among the electors) "who has hitherto been able to squeeze everyone like lemons, and he fancies that he can squeeze me too."

"Indeed!" exclaimed Grigiolo amazed. "Then we are sitting on a fence and don't know which side we may fall."

"Just so, my dear fellow, and that is why I do not draw up a programme which should secure the approval of the Constitutional Association, because, in such a case, that man would desert me. But I don't intend to draw up a programme. I intend to take my stand upon my own position, and not to compete in an examination, so there!"

He began to sip his coffee very slowly. Grigiolò cast a furtive glance at the clock, as though to insinuate his opinion that they ought to finish their business quickly.

Cortis raised his head from his cup, and asked quietly,—

"Are you a Catholic?"

Grigiolo started.

"I?" he answered. But—"

Cortis emptied and put down his cup, and recommenced his remarks in the same thoughtful voice.

"To the electors I am the Deputy Cortis; to my neighbours I am Daniele Cortis, who has written upon bi-metalism and the increase in the number of banks. I am also that provincial Councillor Cortis, who voted with your friends when an attempt was made to introduce politics into the nomination of our president. That must be enough for them. I will draw up no programme; my time is not yet come. Did you notice what those four chatterboxes said this evening? But I shall get their votes all the same. I shall ask for support on the ground that I am at least a gentleman, while my opponent is a swindler; but they must not expect opinions from me. I say to you again honestly, if I refuse to give a public adhesion to the ideas of the Constitutional Association, it is not because I wish to retain the support of one powerful individual, it is simply because those ideas do not coincide with mine."

"Who can understand what this man's ideas are?" thought Grigiolo; "who can tell what sort of a deputy he will make?"

It occurred to him that his friends of the Association might be annoyed with him for not appreciating at its proper value the importance of this interview with Cortis, and for not forcing him to speak out more clearly.

"But," he said, "these views of yours are in reality very far removed from—"

"Not at all, my friend," answered Cortis, in a low voice, standing with his arms folded across his breast, frowning.

"Wait," he said.

He violently pulled the bell which hung near the sofa. It rang loudly.

Saturn rushed to the door, and barked at the night.

"What the devil is he going to do now!" wondered Grigiolo.

The servant appeared.

"Put a table in front of that gentleman," said Cortis, "and then bring pens, ink, paper, and candles immediately."

"But," observed Grigiolo, again looking at the clock. "it is after half-past twelve."

"I shall not sleep to-night," remarked the other drily.

"All very well, if you like it; but—"

"Two candles, pen, and ink," said Cortis to the servant, as he approached with the table.

Grigiolo was dumbfoundered. The servant, grave as a judge, brought all that was required, lighted the candles, and departed at a sign from his master.

I have to write a political letter to-night," said Cortis. "But it is private, you know. I make you my secretary. How old are you?"

"Twenty-seven."

"I am thirty-two. *Ça va.* Write—"

"'Dear Friend,—This friend is an ex-deputy of the Right, a learned man, stuffed full of quotations, who cannot move now because he has swallowed so many books. He has offered me the public support of the Central Constitutional Association.'"

Grigiolo wrote obediently, looked up, and repeated, "*Dear Friend.*"

"'I thank you,'" continued Cortis, dictating, "'but as I consider my success assured—'"

"Oh," murmured Grigiolo, as he wrote, "I understand. Because he has the president of the association on his side. Assured."

"'Without external influences' (forgive me for that remark, Grigiolo), 'therefore it is not necessary that the Central Association should take any steps on behalf of a thinker who is free from your teachings and ideas.' Have you written that?"

"Yes."

"Fresh line. 'I must add that, in entering the Italian Chamber of Deputies, I shall not expect, as so many of you do, oh, my chimerical friends, to find myself in the House of Commons—'"

"What the deuce?" interrupted Grigiolo.

"'In the House of Commons—to find myself in the

House of Commons, seated on a bench that has lasted six hundred years. I do not believe that the English constitutional doctrines are adapted to the Chamber. I do not believe in the advantages of your parliamentary despotism, whatever be the colour of the majority. Ovid might perhaps justify the rapid metamorphosis which has been imposed upon the country, but it would be a more difficult task to justify it by the light of experience. If God—'"

"Phew!" exclaimed Grigiolo, breathlessly writing. "What next?"

"I don't quite know. Go on. 'If God will forgive Signor Sella for not having conciliated the ministerial party, or the others for having prevented such conciliation, it will perhaps be because—'"

"Because," repeated Grigiolo, waiting, pen in air.

"Upon my word, I don't know," answered Cortis. "Put it thus: 'Because from the surroundings of the House of Parliament there was heard no voice summoning a valiant man to raise again royal authority in the name of the Country, or to assemble the whole nation around the Palatine.'"

"The Quirinal, you mean?"

"Yes, you are right; the Quirinal. It would need a man with the great ideas of the September conquerors to shut up the king in a house of priests. Go on writing. 'If one believes that the monarchy is only fit to give balls and dinners, and to decorate our every-day faces with a dash of chivalrous sentimentality, I don't care to suffer on its behalf. But I, my dear friend, think it is still good for something more than that. I believe it is of use to finish the lesson in geography that Victor Emmanuel gave Europe; I believe, above all, that it is of use to inaugurate with that other monarchy, the ecclesiastical, a policy of common sense, and with a prospect of lasting; a policy which, while it shall in no degree put the State below the Church, shall give it force enough to startle the world with our social reforms.'"

"Gently," cried Grigiolo, writing furiously.

"'I should mind very little,'" continued Cortis, his words and his face both getting hotter, "'being called a clerical, or having the whole pack of radicals and *doctrinaires* at my heels—'"

"Gently, for heaven's sake," groaned the secretary, exhausted. But Cortis took no notice.

"'If I could render my country solid and powerful, and obtain for it the honour of leading the way in a well-organised social revolution. But to obtain this we must have neither political superstitions, nor religious scepticism, nor scientific bigotry, nor—"'

Cortis continued his dictation, raising his voice at last to such a pitch, that his dog jumped up and watched him angrily.

Grigiolo threw down his pen.

"Forgive me," he exclaimed, "but how do you expect me to follow you?"

He could stand it no longer.

Cortis dried his forehead without a word, and, having seated himself on the sofa, he read his letter right through down to where it was broken off. That phrase he concluded thus, "nor trembling hearts."

"I write all this," observed honest Grigiolo, "but you know I couldn't sign a word of it."

"Naturally," answered Cortis with a laugh. "There are many people in Italy who would be glad of a chance to enunciate these ideas without having to sign them. We will find one man who will sign for them all. Shall we finish?"

"Gladly."

"Then write. 'You will easily believe that these notions of mine are not likely to attract the priests in my division. Four-fifths of them are openly fighting against me, and the remaining fifth is standing aloof and looking on.' "

"That is true," remarked the secretary, writing.

" 'Because they know that I have always regarded them as blind and ignorant men, which they are; and they know that I, a Catholic—'

"Supposing this letter ever gets into print?" said Grigiolo as he wrote.

"Do you think I should mind? I will say it in the chamber, *coram hominibus*. I want to meet face to face these bold thinkers who laugh at me. Go on writing. 'They know that I, a Catholic, if ever I were to become a minister, should be capable of obliging them to study something more than the *summa contragentes*.' Will you kindly read it all to me again."

Grigiolo did as he was asked.

"I will write the ending myself," he remarked. "What do you think of it?"

"The ideas are good enough," answered the secretary; "but how can they possibly be carried out while we are in the state of transition in which we are living to-day?"

"There's the rub," answered the other. "But are we far off from the realisation?"

Grigiolo rose from his chair.

"Yes," he answered, "far from it; and I have a twenty-minutes' walk before I get to my bed."

"You are right; I have been very thoughtless."

"Not at all!"

"Now, I will send someone home with you."

"Please don't; it really is not necessary."

Cortis rang the bell.

"How is the weather?" he asked, as he ordered the servant to light a lantern, and accompanied Grigiolo into the porch. The white front and the white wings of the villa shone and disappeared again every moment, but no thunder was audible.

"Will you sleep here?" said Cortis, "unless you have any scruples against passing the night under my roof?"

Grigiolo thanked him, and protested against his last speech. He really could not stay. He was not afraid of the weather, and besides, he did not think it was going to rain.

"And you—" he said, "you start to-morrow?"

"Yes, I do."

"Whatever the weather may be?"

"Yes."

They were both silent. Behind them, in the room, the lamps were dying out and beginning to smoke. From the window they could see the silvery jet of the fountain and the white gravel.

The servant came bringing the lantern.

"And so—" began Grigiolo.

The other interrupted him; "I will come part of the way with you," said he, seizing his arm and dragging him down the steps, without giving him any chance of preventing him.

"You consider me a conservative?"

"I don't know; to a certain extent it seems to me that you are."

"And naturally you will say so to your friends; you will tell them, won't you, that I am one of this new growth of fungi? But tell them also to wait before they judge me."

He was silent for a space, then opened his mouth impetuously, but he refrained and said only,—

"Let them wait."

He went on a few steps, and then stopped as if in pain.

"Good God!" he said, "is there nothing left that our poor Italy can teach the world? Has Providence raised her from the dead merely in order to make a bad democracy, and a bad literature which will shortly ruin each other?"

"Do not let us talk about it," answered Grigiolo.

"Do you believe," continued Cortis, "that if it were so, the idea of going into Parliament would have ever entered my head? If you knew the state of my mind you would not think that. Only tell your friends that I may be to be found amongst the ranks of a conservative party, but that I am a motive power. Good-bye."

He left him with a rapid gesture of farewell, and disappeared in the darkness. Grigiolo remained standing, almost petrified, until Saturn, who had been running on in front, suddenly passed by him at full speed. A flash of lightning showed him some distance off, close to his master.

"I will do what I can," thought Grigiolo, "but he is mad!"

CHAPTER IV.

AMONGST THE ROSES.

The little chapel of the Villa Carrè, hidden away in a corner of the garden between the railings and a group of firs, had apparently never ceased during the night of the 29th June from tinkling its bells. The day came, the sun came, the merry north wind came and rustled the leaves of the poplars along the high road, and whispered to the roses which climbed everywhere, even along the iron supports of the awning outside Elena's window; and still the bells tinkled. Elena, who had fallen asleep just before dawn, was aroused by the noise, and lifted her head from the pillow. Had not somebody rung the door bell and brought her a letter from Daniele? Had it not been placed there on the dressing-table? No. On the table her rings and her bracelets were scattered, and her volume of Châteaubriand lay open. A dream: it must have been a dream. She rose and opened the window and let in the sweet air of the trees and the mountains. On her white bed, on the light walls of her room, which was enclosed like a nightingale's nest in a corner of the villa almost hidden by roses and jasmine, she could see the reflection of the blue sky and the pure light of the dawn. "Holiday, holiday," sang the bells. Elena felt a great wish to cry. She was always thus when she first woke, then her heart shut the door upon her passion and kept it a prisoner till the evening, except when Elena, finding herself alone, descended into the depths of her heart, and delighted to feel in herself a flame of passion and of life.

She dressed herself, alone and hastily. Her little room was like sweet music—too sweet! The scent of the roses was too luxurious, their exquisite beauty was too delicate. She suffered there, and her mind lost all its vigour; one ought to be happy to dwell in such a nest, and not to have thoughts in one's mind, such as she had, which accorded ill with the beautiful surroundings. Elena looked for a minute out of the window, through the leaves of the roses blown about by the wind. The tops of the mountains were red; a bluish shadow covered the fields, the shrubs, and the paths of the gardens, which some labourers were raking. She thought that this was the third day since Cortis's departure, and that perhaps she might receive a letter.

Ah! ought she to wish for that letter? She had loved him in secret for how long! But there had been a time when she did not wish him to think of her. A friendly glance, a kind word, any token of kindness were enough for her. And on her side she only wished to show him quiet friendliness; loving and suffering in silence, with the passionate hope of being able to do something for him some day, but she knew not what; of being able to do a little good in the world by that means. Otherwise, childless as she was, divided in her soul from her husband, she would have gone through life like a shadow, here and there comforting some sorrow perhaps, but finally bringing to God, like the servant in the gospel, many useless treasures laid up in her heart.

But now she knew that she was loved, she doubted not that she had been understood by him; at present her whole soul was in a state of restlessness, full of doubt and torment.

She turned from the window and seized the book lying on her table. It was the third volume of Châteaubriand's

Mémoires d'outre Tombe, and had been lent to her by Cortis. The latter had told her that, as a boy, he had conceived a violent passion for Lucile de Châteaubriand, Comtesse de Caud ; and now, with jealous anxiety, she hunted through the memoirs of the great poet for every word that might recal the figure of his sister. She sought to revive from them that beauty full of sadness, that spirit full of mystery and genius, which considered itself superfluous upon earth, and so difficult to know, "tant il y a de diverses pensées dans ma tête," as she herself wrote to Châteaubriand, "tant ma timidité et mon espéce de faiblesse extérieure sont en opposition avec ma force intérieure."

The volume was open at the beginning of the third book, wherein is described the retirement of Madame de Caud to the convent of the Dames Saint Michel in Paris, and in which are enshrined like relics, the last letters she wrote to her brother. Elena, the night before, had reached this passage in an undated letter.

"Quelle pitié que l'attention que je me porte ! Dieu ne peut plus m'affliger qu'en toi. Je le remercie du précieux, bon et cher présent qu'il m'a fait en ta personne et d'avoir conservé ma vie sans tache ; voilà tous mes trésors. Je pourrais prendre pour emblème de ma vie la lune dans un nuage, avec cette devise : souvent obscurcie jamais ternie."

Elena had stopped reading at this point, with tears in her eyes. Had that brother, whom Lucile called the best part of herself and a gift of God, never been a danger to her ? As she read on in this state of mind she came to the description of Renato, where, in the forests of Combourg, she lived only in his heart, and oppressed by unconquerable sadness she translated with him the *Tœdet animam meam vitæ meæ* of Job, or wrote those short prose lyrics to the dawn and to the moon, so melancholy and so sweet in their design, so softly musical in their expression. As Elena read the letter, she put herself in the place of the writer; she herself was speaking to Daniele.

She began to read again, but her head was hot and excited, her chest so weighed down that she could not continue. She felt that she must have air and movement. She took up the volume and passed through the anteroom smelling of cigars, walking on tiptoe so as not to wake the baron, who was sleeping noisily in the room next her own, with his door open.

She went into the garden and followed the path which leads by the evergreen shrubs, to the chapel of Saint Peter, and to the gate which opens on to the high road. She met a messenger with a telegram for the Baron Senator Di Santa Giulia; and having told him to take it without delay to her husband, she passed through the gate, turned to the right, and walked along the road, bordered by poplars, leading to the poor cottages of Passo di Rovese and the river. She thought of Lugano, in which she had spent two days once some years before. She saw a sheet of blue water, a long row of white, yellow, and grey houses, a crown of hills green up to their very summit. Where was Daniele? Her fancy changed his whereabouts every moment. He was at his window in the Hotel du Parc, or now he was in a somewhat gloomy villa on the lake which she remembered, or else he was in that red and yellow villa up on the hill. And she pictured to herself a person about him, who who took all sorts of shapes, sometimes deserving pity, and sometimes repulsive; an old woman in all the appearances of grief, either real or false. Daniele must have had his first meeting with his mother two days ago. Another day could not pass without a letter from him. The post did not come in until the evening.

"Twelve hours more!" thought Elena, stopping on

the little wooden bridge to watch the shadowy waters of the Rovese, and to drink in the health-giving air which bore in it the scent of the Alpine meadows and the fir trees. The owner of the neighbouring hydraulic saw-mill passed, and took off his hat to the "little countess," as she was still called all round the neighbourhood. She kept him in conversation, and, half seriously and half laughing, led him on to talk of the elections. The man, an influential elector, had been talked over by the Baron di Santa Giulia, and his mysterious answers, combined with his cunning smile, at first troubled Elena. However, she soon penetrated his secret, and dispersed all the baron's electoral cobwebs. She told him with a smile, that in politics she and her husband disagreed, and added, that Count Lao was very anxious for the success of Cortis. That was an important consideration, as the Carrò family voluntarily paid half the cost of the maintenance of the bridge on which they were standing, and which had been made by the owner of the saw-mill. The latter, contrite, promised that he would vote for Signor Daniele, "now that you put it to me in that light!" and with a profound sweep of his hat, he passed on his way.

Elena walked along the left bank of the Rovese, among the alders that hid the river from the meadows. Now the thick wood is bathed in the river; farther on, a grassy projection from the bank stops the water, which runs slowly round it, with whirling current. Elena stopped with her closed book in her hands, and watched the stream, while on the other side she could see the old fir trees belonging to her own home. There was no living creature on the bank or in the meadows; white clouds flying over the tops of the trees veiled the sky. How sweet it would be, she dreamed, to hide herself away with him for ever, in some secluded green retreat. "No!" she muttered half aloud, "no, no!" She continued her way, sighing, opened the Chateaubriand at the last few pages, far from Madame de Caud's letter, read a few lines about Buonaparte, and closed the book again. As she passed near a large poplar, she remembered that a few years before she had cut upon it the name of a girl-friend. She sought for it and found nothing; no trace of that happy time was left to her. Where were they all now, those mad joys, those fantastic hopes, those melancholy feelings of a day, those deep sorrows of an hour? Her friend was now living in some out-of-the-way little town in Piedmont. She had lost her only child and would not be comforted; she had even ceased to answer Elena's letters.

She had cut her name there in the Autumn of 1869, a few months after she had first known Cortis. She was about seventeen at the time, he was nearly twenty. She remembered the first visit of her uncle and his son, in the May of that year. It was only after her marriage that Elena had become aware that old Doctor Cortis, who had for some time lived in Piedmont, had always refused to return to Friuli, after his domestic catastrophe; and that he had been induced by his sister Tarquinia to buy Villascura. How long a time had passed since then, and how many things? The resounding current of the Rovese seemed to her like an echo, and pained her.

"What a child I was!" thought Elena. Her cousin, a good-looking young man, full of cleverness and life, used to like watching her, but she, as she looked back now, remembered that she had taken no notice of him, till some time later; and then old Cortis had died, and Daniele had gone away into the world with the stream.

He had travelled for many years, had studied political economy at Berlin, and taught it at Florence, and now, after seven long years, he had returned to Villascura, to carve out a political career for himself. What years those had been for her! Elena opened her book, sat down by the way-side, read a few lines without understanding them, and finally let herself drift with the rush of painful thoughts that assailed her.

Every now and then she opened her heart to them in desperation, so as to get a moment's respite from the pain of fighting them. She heard her mother introducing to her Colonel Baron di Santa Giulia, she saw his slight bow as he took her hand. Then she saw herself again in her girlish bed, one long December night, debating with herself, whether she could remain in that house which had become hateful to her, through certain fancied evidences of sin, or whether she should say that painfully bitter, "Yes." Her hands grasped the book, her eyes fixed themselves upon the pages; she forced herself to read a few lines in order to rid herself of those fancies. She chanced upon these words,—

"Il n'y a qu'un déplaisir auquel je crains de mourir difficilement, c'est de heurter en passant, sans le vouloir, la destinée de quelque autre."

It was only after reading two or three lines further on, that she perceived how applicable this paragraph was to herself.

Then she returned to it with avidity, and forgot herself in it until the sun, coming up between the shoulders of the overhanging mountains, shone upon her book. She seated herself on a low wall at the edge of the wood, whence the road ran down to the river, which displayed its glittering pebbles and its bright banks in the sunlight.

She passed through a moment of mortal hopelessness. Always that same doubt, that same remorse, that shadow that haunted her. She was hurting him, although no word of love had ever passed between them, she was a hindrance and an impediment in his life. She laid the book down upon the wall, and ceased thinking, lulled by the sun and the murmur of the Rovese. After a time she took up the book again, and hunted slowly through it with icy fingers, for the passage, "Il n'y a qu'un déplaisir." She closed it again hastily, got down off the wall, with eyes full of tears, and slowly turned towards the house.

As she passed under the windows of Count Lao, she saw him making signs of greeting to her, from behind the panes. She signalled to him to open, but in return she received nothing but a gesture of horror, and a finger was pointed to call her attention to the trees which were swaying in the wind. Malcanton and Perlotti were going round the garden with the bailiff; they were giving orders, taking measurements, and studying the ground, as though they were about to fortify a camp in presence of a hostile army. They had to decide where the band should be placed, and where the fireworks should be arranged. Malcanton had been specially charged to lay out the lawn-tennis ground before the arrival of the guests, who were expected from the neighbouring town. As soon as he saw Elena in the distance, he began waving a letter above his head, crying out,—

"*Laan, laan!*"

Elena started and hastened towards him.

"Has the post come?" she asked.

"Yes, that idiot of a postman thought fit to keep the letters in his pocket all last night. There is one for you. The rules have arrived, and they say that it ought to be pronounced '*laan*,' as you said. See, here it is, I will read it to you."

While Malcanton was hastily beginning to read the rules for the game of lawn-tennis, Elena turned her back on him.

"Here!" he cried; "Elena!" but she was already in the house, and he, poor man, grumbling a little, returned to his work.

She found her husband fuming and raging in his shirtsleeves, furious with her for her absurd passion for going out before sunrise.

Elena did not wait till he had done, but pushed the door too in his face. He, however, kicked it open, and, just as he was, came into the passage.

"This is no joke," said he. "I have very serious matters to talk to you about."

"Say what you please," answered Elena, "but not in that manner."

"Go in," replied the baron, holding the door open; "we will put on our best manners to please your ladyship. Will you kindly come in?"

Elena entered; her husband closed and locked the door with a grunt of satisfaction, and muttered, 'What susceptibility!"

"Be quiet," he said, seeing that Elena wished to put in a word. "We must start to-night. Do you hear?"

"Why? Yes, I hear perfectly. Is there anything else?"

"There is this, that we cannot start thus."

Elena seated herself in an arm-chair, and began to read her Chateaubriand.

"Damn your books!" exclaimed the baron. "Have the goodness to listen to me. I tell you that we cannot start thus."

"But what can I do, if I know nothing and understand nothing. What prevents us from starting?"

"You spend your life a thousand miles above the clouds. Do you imagine that I came for my own pleasure into this infernal country of yours, this land of rheumatism and ice, where one freezes in June, and where it rains sixty times a day? I didn't come here to sleep in a nutshell like this, where my feet stick out of the door. You know that, I suppose?"

"If I had not known it I might have guessed it."

"You need not be so witty. I have said it."

"And what next?"

"Why." The baron lowered his voice, and with an obscene oath, said that he had got nothing of what he expected.

"And this is what you want me for, is it?" asked Elena, rising and putting her hand on the door-handle.

"What the devil should I want you for otherwise?"

"But is this money my business, pray?"

"Certainly it is. You spend most of it!"

Elena knew perfectly well the various secret means which the baron had for getting rid of his money, but she disdained to retort, and only said, "And therefore?"

"And therefore, if that skinflint of an uncle of yours—"

Elena, in an instant, rushed into her room; but before she could close the door her husband followed her crying,—

"Come now, what—"

"Leave my room," she said, turning towards him.

His voice dropped, he was abashed by the glittering eyes that were fixed upon him, he hesitated a moment and finally withdrew, slamming the door violently behind him.

Elena saw a letter on her table and seized it with a beating heart. It was from Cortis, dated from Lugano. She waited an instant, then opened it and read,—

"DEAR ELENA,—I shall probably start for home to-morrow evening, and pray heaven that I may still find you. I have great need of you. I will tell you all when we meet. I am worn out. As hitherto my heart has no resting place but you, it shall never have any other.

"DANIELE."

She did not know how long she remained standing with the letter in her hand, when her husband entered fastening his necktie.

"What has happened to you?" he asked.

She placed the letter openly on the table, unconcernedly, and answered quietly,—

"What do you want with me?"

"What I want? I want to tell you this, that I must have money, and that if I don't, you will regret it, for I will shut you up at Cefalù for ever and a day, and not all the powers of Rome, or Venice, or heaven itself, will get you out of it. You see that I will get it!"

"How will you get it?"

"Now, at once, from your uncle. If not the money itself, I will get a little bit of writing, or even a verbal promise, because I am a good fellow, they know they can trust me. It will do if the money reaches me in Rome in a week's time. Do you think I am afraid of your uncle? I am going straight to his room, and I will offer him the alternative; either Cefalù or the money. If he cries out, I will cry out too."

He took his long yellow beard and pulled it through his hands.

Elena studied his face in order to discover whether he had really meant what he said, or whether he only meant to frighten her into interfering. To say the truth, the baron had a certain amount of military sincerity, and his forehead was undisturbed.

"I will do it," she said; and she noticed a look of satisfaction in his eyes. "I will do it, on one condition."

"What condition?"

"That you do not say one word. Do you hear? One word, and I will do nothing."

"I will not speak."

"To nobody?"

"To nobody."

"Now go, and shut the door."

The noble baron had noticed the letter on the table. but left the room without any comment on it. He suddenly reappeared at the door, however, and said,—

"You must ask your uncle to advance to you some of the money he always gives you, Fifteen thousand lire will be enough for the present. You may tell him I need it to pay the last instalment of the mortgage upon Cefalù, And you may add, that if I have to borrow it elsewhere, I shall take every one belonging to me to Cefalù and put them on half rations. Do you understand? Either the money or Cefalù."

Elena was reading her letter a second time, and answered without looking up,—

"Very good."

The door closed; she was alone. Then she laid down the letter and seated herself on her bed, which was not yet made, and looked out of the window to the west, through the roses, upon a green meadow bathed in sunlight. Many thoughts rose in her heart, designs and plans formed themselves slowly in her brain. Her lips moved as though uttering words, but no sound came from them. At last she rose, went to the window, and, hidden behind the roses, she wept.

CHAPTER V.

FOR HIM! FOR HIM!

MALCANTON and Count Perlotti were standing under the window of Elena's room, and were knocking at Doctor Grigiolo's closed shutters; he was fast asleep. Elena passed them boldly, put on her hat and gloves, and went to her mother, who was still sleeping, and, without much preamble, announced that her departure was fixed for that evening. The countess's thoughts immediately flew to the money required by her son-in-law, and she was terrified at the idea of a scene on that day of all others, when her house was full of guests. Imagine Lao with his temperament! She wished that money and excitable people were all at the bottom of the sea together.

"You, my child," she said, "had better not mix yourself up in it at all. Let your uncle do as he pleases."

She told her of all she had suffered during the last fortnight, between the ill-temper of her son-in-law and the scoldings of her brother-in-law.

"And you would never let me talk to you about it."

Elena interrupted her, told her that everything was settled, and, without further explanation, begged her to allow her maid to pack her trunks.

"Everything settled? How? When?"

Countess Tarquinia was beside herself with surprise, but she could obtain no explanation from her daughter, who embraced her, begging her not to make herself miserable about it any more, and then departed. The countess rang her bell violently, and sent for Elena again. She did not know where they were going, whether to Rome or to Aix-les-Bains. Elena then admitted that she did not know herself. Her husband had not told her, and she had not enquired. Probably it would be Rome, however, because a telegram had come, and Di Santa Giulia was expecting to be summoned to a meeting of the Senate.

Countess Tarquinia would have desired greater certainty, but Elena ran away, and went straight to Count Lao, who, having got up for a minute to look at the weather, had betaken himself back to bed. When Elena, in hat and gloves, suddenly burst into his room, and said, "I am going away," he fancied that she was on the point of starting and sat up in bed. The twelve hours' delay appeared to him a clear gain; at least they could talk it over. He rained questions upon his niece. Could she not do this? Could she not do that? Surely the baron could go by himself to Rome, or even farther. It did not occur to him to propose to accompany her himself, but he mentioned the steward, and that fool Malcanton who, as he said, was good for nothing else. When he saw he could not move her, he flew into a passion, turned his face to the wall, huddled himself up in the bedclothes, and screamed to his niece to go away, and at once, that he did not care a pin whether she went to Rome, or Sicily, or Africa, or anywhere else she pleased, and that she need be in no hurry to return.

Elena moved, approached the bed quietly and leant over it; the face, which was half-hidden between the pillows and the sheets, was moved also.

"Ugh!" said Count Lao in a rough voice, as if to ward off any demonstrations of tenderness or affection. Suddenly Elena kissed his forehead.

"It is my duty," she said softly.

Then she spoke to him about the money. Lao gradually turned towards her, listening attentively. Elena, laughing, told him not to be afraid, and ordered him to reply merely to her mother, should she question him, that he and Elena had come to an understanding; he was not to say anything more. Her uncle did not understand, and demanded explanations. She gave him another kiss, and, excusing herself on the plea that she had to go to mass (although it would not begin for another hour or more), she left him.

She ordered a carriage and drove to Villascura, where she stopped at the priest's house. He was in church, but a pleasant housekeeper begged the "little countess" to wait a moment and retired discreetly, just as the priest himself entered and greeted her with a manner in which were mingled respect, surprise and expectation. Elena had come to take leave of him. He expressed his regrets, which were perhaps increased by the fact that he had several times been the channel through which passed her secret charities. This time also she wanted to lay a similar burden upon him, but she also wanted to be advised and assisted. The priest exhausted himself in thanking her in the name of his poor. He also hoped to obtain the support of the senator in some difficulty which had arisen between him and the Commissioners of the Crown Lands. The baroness gave him to understand that her husband could not help him much, but that she thought that it was in her power to be of use to him; and as she said good-bye, she begged him with a smile to be good enough to bless the crops of those who voted for Daniele Cortis. The priest grew very red, and protested that he had never refused his blessing from political motives. But there was a story which was not without foundation in fact, that he had refused his assistance to keep the caterpillars off the cabbages belonging to some of the supporters of Cortis. Elena comforted him. Now was the time, she said, to remedy the evil. The priest had not known Cortis well when he had done this; but now he could conscientiously state to the electors that Cortis was by no means an enemy of religion; quite the contrary; she would answer for him. The priest promised to do all that her ladyship wished, even to adapting his political convictions to those of Countess Tarquinia, and, with bare head, he accompanied the baroness to her carriage.

"Villa Cortis," said Elena to the coachman as she got in.

When the last cottages of the village were passed, she saw the wall surrounding the French garden, and above it the gleaming fountain and the dark-wooded sides of the hills. With pale and sad countenance she went up to the little grass lawn in front of the house, passed through the court-yard, and turning off by the garden railings, disappeared in the wood. She lost herself in the mystery of the shadows which cast around their silent invitation, and which in a short time become thick and dense, lying darkly over the paths that wind in and out among them. Within those woods are hills and valleys perpetually shaded; lakes, ponds, and glades, girt round by overshadowing trees, and there may be heard, too, the voices of invisible springs. The branches of the lofty trees, growing around the garden gate, by their waving and murmuring in the wind, suggest a poem of shadow and of life, and give one a foretaste of its sombre magnificence.

Elena entered by the broad path to the left.

It might have been possible for a quick ear to distinguish her light footfall as she walked; but had any one followed her cautiously and lost sight of her after the first bend in the path, he would have listened vainly for her step.

She descended into the valley which opened on her left immediately after this turning, a narrow valley through which a stream covered with water-lilies trickled; the grass grew thickly over the path, and overhead the branches of the acacias on either side mingled, and cast a golden green shadow. Thence she mounted to a quiet opening in the hills, and there, among the trees on a grassy plateau, stood a column of ancient marble, brought from the baths of Caracalla to this other solitude, and bearing on its base two clasped hands carved in relief, and the following words:—

Hyeme et Æstate
Et prope et procul
Usque dum vivam et ultra.

Elena reappeared half-an-hour later still paler. She closed the garden gate behind her, leaning her head against it for a last look at the dear flowers, and to say to them, "Shall I ever see you again?" The trees could not hear her, they were too high, but they still swayed and murmured in the wind, offering her the poem of life and shadow, the sweet day-dreams of love. But she would not hearken to them. She turned away with a sigh, and walked away with bowed head, and with the words of the old column in her heart: "In winter and in summer, from near and from far, as long as I live, and beyond that again."

She stopped at Villascura for mass. Coming out of church she found Pitantoi and Don Bartolo in friendly conversation with the coachman. Little Don Bartolo came forward with his somewhat comic familiarity and reproved the contessina for leaving them so quickly.

"Contessina," said Pitantoi, remaining respectfully in the background, "it will be all right for Signor Daniele, even though the good priest here does dislike it."

"What, what, what!" exclaimed Don Bartolo, turning round quickly and grasping his knobbed stick. Elena took no notice of him, but she nodded pleasantly to the other.

"Good-bye," she said, as the horses started at full speed, covering with dust the two combatants.

Countess Tarquinia was in the garden with the Perlottis. Malcanton, red and perspiring like a porter, had not yet succeeded in marking out the lawn-tennis ground, notwithstanding the help of the bailiff; Doctor Grigiolo was upstairs in a small room preparing fire balloons for the evening, and at that moment was leaning out of window shouting, "Paste, paste!" As soon as he saw the carriage return, he rushed down from his laboratory and joined the Perlottis and Malcanton, who had gone to meet Elena to express to her their regrets at her intended departure. Signora Perlotti told her that she and her husband had arranged with the baron that they should all start at half-past ten, after the illuminations and fireworks. Countess Tarquinia, guessing what they were talking about, began to exclaim, "No, no," from a distance, and made gestures of dissent with her fan.

"Your mamma won't hear of it," said Signora Perlotti; "she is always so good, poor dear. But we really must go!"

"We really must," repeated her husband, notwithstanding some expressed doubts of Malcanton and Doctor Grigiolo.

"I am selfish," said Elena smiling. "I shall be glad to start with you."

They all turned towards Countess Tarquinia, who, with her parasol, was beckoning to them to come into the shade between the house and the dead cypress tree clothed in wisteria. The baron soon joined them there. His mother-in-law rallied him in a friendly manner about his sudden flight, and again begged the Perlottis to stay on at the villa. The baron looked sulky, and seemed to ask, "What is the good of this comedy?" Elena was silent, and let her mother talk on undisturbed. All at once the hall door opened, and Count Lao, who was received with acclamation, appeared. It was very seldom that he came out of his room so early in the day. He answered with a nod to the surly "good-morning" of the baron, and quickly gave the rest of the party to understand, that he wanted none of them except Elena, who meanwhile found an opportunity of telling her mother not to press the Perlottis to stay.

It was time for mass, and all the group, except Elena and her uncle, moved, more or less willingly, in the direction of the little church, the baron going last, and turning round now and then to watch the two who were standing together.

Perlotti asked the Countess whether Lao never went to church.

"Oh!" she said, "the Carrés have always been infidels, one and all. Did you not know that?"

And they entered the church under the fir trees. Then Lao took his niece's arm.

"Now, explain all this to me," he said.

"What, uncle?"

She looked at him with her two honest eyes, arching her brows and smiling; then she exclaimed, "Oh, yes!" as if she had suddenly remembered.

"You are always in the moon, and it takes you some time to travel down to the earth," said Lao crossly. "Do you imagine that she has waited all this time without coming to find out from me what was the matter?"

Lao hardly ever mentioned his sister-in-law by name; he merely called her "she."

"And what did you answer?"

"I was, I am, and always shall be, a fool. I answered her as you wished, that everything was settled between you and me, that that was enough for her, and that she was not to bother me any more. You may tell her anything you please, I don't care what you say to her; but you must explain matters to me."

"But if everything is settled!" Elena broke in, laughing, "what is there for me to explain? Let us go for a little walk, dear uncle."

She proposed that they should take a turn in the garden, and offered him her arm, but he would not hear of it, demanded these explanations, and was quite angry with her for being in such good spirits.

"Oh, uncle! she said, laying her hand on his shoulder, and looking quite gravely at him.

"Forgive me," said Lao, recovering his temper; "but you ought to see that it is necessary for me to have this cleared up."

Elena looked into his face for an instant without a word, then, taking his arm, she said,—"Come along," and drew him off towards the agent's office—a pretty little house at a short distance from the villa, its northern side curiously sheltered by some mediæval ruins, and its eastern side covered with creepers and roses up to the roof. Elena entered it by the southern door, which led into the little room that had been her sitting-room as a girl, a nest hidden behind vines and roses, facing the open country towards Villascura and the mountains of Passo Grande.

"What in the world have you brought me into this box for?" grumbled Lao, stooping under the doorway.

"Listen, everybody," she answered, "to this bear without taste or feeling!"

She compelled him to sit down on the little sofa, and to admire the view of meadows and mountains, and her coquettish little nest, perfect from its flooring of walnut-wood, up to the gilded dove which supported in her beak the hangings of red and white silk, wherewith the walls and ceiling were draped.

"Yes, yes," growled Lao, "an old sweetmeat box, empty and greasy. And what next?"

"Have you no confidence in me, uncle? Need I give

you so many reasons before you will do anything for me? Come now, don't be angry! I will tell you all about it, and explain it all to you. Only you must be kind to me during these, the last few hours that I have to spend here."

"And you still keep up these mysteries," exclaimed the Count, throwing down his hat. You will keep on putting me off for the next hundred years."

"Gently, gently," said Elena, "I am going to tell you all about it. A fine secret, indeed! There is no secret! Don't you understand? I have talked it over with my husband this morning, and he will say no more about it."

"Very good. But pray, why am I given any part in the comedy?"

Elena tapped the ground with her foot.

"How dense you are, uncle. Can't you understand?"

"Very dense, indeed," answered Lao. "I can understand nothing at all; I am still waiting for the key."

"But for mamma's sake! You see my husband has always been to mamma about these matters, and has always told her that he would not go without this money, of which he is in great need; and now it seems to me that we must save her feelings, and, in order to do that, she must be allowed to believe that everything has been arranged according to his wishes."

"And has he made up his mind not to ask for any more?"

"That is more than I can tell you."

Count Lao was silent, and looked at his niece in such a way as to make her blush.

"All right," he said at last. "And what are your plans after you have been to Rome?"

She did not like the conversation to be thus abruptly broken off. She feared that he had some suspicion, but she dared not clear up her doubts. They talked of what they would do in October when Elena, according to custom, would be coming home for a month. A fresh coldness had sprung up between them; they talked without looking at each other, without any regret in their voices; and, displeased with each other, they soon relapsed into silence.

"How much does your husband require?" suddenly asked Lao.

"I don't know," answered Elena, without surprise, as though she had seen from the first whither her uncle's thoughts were tending. "He talked about fifteen thousand lire."

She opened the drawer of the little table standing by the sofa, and taking from it a pencil, she wrote, under a line of other dates, "29th June 1881?" For many years she had always written in that drawer the dates of her arrival and departure. This time she added a note of interrogation, and closed the book.

"What are you about?" asked Lao.

"Take a wife, uncle," she answered.

"Silly child!"

At these words the cold and strained feelings which were weighing upon them vanished. Elena laughed, took one of her uncle's hands, and preached him a little sermon, in joke, upon the subject of an ideal aunt, a mature and majestic beauty.

"Mercy!" exclaimed Count Lao, at this description, now quite amused at the idea, notwithstanding the "silly child!" with which he had at first received the idea, "I know what you are driving at. Many thanks. A nice barge to take in tow."

Having joked about this for a time, they returned arm-in-arm to the garden, and there they found a fly-driver, who had been ordered by Di Santa Giulia from Villascura. Countess Tarquinia could not let Elena have the horses from the Villa that evening, as they would be wanted the next day to take her over to pay a visit at a neighbouring country house.

Count Lao flew into a passion, declared to Elena that the horses belonging to the house should be at her disposal, and warned her not to say a word against his arrangements; then, turning to the driver, he told him to go to Countess Tarquinia, and to take his orders respecting the next day's visit from her. At this moment the Countess and her guests advanced towards them from the church under the fir trees. The baron was listening inattentively to Count Perlotti, while he watched his wife and Lao closely. He had not yet been alone with his mother-in-law, and therefore he did not know what Elena had said to her about the money. But Elena must certainly have talked about it to her uncle while all the rest were at mass. With what results? They both seemed to be in good humour; his spirits revived. Just then a servant came and announced the arrival of a party of guests from the town.

"Elena, Elena!" cried her mother, dismayed, "come and help me with the luncheon, do try to be of some use. God bless these people; fancy coming at this hour!"

She hurried forward, with Malcanton, Perlotti, and Grigiolo, to greet the new-comers. Di Santa Giulia, in the confusion, succeeded in whispering to his wife,—

"Have you spoken?"

"It's all settled," answered she, hurrying towards the house.

Di Santa Giulia remained alone with Count Lao for a moment, because Elena, on reaching the house, turned round and called the latter. The baron stretched out his hand.

"Thank you," he said.

"No need," said Lao drily, thinking that he was being thanked for the horses; and he called to Elena, "I am coming."

The baron let him go, and walked with long strides, with his hat on the back of his head, and his beard flying in the wind, towards the stables, where a stack of umbrellas and parasols denoted the advent of at least eight or ten persons.

Count Lao did that day a thing most extraordinary for him. He came to luncheon, although it had been postponed a whole hour in consequence of the new arrivals. These all talked loudly and complainingly of Elena's departure.

"By the way, Countess Tarquinia," said the baron, "have you arranged with the fly-driver?"

"Yes," she replied, in a cross voice; "did not my brother-in-law tell you that you could have our horses?"

Di Santa Giulia slightly turned his head towards Lao, and mumbled a few words of thanks.

"But—" began Lao, surprised that he did not know of the arrangement about the carriage; and then he stopped short. Countess Tarquinia asked Elena, as soon as she found an opportunity, whether she were a witch. Everything seemed settled, and everyone pleased and satisfied. She even managed to whisper to her son-in-law, "You will be contented now," to which he answered aloud, "Certainly."

She proposed that the party should adjourn to the billiard-room after luncheon, but Elena suggested that they should walk in the gardens of the Villa Cortis, and sent her husband in her place, excusing herself on the score of her packing. The baron would have gladly remained behind in order to learn from his wife what had really been the result of her interview with Lao, but, feeling certain that it was good, he determined to show himself in an amiable light, and therefore went with the rest of the party. Grigiolo alone remained behind, in order to arrange the supports for the illumination of the grounds, the house, and the agent's office.

"Now, explain this to me," said Count Lao to his niece as soon as the party had started.

"What?"

"Your good-for-nothing husband came up to me after church this morning, and thanked me as warmly as though I had saved his life, which I certainly would not do!"

"Uncle!"

"No, I certainly would not! But I want to know the reason for this gratitude."

"For the loan of the horses, perhaps."

"The horses! nonsense; he knew nothing about them then. Did you not hear what passed at luncheon?"

"Perhaps it was for the hospitality you have shown him during these three weeks."

The uncle was silent, and looked at Elena as he had looked at her in her little sitting-room at the agent's cottage. She did not blush this time, but pretended indifference. She remained talking for a few minutes, and then said that she must go upstairs to see to her trunks.

"And Cortis?" cried Lao, as she was going upstairs.

Elena started at the sound of that name, and stopped short without turning round. She had not talked of Cortis to her uncle since she had repeated to him those three words: a grave matter.

"Has he not come back yet?" asked the count.

"I do not think so," answered Elena, with a trembling voice.

"I wonder how this election will go?" said the count.

Elena slowly went up the stairs without answering. As the hour of her departure grew nearer, she felt more clearly how difficult it was to talk of him, or to restrain her own feelings.

She hastily finished her packing with the help of her mother's maid, and then went out to say good-bye to the bailiff's wife and to two or three other peasants. As she was coming back to the house, her uncle called to her from his window, and begged her to go up to him.

"Look here," he said, "do you want any money?"

On hearing from Elena that she did not, he insisted, begging her to speak clearly, and ask him if she wanted anything for herself. After all, everything that he possessed would be hers one day or the other. Elena hesitated a minute, and then refused. Lao said no more about it.

"Let us say good-bye now," he continued, pressing her to his heart "This evening, with so many tiresome people about, I shall not have an instant alone with you. And remember this, whensoever, wheresoever, and for whatsoever purpose you want me, I do it for your sake, and also," he kissed her forehead, "for your father's," he added, raising his face.

Elena looked at him with tears in her eyes, and grasped his hands tightly. Her father and Count Lao had been brothers, but not friends; that was one of the reasons why the latter had lived away from his own country for so long. His health having broken down, and his brother being ill with the malady which finally killed him, they had become reconciled, and Lao, at the express wish of his brother, had taken his place as head of the family.

The party that had gone to Villascura was to return shortly before dinner. Elena ordered that meal to be sent up a few minutes earlier than usual, and told her mother that she had done so when she came home; neither the countess nor the baron had any opportunity of finding out exactly what had passed between her and her uncle.

Towards the end of dinner, the band from Villascura entered the garden, playing as it came, and Malcanton, the factotum, rushed out to receive it, and to place it in the corner reserved for it between the agent's house and the laurels which bordered the garden on the west. Following the band came several people; the Zirisèlas, the Picutis, and all the society of Villascura and Passo di

Rovese. A moment later Countess Tarquinia went out of doors with the whole of the party except Lao, who hurried to his room, where he shut himself up. When the countess appeared, the band struck up a fantasia on the "Sicilian Vespers," the Zirisèlas and Picutis, in their best clothes, came forward to greet their hostess, and a number of people stood about under the trees, which were gilded by the rays of the setting sun. Baron di Santa Giulia took his wife's arm, and led her away from the rest.

"The devil take you!" he said; "can't you speak to me? Tell me what has happened? First of all, how much?"

"Wait," answered Elena, stopping short. and looking over her shoulder. "Excuse me," she added, shaking off his hand, "those ladies have come on purpose to see me. How can you expect me to leave them?" and with these words she ran to greet Signora Zirisèla.

Before they went into the garden, Countess Tarquinia had said to her son-in-law, "You will be satisfied now!" therefore there could be no doubt that things had been settled, but the baron would have preferred to have more definite information.

The shadows were growing longer and longer, the wine ran freely in the corner between the cottage and the laurel-bushes, and inspired the musicians of Villascura to play with still more diabolical vigour. In front of the band, on the grass, the gentlefolk were dancing; the peasants were dancing too, but in the background. The indefatigable Perlotti, bathed in perspiration, wanted, at all hazards, to make Elena dance with him, and made her a thousand ridiculous speeches. Elena, annoyed, tried to free herself from him with a sharp speech, when her mother interposed.

"Leave her with me a little," she said. "I lose her to-night."

Mother and daughter moved away together along a little path that ran by the side of a stream between the agent's cottage and the fields.

When other people were present, the countess was all tenderness towards her daughter, although the latter replied but coldly to her advances; when they were alone there was much reserve between them, the countess not having any ideas, inclinations, or feelings in common with Elena, knowing that the latter was her superior both morally and intellectually, and conscious of certain previous gallantries which, although the countess freely forgave them in herself, she knew would be very differently regarded by her puritanical daughter. She complained to Elena that she could not spend these last few hours alone, quite alone, with her; but how was it possible with a house full of guests, on such a day? She would make up for it in October. She begged Elena to come back quickly, and not to allow herself to be carried off into Sicily; and she added that if they were to pass the summer by the sea, it would not be prudent to go to Naples. If her husband absolutely declined to come to Venice, there were Leghorn, Genoa, many other places more suitable than Naples. Or why not Dieppe or Ostend? But if they did not go to the sea, she thought they could not do better than try Aix. Di Santa Giulia had talked of Aix at first, if only he could raise the money. Now Elena could remind him of what he had said, and keep him to his word. And when she went to Aix, or wherever it might be, she must take a maid with her, she must insist upon that. Now he could not pretend that economy was necessary.

"By-the-bye," said the countess at this point, "how did you succeed in converting your uncle, and what did you settle?"

"You know quite well," answered Elena, "what my husband wanted."

"Yes, he wanted at least fifteen thousand lire, which, after all, would not ruin one, and I can't help thinking that your uncle might have made less fuss about giving it."

"What did my husband once say to you, mamma? Did he not say that if he failed to get this money he would imprison me at Cefalù for ever and a day?"

"The wretch!" exclaimed the countess. "Yes, he did!"

"Well, now it is settled that I shall not go to Cefalù unless I choose."

"Thank God for that; but—"

A shiver ran through Elena, and shook her whole body.

"What is the matter," exclaimed her mother, "what has happened?"

In a moment Elena regained her self-control.

"Nothing," she answered; "really nothing."

The countess, genuinely uneasy, insisted, but without avail. At this moment, Malcanton came up to ask whether, during the religious functions, the band might rest in the house instead of going to play in the church, as the priests had requested. Elena left the two to consider this weighty matter, and wended her way to the stables, to see whether her luggage had been taken in the cart, and whether everything were ready for their start; but as her husband chanced to come out of the house at that moment calling to a servant, "Is the baroness there?" Elena turned back. Now she wanted to avoid her mother, who, having got rid of Malcanton, was coming in search of her. She went in-doors, and took refuge with Count Lao. As she knocked at his door, she remembered that stormy evening when the rain had clouded every window, and she had knocked at the same door with a presentiment of a new and unknown danger. Now the quiet evening light lay on the floor; the church-bells were ringing in the clear sky; merry voices floated through the open windows from the garden; all seemed to say, "Go away thou of the sad thoughts."

A lamp was already burning in Count Lao's room, and he was writing.

"Is it you?" he said. "What time is it?"

"About nine, uncle."

"So you still have an hour? Excuse me if I go on writing this letter, which it is important for me to finish."

Elena sat in silence near the window. A thread of light filtered through the trees from the tower of the church. Other lights were moving about the garden, and the chattering increased momentarily. She could hear Doctor Grigiolo's voice as he screamed out his directions for the illuminations.

A servant came in search of Elena. The countess wanted her at once. She was waiting for her daughter just outside the house near the dark billiard-room. Countess Tarquinia did not pretend to be a saint, but she was convinced that her heart was good, and she wished to prove it to Elena. She implored her to speak, to confide in her if she had anything on her mind.

"I have not your virtues," she said with humility, "nor your talents; but I am your mother after all."

Elena was moved, and embraced her with more affection than she had exhibited towards her for a long time.

"It was nothing," said she; "but when you said 'thank God!' a stupid thought passed through my mind—a fear lest I should never come back here, and I shivered—that was all."

Her mother kissed her, and scolded her for giving way to such foolish thoughts. In her heart of hearts she was not at all comforted, for she knew that Elena was most unlikely to give way to empty dreams.

Their conversation was interrupted by the Perlottis, who came out of their room in travelling costume.

"It is early," said the countess.

"Yes, dear; I know we have nearly an hour," answered her friend; "but Grigiolo begged us to miss as little as possible of the illuminations!"

They went out together. Festoons of coloured lamps hung from tree to tree, and from the windows of the house to those of the cottage. There they stopped, but they encircled the dead cypress nearly to the top, and in the darkness it rose up like an obelisk of fire. The people cheered and clapped their hands. Then the band struck up, and marched through the trees and round the grounds, and took up its position on the lawn. A rocket cleaved the darkness from the far side of the field; then another and another; stars of every colour fell from the sky. The crowd ran from all parts of the ground. The baron, who had been hunting high and low for his wife, cursing between his teeth, found her at last, with her mother and the Perlottis, on the steps of the porch facing the field.

"Elena," said he, "I want you a moment."

He called her indoors near the billiard-table. He was furious at not having yet been able to speak to her.

The money! Had she got it? Had she a letter, or a promise by word of mouth, perhaps? Had she allowed herself to be put off with that?

Elena replied contemptuously that he had said himself that he would be satisfied with a promise, and that her uncle's word was as good as his bond, or his gold either. Then she desired him to have the horses put to the carriage, and turned back to her mother and the Perlottis, who were calling her.

After the rocket, a balloon went up filled with crackers and squibs, that fizzed and exploded in the air.

"Long live Grigiolo!" screamed Perlotti.

The baron, instead of ordering the carriage, went up to Count Lao's room. He met him coming downstairs with a letter in his hand, and said that he was come to say good-bye, and to thank him.

"There is no need," said the count shortly.

"I am sorry," continued Di Santa Giulia, "that, owing to the payment of this interest, I should be obliged—"

"What payment of interest?"

Lao scratched his head as if trying to remember something.

"Well," exclaimed the baron, losing his temper, "Elena must have told you of the reasons which oblige me—" he concluded the sentence by an expressive noise in his throat.

The count was silent, and looked hard at him; then he said,—

"I know; all right."

He departed, leaving the baron not overpleased.

"What the deuce has happened to all these people to-day?" said the latter to himself, as he went to order the carriage.

Count Lao, wrapped in his great-coat, with its cape well buttoned, and collar turned up, joined the group in which his niece was standing, on the south side of the billiard-room. Two minutes later Doctor Grigiolo rushed up, quite out of breath, watch in hand.

"Oh, Baroness Elena, it is only just nine o'clock, and you are already having the horses put to the carriage; for pity's sake, baroness, don't go yet; the most beautiful show of all is just coming!"

"Let us be off," said the baron, coming up at the moment. "The best of all is not to miss the train; I must be in Rome to-morrow evening."

"Ten minutes, only ten minutes more!" implored Grigiolo.

"Five!" roared the baron.

A rocket went up, and at the same moment there burst out Bengal lights which illuminated the whole villa and grounds, the tower of the church at Villascura, and even the woods of Passo Grande. The air resounded with exclamations of applause. Then other white lights blazed over the fields to the right and left, throwing a silvery light over the gravel and the grass, and over the black croud of spectators. The band played the chorus from "Nebuchadnezzar." Elena, the countess, Lao, and the baron stood together in a group on the thorns of hidden uneasiness.

"I am sorry that we have had to hurry it all so much," said Grigiolo, turning round, humble in his glory.

The carriage was announced.

"Come along," growled the baron.

Lao squeezed his niece's hand, and returned to the house.

Notwithstanding the brilliancy of the illuminations, it was not possible to see much near the carriage, drawn up as it was between the stables and the thick magnolias which grew on that side of the garden. Peasants, servants, boys, all crowded round the horses. There was a moment of confusion. Signora Perlotti could not find her travelling-bag, and feared it had fallen under the wheels.

"I will light a Bengal fire!" exclaimed Grigiolo.

"Please don't," begged Elena, her voice full of terror, and seizing his arm.

Then came the kisses and the good-byes. Elena's old nurse, now the wife of the bailiff, sobbed aloud. All were in their places and ready to start except Signora Perlotti, who could not find her bag. At last it was found to have been sent on with Elena's luggage, which had started an hour previously.

"Let us be off," said the baron. "Good-bye, gentlemen!"

The horses started; the gravel creaked under the heavy wheels. As they drove under the portico, Perlotti waved his cap, and his wife her handkerchief; the wheels and the iron hoofs of the horses clanged for an instant over the pavement; and then all at once the sound died away, and was lost in the distance.

But Grigiolo and one of his assistants ran up to the colossal fir-tree that, from the plateau above the road, extends its black fringes over the country. As the carriage passed underneath it, by the side of the Rovese, a white Bengal light, like a ray of sunshine in the darkness, discovered to Elena the old tree leaning over the slope of the hill.

"Safe journey!" shouted Grigiolo at the top of his voice.

Elena leaned back in the carriage, as though she would carry away in her heart that last sight.

"That fellow is mad," said the baron.

Everything became dark again, and nothing was heard save the roaring of the Rovese torrent and the measured trot of the horses. The Perlottis began by making an attempt at conversation, but, finding that they could awake no response, they both quickly fell asleep. It is a good three hours' drive from Passo di Rovese to the town at which the Di Santa Giulias were to take the train for Rome.

The baron neither spoke nor slept. Wrapped in a shawl of his wife's, he grumbled curses between his teeth at the abominable dampness of the night, and at the rheumatic horses of the countess. Elena, leaning as far back as possible in one corner of the carriage, was silent, and kept her eyes fixed upon the road.

At the station the Perlottis found their bag, and then insisted upon remaining with Elena, so that they might write to her mother the next day that they had actually seen her into the train. While Di Santa Giulia was looking after the luggage, the servant, who had come from the house with them, gave Elena a letter from Count Lao.

"Is it for the post?" she inquired.

On looking at it, however, she saw that it was addressed to herself, and put it into her pocket, saying only, "Very good."

After a quarter of an hour, the train arrived full of people. Di Santa Giulia made such a noisy use of his titles, parliamentary and otherwise, that an extra first-class carriage was attached to the train, so that the honourable senator and his wife might travel alone.

"At last," said he, throwing himself at full length upon the cushions, with his knees in the air, and his hands under his head, "at last we have got rid of those bores! Now tell me all about the money. What did you settle?"

"I settled it according to your wish."

"Fifteen?"

This question was answered by the whistle of the engine as the train moved out of the station.

"Fifteen?" repeated he..

Elena hesitated a moment, keeping her head out of the window, until all the lights and the offices of the station had disappeared from sight.

"No," she said, drawing in her head; "I chose the other course."

"What do you mean?" exclaimed the baron, sitting bolt upright and facing his wife. "The other course?"

"You told me," answered Elena, raising her voice so as to be heard above the noise of the train, now rushing at full speed, "that unless you got the money you would send me into Sicily, and that I should hear no more of either Venice or Rome. You told me distinctly that I should put the case thus before Uncle Lao: 'Either the money or Cefalù.' Well, as it depended upon myself, I thought that I had a perfect right to decide, and I have chosen Cefalù."

During this speech a change had come over the baron's face. At the last words he seized her knees, leaning forwards to her.

"So," he said, through his clenched teeth, "you mean me to understand that you said nothing at all about the money?"

Elena neither spoke nor moved.

"Did you not speak?" he repeated violently, squeezing and shaking her knees.

"No, certainly I did not speak," she replied.

The baron thought she was telling a lie, and that she, her uncle, and her mother had all combined to make a fool of him; in a frenzy of rage he lifted his hand.

"Courage," she murmured quietly, without flinching.

He did not dare to strike her.

"Ah!" he said, "you did not speak?"

The train at this moment entered a tunnel. Elena saw her husband gesticulating furiously; she heard him screaming, but without being able to catch what he said. She did distinguish, however, the word "hypocrite." Her eyes flashed. She pointed at her husband, in answer, with the forefinger of her right hand.

"I?" screamed the man.

He was silent, and so was Elena, until the train left the tunnel, and the noise became less in consequence.

"What do you want the money for?" she asked.

He answered brutally that he wanted it for his own purposes. It was not true; he wanted it in order to enable him to meet formidable engagements, but he wished to insult her. He added that she had been the first to play the hypocrite, for she had deceived him at the altar with her false "I will," which she did not mean.

Elena's heart ached at this. It was true, quite true; she recognised her own fault, the selfishness of the resolution she had made to quit the paternal roof. She disdained to answer that; even if she did not believe in God, she would die sooner than belie her "I will," however much she might grieve for it. She must suffer the penalty alone, in silence, until the end.

Her husband asked if she thought that he had threatened Cefalù as a joke.

"I hope not," she replied.

"I hope," retorted the baron with a sneer, "I hope those two other people will laugh at me now," he added, "but may God crush me if ever I look upon their faces again, or if ever I receive from them a drop of water, even though I die of thirst."

To Elena's protestations that her relations knew nothing about it, he made no reply, and, huddling himself up in the opposite corner of the carriage, he relapsed into silence.

They watched each other, each from his own corner --he surly, she grave—in the cold and darkness which blew in at the windows, and made the lamps flicker as though they were afraid of it. Suddenly Elena remembered her uncle's letter, and read it secretly. Count Lao said, in very few words, that he did not altogether believe what she had told him, and, fearing some sentimental foolishness, he had sent to the National Bank at Rome for her the sum of fifteen thousand lire, that she might repay him in October, if she really did not need it. Elena replaced the letter in her pocket, and looked out of the window.

Little by little the noise of the train became to her like the continual beating of the waves, then it seemed to be like a tumult, with the shouts of many people; the dark country looked to her like a sea, and the fixed eyes of three distant planets seemed to call her to themselves, as if they knew her secret thought: "For him, for his sake, so as not to sadden his life!" The rare stoppages of the train interrupted these thoughts. Travellers got in and out unnoticed by her. Towards daybreak the train passed, with a great noise, over a bridge with high sides of iron lattice-work, through which were visible a large sheet of water, and the reflection of the waning stars. Someone said, in a low voice,—

"The river Po."

Elena roused herself from her thoughts; she was sorry to see the first glimmer of dawn, and she closed her eyes again to the vanishing bank of the river, and revived in her passionate imagination the words engraved upon the poor stone hidden far away on the horizon in the gardens of the Villa Cortis: "In winter and in summer—from near and from far—as long as I live, and beyond that again."

CHAPTER VI.

SIGNORA FIAMMA.

Cortis arrived late in the evening at Lugano, and went to the modest *Pension du Panorama*, one of the houses which dignify with the name of Paradise that edge of the lake in the curved hollow far from the town, and from behind which rise the steep slopes of San Salvatore. He left his inn immediately, and took the path that led upwards to Pazzallo. His mother's friend, Signora Leonora Fiamma, had written to him that they lived in a little house between Paradise and Pazzallo, on the left-hand side of the road, somewhat below a tavern, almost hidden under the shade of a thickly-wooded slope. He was to ring a bell which he would find in the red railings between two mulberry trees.

Cortis found and rang the bell. He had announced his coming by telegraph, so that he knew he would be expected.

A maid servant came to the gate.

"Is Signora Fiamma living here?" he asked.

"Yes, sir."

"How is the other lady?"

The maid hesitated for a moment.

"Are you," she inquired, "the gentleman who sent a telegram?"

"Yes."

"Good. The lady is much the same as she was.'

"Ill?"

"The same."

"Have the goodness to answer me," said Cortis sharply. "Is she ill or not?"

"My mistress will tell you," she replied impertinently, as she opened, with very bad grace, the door of a little drawing-room on the ground floor.

"Here is that gentleman," she announced, looking towards the opposite corner of the room.

Cortis entered. High up in the corner he saw a lamp; under the lamp, and in the shade of a large easy-chair, he saw some shining black hair, and the face of a woman which in that light looked faded and tired.

"Signora Fiamma?" he said.

The glossy head made an affirmative motion, and after a pause, a voice, neither youthful nor sweet, but rather languid and sad, said gently,—

"And you are Signor Cortis?"

The reception and the voice displeased Cortis, who did not return a direct answer.

"And your friend," he asked, "how is she?"

"Still in the same sad state," was the answer. "Pray sit down. It will be impossible for you to see her this evening, as the doctor does not think it would be safe. I must apologise to you," she went on, "if my reception of you seems cold, and if I do not express all the gratitude that I ought to feel, and that I do feel, for you; but I myself am far from well."

Signora Fiamma pronounced these last words as if with her last breath, and rested her head on the back of her chair. As the lamp light fell upon her, it displayed a forehead deeply marked with wrinkles, and a large and tragical nose. Her eyes looked passionate and untrustworthy.

She heaved a sigh so deep that it was almost a groan; and turned her head, without raising it from the cushion, towards Cortis.

"You see," she said, "I can do no more."

"Listen to me," said Cortis; "in no case did I wish to see your friend this evening, unless it were of vital importance that I should. You must forgive me, signora, if I speak to you very frankly, as is my custom. I have always believed my mother was dead. You tell me she is living."

"You want proofs?" sighed Signora Leonora. "Does not your heart tell you," she continued, in a dramatic voice, "that under this roof—"

"Please leave my heart out of the question, signora," broke in Cortis. "I shall be grateful if you will show me the proofs of what you have stated."

"It will be a great blow to Signora Cortis," she murmured, raising her eyes to heaven, "but it is just, it is only just! We were prepared for this! Now I will show you my friend's papers."

She wiped her eyes several times with a scented pocket-handkerchief, which she afterwards gazed at as though to assure herself that she had not shed tears of blood. She begged Cortis to ring the bell, ordered a candle to be brought, and raised herself with an evident effort. She was tall and thin, a long, yellowish neck showed above her collar of black tulle; her large black eyes were surrounded by a yellowish rim. She wore a very well-made black gown, with a long train, and her walk was rather like that of Lady Macbeth when she appears upon the stage asleep, bearing the light in her hand.

As soon as she had gone, Cortis made a hurried examination of the room; he noticed two oil pictures, a Magdalen and a Saint Cecilia, evidently copies, the photographs of an old lady and of an old man covered with decorations, and with an inscription underneath in German; a few ascetic books, a small basket crammed with visiting-cards, and an album of water-colour sketches, which bore on its first page the name of Signora Leonora Fiamma, artist in ordinary to H.R.H. the Grand-

Duke Leopold of ——. A dusty harp stood in one corner.

The signora returned in a few minutes, placed the candle and a small portfolio on a little oval table which stood near her arm-chair, and told Cortis that her friend wanted her at that moment, but that he was at liberty to open the portfolio and see for himself. She would come back later.

Cortis, when he was alone, had to exercise all his self-command, for, before opening the portfolio, he buried his face in his hands, and drove away, with a violent shake of his head, every thought of weakness that might disturb his judgment. When he uncovered his face he was grave, but calm.

The first paper that he lighted upon was a letter from a Doctor P——, an old friend of his father. It appeared from this letter that in 1857, more than a year after she had quitted her husband's roof, Signora Cortis had written to him imploring his forgiveness. Doctor P—— had been charged to answer her appeal, and had been told to say that there was no chance of it being granted; and he had added, on his own account, to this bitter message, a long and friendly letter of encouragement, good advice, and vague hopes for the future. This doctor had been a colleague of the elder Cortis in the Crimean war, while the signora was allowing herself to be led astray at Alessandria. On his return, her husband discovered her infidelity, and she had then accused an artillery officer, who had died a few days previously. P—— gave her to understand that her husband did not much believe this story of the officer, and that this doubt of her truth was doing her still greater injury in his mind.

While Cortis was reading, groans and sobs resounded above his head in the silent house. He seized the candle to go and see whence they came, but he heard a step, a quiet voice, and all was silent again. He put down the candle, and finished his reading in a very agitated frame of mind.

He next opened a little gold locket, and found therein the portraits of his maternal grandparents, Charles and Magdalen Zarutti di Cividale. As a child, he had twice passed the autumn with them at Cividale. There was his grandfather, that dear old man who used to come to Alessandria to fetch him away in September, and bring him back at the end of October. There he was, smiling! And his grandmother too, poor old lady, how happy she looked! They died of broken hearts within a year of each other, and now, as they looked at him, they seemed to say, "Dear boy, we are your grandparents!" Cortis looked no further, but hurried out of the room in search of the signora. He called, opened a door that he came upon by chance, and found himself in a studio, filled with easels and chairs, and reeking of paint and tobacco. On a table lay a copy of *Nana*, between a bottle and a pile of cigars. A moment later the maid-servant appeared, breathless.

"What do you want?" she asked crossly; "what are you looking for?"

"That Signora Fiamma," answered Cortis; "go upstairs and tell her to come down."

His voice and manner expressed disgust rather than good-will towards "that Signora Fiamma."

The woman pushed past him, and hastily shut the door of the studio.

"I cannot at this moment," she said.

"Very well; then I will go myself," declared Cortis.

"Oh, for mercy's sake, don't. It is strictly forbidden."

Cortis took one of his cards out of his pocket, scribbled a few words on it in haste, and then tore it up.

"Go," he said, "tell her that I am waiting," and he returned to the drawing-room.

The maid reappeared presently with these words written by Signora Fiamma,—

"Your mother is so upset at this moment that it is impossible for me to come down to you. Come to-morrow morning at eight. Take the portfolio away with you."

"Good God!" exclaimed Cortis, "but may I not even be told how this other lady is, or what she is, suffering from? Why can I not see her this evening? When will the doctor come? Who is the doctor? Do you not know that I must see him? Come, speak, say something! Don't you belong to the house? Are you dumb? Can't you answer? Speak, I tell you!"

"Hush," said the woman, "her illness is all nerves—a woman's illness; I don't believe there is any danger. But if she has said that she cannot see you this evening, it's no use to wait. Come to-morrow."

"But what is this doctor's name? Where does he live?"

The servant named a certain doctor who, she said, lived outside Lugano, and who would probably not come again before the following evening.

Cortis took the portfolio.

"You will say to your mistress," he began— "but, by the way, who is your mistress?"

"What do you mean by who is she?"

"Is she Signora Fiamma, or the other?"

"Oh, Signora Fiamma."

"And the other? How comes it that they live together?"

"I don't know. I have only been here two months: I think they have always been together."

"How long have they lived in Lugano?"

"Three or four months."

"And how long has this other lady been ill?"

"She is neve well. She has always been poorly ever since I came."

Cortis could get nothing more out of the maid.

"Well, then," he continued, "tell your mistress that I should have much liked to see her again this evening, that I will bring back her papers to-morrow."

The servant took a light, and accompanied him as far as the garden gate.

"My mistress wished me to ask you where you are staying?"

"At the '*Panorama.*'"

She answered by a contemptuous grimace that was full of eloquence, and closed the gate.

Cortis walked hastily away, torn by his feelings, which could only find vent in active exercise. What a repulsive face that artist of the Grand Duke had! What a perfume of lies there was in that house, and what a stench underlay it!

And his mother—his mother! The anxious doubts that had been raised by the rigmarole written to him by Signora Fiamma rose again in his mind more painfully than ever. How could she be the friend of such a woman! Nevertheless, Doctor P—— had evidently some esteem and friendly feeling for her when he wrote to her. And she, at least at that time, had wept, and prayed, and suffered. There was still hope for her! But how could she have deceived such a man as his father?

When these two opposite opinions clashed in his mind, Cortis stopped short, and spoke aloud in the darkness; then, when he had vented his feelings, he looked upon the lights of Lugano, the austere, dumb passion of the mountains which raised their black masses against the sky, and still further in the background, the mysterious lake, of which he could see neither the beginning nor the end. His recollections of Lugano were of bright sunshine amongst the hills and sparkling water; but it was very different now. That dolomite peak, far away to the east, menacing heaven with its lofty head, seemed new to him.

He had not seen that previously. Before going back to his inn, he walked along the lake into the town. Everything was deserted. The silent steamboats lay at anchor in front of the dark houses. A few foreigners were still talking and smoking on the terrace of the *Washington Hotel*, where Cortis had stayed with his father in the September of 1868. He stepped on to the little steamboat pier, and watched the grey, motionless lake, and the lofty ghost of San Salvatore. He had arrived there thirteen years before with a crowd of pleasure-seeking people; the day had been very bright and very windy. He ran away, and returned exhausted, as he hoped he would, to his hotel.

That night, in his few snatches of sleep, he dreamed that Elena led his mother to him by the hand, saying, "Comfort her!" His mother was small and fair, with blue eyes; she did not speak—she only wept.

He rose a little before six, and went out into the hotel garden, where an old man was watering the flowers. The sky was clear; on the lake and mountain lay the oblique lights and long shadows of early morning, and far away to the east the dolomite peak, now bathed in blue mist, no longer looked threatening. Cortis asked the old gardener if he could tell him anything of two ladies, who had lived in a villa near Pazzallo for some few months? He did not know them; he had known one lady who used to paint, and who lived somewhere in that direction. She came to luncheon several times at the *Panorama*, but now the proprietor would not let her come any more, as he had not been paid, after the first two or three visits. More than this Cortis could not discover. He felt that he could wait no longer, and took the road up the hill, determined to get some information before eight o'clock. He met some peasants coming down into the town with vegetables and fruit, and inquired of them; but they could tell him nothing. He had reached the red railings, when he saw a milk-woman coming out of the gate. He stopped her, and asked for a glass of milk. The woman, smiling, asked if he were going up San Salvatore. Cortis drank, and made no reply.

"Listen,' said he; "is it you who generally brings the milk to this house?"

"Always."

"So of course you know the ladies who live here?"

"To be sure."

"What are their names?"

"Why, the servant is Miss Barbara, and the mistress has a name that I have never been properly able to master."

"And the other lady?"

"Which one?"

"The other, the friend of the mistress of the house?"

"My good sir," said the woman in surprise, "I don't know her at all."

"But they live together!"

"Indeed not, sir; there is only one lady here."

"What do you mean?" he asked. "Don't you know that there is a sick lady here?"

"That there painter lady is always queer, but there is no other lady in the house, unless she arrived yesterday. The day before yesterday I was working in the garden the whole day."

The woman's face was honest and open, and her words rung like truth.

"Thank you," said Cortis with a pale face, "that will do."

He rang the bell. The door of the drawing-room was opened slightly and then shut again. No one appeared.

Cortis rang a second and a third time, always more loudly, and always without result.

A peasant who passed stopped to look on.

"You may pull that bell all day," he said, "if they

don't choose to answer. That's what always happens with these here swindlers."

"Do you know these people?" inquired Cortis.

The peasant replied that he knew the artist lady very well indeed. She lived alone, looked like a witch, and paid nobody.

Cortis rang for the fourth time. At last the maid appeared.

"It is only seven o'clock," said she, "we were all in bed."

He entered without speaking, but gave her such a look that she turned pale, and was silent.

"Your mistress?" he said, "where is your mistress? Why do you look at me like that? Why don't you answer me? Is she in bed? I must speak to her. Come here," he exclaimed, as the woman was retreating, "how is the other lady?"

The servant drooped her eyes and began,—

"It is not my fault—"

"Let me in," said Cortis.

"It is not my fault," she continued. "I only say what I am told."

Cortis ordered her to be silent, and to lead the way.

As they reached the drawing-room, the woman said in a whisper,—

"It is three months since I have had a penny of my wages."

"In that case you tell lies for your own pleasure," said Cortis. "Your mistress is up; she is not in bed."

Some one could be heard moving about overhead. At the same moment a bell rang.

"I am wanted," said the servant, going towards the door.

Cortis stopped her.

"One minute," he said. "Is her real name Fiamma or not?"

Barbara looked at him open-mouthed.

"Why? Didn't you understand? No, no! that's a name that the lady invented for herself. She is really your mamma!"

And she turned to go upstairs.

"I will go," said he; "where is the staircase?"

He found it at the end of a short passage, where a petroleum lamp was burning before various images of saints and madonnas of every kind and colour. He had reached the last step, when a door in front of him was thrown open, and Signora Fiamma, dishevelled and untidy, appeared on the landing with a cry.

"Ah! I see!" she exclaimed, "your heart has told you!"

She clasped her hands, and would have thrown herself on her knees, but Cortis seized her by the arm, dragged her into the room, and shut the door behind him. She fought and struggled to go down upon her knees, pushing her arm against the back of her son, jerking herself backwards, and shaking her head violently. At length she fell exhausted into the arm-chair towards which Cortis pushed her.

"I lied to you," she said panting, and out of breath, "I have deceived you, I had not courage to tell you all at once; I wanted to see you, to hear you for one hour in peace."

Cortis, leaning over her, interrupted her first words, placed his hand over her eyes, kissed her, as though impelled to do so, and quickly withdrew himself from the arms which she had twined round his neck. She remained with her hands in the air, stupefied with joy.

"Daniele!" she said.

She no longer saw him standing in front of her, but she heard his voice from behind her chair; his manly voice broken with sorrow.

"Forgive me; I kissed my mother and did not wish you to see me."

Signora Fiamma was silent for a moment, and then, in a low, complaining voice, she answered,—

"I don't know what you mean."

Cortis sighed and made no reply. Some minutes passed.

"Here is your portfolio," he said at last, drily.

"Oh, Daniele, Daniele!" groaned the signora, "do not speak to me like that!" and she burst into tears. "I only half deceived you," she went on; "I am suffering so much. I have only a short time to live, do you know, Daniele? Had I not known that, I should never have dared to write to you. God is merciful. He has purified me with an accumulation of indescribable troubles and sorrows. Now I can bear no more, I can bear no more. You have been good enough to come to me; search in your heart for one word, after hearing which I may die happy."

"But, don't you see," broke in Cortis, "don't you understand that I do not—"

That I do not believe you, he was going to have said. The signora waited, pale and staring, for the words which were not pronounced. Her voice died on her half-open lips. Daniele took a chair, and, moving it close to his mother, planted it on the ground with such force as almost to break its legs.

"Tell me everything," he said, throwing himself heavily into it. "Everything, from that day till this. You cannot!" he cried, with sparkling eyes, as his mother hesitated.

"I can, indeed I can," said the signora, with a theatrical gesture. "It will be painful, but I can do it. It is my duty, and I will speak."

Cortis seemed in that moment to recognise his mother better than he had done by the papers in the portfolio, better than by the dim memory that had remained to him from his childhood. He fancied that there was some electricity in both their veins, although his mother used hers only for theatrical experiments, while he reserved his for real thunder and lightning.

She told a long, rambling, sentimental story, bathing her worn-out sentences with tears, in hopes of making them seem fresh.

Her purification had begun on the very day of her well-deserved punishment. Grief, good resolutions, hope—yes, even hope itself—had never abandoned her thenceforth. On leaving her husband's roof, she had implored the compassion of some kind relations, who had taken her to their house. But her life with them had been made too luxurious by their tenderness and affection ; it was no expiation ! On that account, she had quitted the dear creatures, to whom she hoped God would show mercy, as they had shown it to her ! Signora Cortis laid great stress upon this detail, being afraid of a certain calumnious report, according to which the "dear creatures" had driven her, after three months' trial, away from their tenderness and affection. Then God had whispered to her, "You can paint," and she had turned to art, and said, "Save me !"

She had betaken herself to Rome, in order to copy in the galleries for money. While there, the Grand Duchess of —— had appointed her to be her painter-in-ordinary. Unkind people might have said the *Grand Duke*—she said the *Grand Duchess.* Of the Grand Duke, she said only that he had died a few years later, and she added that his afflicted widow had lost her love of art, and no longer desired painters-in-ordinary at the court. She had been speaking for an hour when she reached this point. It may have been from fatigue and excitement, or it may have been that the latter part of her story was more difficult to tell than the former, but it is certain that she now began to lose her self-control, and to interrupt her narrative with sighs and groans. Long, long years of suffering passed confusedly before the eyes of Cortis, who sat silent and frowning. He heard all the wails, he saw all the fatigues and the privations of her wandering life, he understood all the ills that no doctor had ever been able to comprehend, and which arose therefrom.

She had come to Lugano from Düsseldorf a few months previously, because her doctors had recommended her to return to the Italian climate. Her sufferings, allayed for a time, had reasserted themselves with renewed force. Work had become almost impossible to her. And then, feeling herself less able to cope with the wretchedness that had lasted more than five-and-twenty years, and seeing that her last day would dawn in gloom and misery, she asked God whether the bitter cup were not yet emptied, and whether she might see her son again before her death. God had given her permission to write, but not the courage. Not daring to say, "I am your mother," fearing to be disbelieved, or worse, she had written to him as a friend of her own, under her artistic pseudonym; that was an inviolate name, indeed it was!

She paused and wept. Cortis looked rather black than sympathetic.

"Help?" he said. "Never? From my father, I mean?"

"No, never anything. Indeed I had not!"

Cortis frowned. She had said "Indeed I had not" in a tone which seemed as if she would imply a reproach, but without quite daring to do so.

"What do you mean?" he asked. "That he should have helped you?"

"Oh, no, no," said the signora, sobbing.

"My father had already done much for you," continued Cortis. "When you left his house he restored to you your whole private fortune. Is not that so?"

"It was very little," she said.

A flush rose to Cortis's cheek. He saw and felt over

him the eye of his father; not severe, but vigilant; and he was now more conscious than ever of all the sorrow, all the trouble that that just and firm man had intended to conceal from him.

"My father was generous to you," he said. "Besides, there are several things in your story that I find difficult to explain."

She was seized with a violent fit of convulsions, and from them passed into a condition of such exhaustion that she could not either speak nor hear. Cortis called Barbara, and, with austere face and in silence, assisted her to do what was necessary for his mother.

CHAPTER VII.

READY!

Signora Cortis did not recover during the whole day, in spite of the assistance of her homœopathic medicine-chest, and of several glasses of rum, the most efficacious, according to her, of all medicines. Late in the evening she fell asleep. Then Daniele, who had barely found time to dine and write a note to Elena, went down to Lugano. Before leaving the house he made Barbara open the studio for him; neither the book, the bottle, nor the cigars were there.

"Does any one come to see her?" asked Cortis.

"Next to nobody," answered the maid. "Sometimes a Russian lady comes."

"Who is she?"

"I think she is a lady from the theatre. But she is as old as my mistress. She had written her name in a book. It was lying here yesterday, but I don't see it now. My mistress must have taken it away last night."

Cortis looked at a study of Monte Rosa, from Pazzallo, and at the portrait of a man, the only pictures which were begun. The man was a local doctor, who, after the first few visits and sittings, had not reappeared.

"Did you know," asked Cortis, as he left the studio, "that the signora had written to me?"

"Yes, sir," answered the servant, in a low voice, and with an air of mystery. "She told me the other day that she had done so, when your telegram arrived. She told me so many things, and cried. You should have seen how she cried."

"What did she tell you?"

"I can't remember. So many things. That she had not been able to live with her poor husband, and that she had a son, a gentleman, to use her own words, and that this son was coming to join her, and that she did not wish to be known all at once, and that she had written so and so. And then she told me that if you came and asked after the lady who was ill, I was not to look surprised, and to say that she was still the same."

"And what was that you told me this morning? That you don't get your wages?"

"Certainly. It is three months since I have had a penny."

"And what does the signora say?"

"That at present she has no money, but that she expects some soon. She tells the same tale to everybody."

"What do you mean by 'to everybody'?"

"Ah, sir, if things go on as they are at present, I shall run away. Every moment of the day there is some one here, first one and then another, asking to be paid; either the landlord, or the butcher, or the pork butcher, or the chemist. And there is no money for them; and then, you see, they are mostly uneducated people, and they speak out their minds about it. I tell you this because I think, in some cases, it is better—"

Barbara broke off at this point in order to follow Cortis with a light. He had turned his back upon her, caring little about her conclusions.

The following morning he returned to the house and found his mother up and dressed. He said no more about the past; he only wished to know how she had got knowledge of his address at Villascura. She mentioned no names, but told him that she had always had the most exact information of the doings of her dearly loved son, and that her thoughts and her heart had always followed him. She spoke to him about Countess Tarquinia and Villascura. She knew that his house was large and ill-kept, and she had often thought how lonely her poor Daniele must be there. Cortis encouraged her to talk of the present, and of her own necessities, and she recounted a whole iliad of troubles. But what were her privations compared to the anguish of solitude? It was just, nay, it was pleasant, that suffering should come to any one who, like herself, had committed a fault, a single fault; a fault —if all were known! if the whole story could be told!— that was, so to speak, involuntary; but to suffer alone, cut off from all affection or pity, no, that was unendurable; she could bear that no longer!

At this point she burst into a flood of tears. Cortis was silent.

"Last night—I had—a dream!" said the signora, struggling with her sobs.

Cortis did not utter.

"It was too beautiful," she murmured, half closing her eyes, and dangling an arm over the side of her chair. "Too beautiful!"

She slowly shook her head, which was leaning over towards her left shoulder, and sighed again, "too beautiful."

Cortis did not display the slightest desire to know what it was.

"There is a kind of misery which ought not to come near you," he said. "I will see to it."

"Thank you," said the signora, "thank you."

She opened her mouth as if to continue speaking, but apparently she suddenly changed her mind.

"I pray God," she said, after a short silence, "that He will grant me the favour of being as little trouble to you as possible. It was He who inspired me to settle at Lugano. I have here found the air that will most rapidly kill me."

Daniele in vain repeated to her that she might search from the Alps to the sea without finding a climate more suited to the state of her nerves. She reiterated each time with more contrition and more resignation the same tragic refrain.

If the signora fondly dreamed that, after so many vicissitudes of storm and fine weather, she was going to brighten up her miserable afternoon with a ray of sunshine, and that her sun would finally set in dignity and peace in the drawing-room of Cortis's house, she was very much mistaken; and it was pitiful to see her beating again and again, stealthily, with vulgar artifice, at a door that remained deaf and dumb.

Later on they went down into the little drawing-room, and talked business. Daniele wished to discover the amount of his mother's debts, and it was by no means easy to do, as, according to her, not a quarter of the things had ever come into her house which the lying shopkeepers had written down on their bills. Fortunately for the latter, Barbara had a better memory, and, after a long wrangle over every item and every figure between mistress and maid, Daniele arrived at a conclusion not far from correct.

When he was again alone with his mother, he told her that he meant to leave the next morning, and that in a few days' time he would send her money, and tell her in what manner he would provide for her maintenance in the future. The signora asked when she would see him again, but Daniele could not answer this question. It depended on so many things, upon the result of his election, and upon other private affairs. Then she began to say, weeping again, that he had every reason for not caring about her, that she would come into his house as a servant, a scullery-maid, but that she knew she was unworthy to be under the same roof as he: oh, yes, indeed she was unworthy.

"I do not think," he said, "that such an arrangement would suit either you or me."

His mother said nothing for a minute, and then, raising her handkerchief to her streaming eyes, she murmured,—

"I offer this sacrifice to the blessed Virgin."

Cortis, fuming with anger, went to the window of the room to get some fresh air. Suddenly a wailing voice said in his ear,—

"Have I offended you?"

He pretended not to hear. Through the shining mulberry trees he was looking at the garden gate, the white road bathed in sunlight, and beyond, the parapet, the calm, deep lake, and the purple mountains of Val Colla. That pure air, that glimpse of innocent life, were a restorative to him. At that moment the train from Milan passed, thundering and whistling under the heights of San Salvatore.

Cortis looked at the clock, and asked his mother if she knew the exact time of the first train.

"Heavens!" she said, "what are you thinking of? Come here, Daniele, I beg you," she added, after a moment. "It is true that I cannot speak to you like a mother, but you, who are an angel, will perhaps allow me to ask you if there be any dear, good girl—"

"No," said Cortis, without turning round.

"I should have been so glad," exclaimed the signora with a sigh. "But, then, I did not expect it!"

"Why?" asked Daniele, surprised.

"Oh, nothing. I thought that you could never find a woman worthy of you."

Cortis leaped out of the drawing-room window, and hid himself between the mulberry trees and the Indian corn, out of sight of his mother.

The latter took hold of the corners of the white handkerchief that she held, and gave it such a violent pull that she tore it across.

"I vow I will not stay in this cursed place," she muttered between her teeth.

She hated Lugano, because, at the age of fifty-two, she had fallen in love with a young doctor; and he, disgusted, would not go near her again. She rose from her chair, and opening a cupboard in the wall, plunged her hand into it, swallowed something hurriedly, and then closed the door very gently, keeping one eye on the window all the time; then, grumbling to herself, "Now I will go and speak to him," she went in search of Daniele. She soon met him.

"Daniele," she said, "bear with me. I have a favour—one only favour—to ask of you."

"What is it?"

"Come farther away," whispered the signora, looking up at the open windows.

They entered a trellised walk to the left of the house. Cortis did not seem the least anxious to know his mother's last whim, but walked beside her, watching the train below him, which was still visible through an opening in the hills.

"That Villascura, Daniele!" said she, "that Villascura!" She stopped, and covered her eyes with her hand.

"What do you mean with 'that Villascura?'" asked Daniele puzzled.

"Leave it, for Heaven's sake!" exclaimed his mother. "Live at Rome, or at Udine, or where you please, but not there."

"Why?"

The signora dropped her eyes, and answered, in a low voice,—

"It is impossible for me to tell you."

"In that case—" said Daniele, as though he considered the conversation at an end.

"Not to please me?" insisted his mother.

Daniele did not understand.

"But why?" he asked, looking at the clock. He had thought of going down to the hotel presently to inquire if any letters or telegrams had arrived.

"At any rate," exclaimed Signora Cortis, with sudden energy, "do not go to the Carrè's Villa."

Cortis frowned, and his face flushed.

"Why not?" he asked, in a voice which trembled with anger. "I shall always go to the Carrè's house."

"Oh, Daniele! not, in any case, while the Di Santa Giulias are there!" As she said this, the signora's face and voice really seemed sincere.

"Very good," returned Cortis, with bitterness; "tell your correspondent, whoever he may be, that he is a liar and a fool, and that the lady in question and I are too far above him to be hurt by his poison."

There had been ill-natured reports at Villascura, and Cortis knew it.

"The lady?" said the signora, with flashing eyes. "I know nothing of the lady."

Cortis, who was looking away, turned his head sharply round, and fixed his eyes on her face, waiting for further explanations. But she said no more.

"Well?" he said.

"Nothing," she replied, with a sigh.

Cortis insisted.

"What has been written to you?" he asked.

His mother laid one hand on his shoulder, and with the other beat her own forehead, saying,—

"It is written here. No one has told me. It is all written here."

Daniele lost his patience.

"Speak plainly," said he; "I can't read what is there."

"If I were to speak plainly," whispered the signora, raising her face with its large eyes, and extending the forefinger of her right hand, "you would experience everlasting remorse for having taken the accursed hand (here the finger was raised towards the sky) of that man!"

"What has he done?" asked Daniele, in amazement.

She clenched her hands, emitted a deep groan from between her closed lips, turned hastily round, and ran away with her head down. When she reached the steps leading to the door, she picked up her petticoats in both hands, and rushed into the house.

Daniele followed her, but before he had time to interrogate her, she flew into a violent rage, begged him not to question her, and promised to tell him all at a more quiet opportunity. Nevertheless, it was his duty to leave Villascura and go far, far away.

"I hope," she said, "that they will make you deputy, and then you can establish yourself at Rome. Then I will come to Rome too. It is the city of my heart. Oh! if only I could die at Rome. I should often see you there, if it were only from the gallery of the Chamber. Should I not, Daniele?"

"What has Di Santa Giulia done?" he asked.

"Heavens! why should you go on tormenting me? Surely your father must have spoken to you about him?"

"Yes, I know that he made his acquaintance in Piedmont when he went thither to join the military academy, that he brought letters of introduction to him from a Sicilian doctor, but that he very seldom came to our house, that he was not a bad soldier, that he gambled a great deal nevertheless, and never studied a bit."

"And now they have made him a senator!" muttered the signora to herself.

"They made him a senator immediately after his retirement from the army, because they wanted a senator from his province, and he possessed a fine name, a good military rank, and great interest. Surely you are not making a crime of that? My father never told me anything more about him. What else should he have had to tell?"

"Nothing, nothing; he could not have said any more."

Cortis shrugged his shoulders, glanced at the clock for the second time, and said,—

"I am going."

His mother had no intention of letting him go so easily.

"You start by the first train to-morrow morning, don't you?" she asked. "At six o'clock?"

"Yes."

"I hope that you will come here again."

"Yes, yes," answered her son indifferently, as he hunted for his hat.

"Then we will talk further this evening."

It appeared that these few words had only been said by a painful effort on the part of Signora Cortis, for she bowed her head on to her breast, and closed her eyes.

Before leaving the room, Daniele turned to look at her. Now that the false eyes were hidden, and the harsh voice was mute, he felt how dear she might have been to him. Suddenly a flash of memory recalled to him his father on his knees teaching him to pray for the repose of the soul of his dear mamma.

"It was better so!" he exclaimed, seizing his hat.

The signora, startled, raised her head.

"What?" she asked.

"Nothing," answered he, and went away without another word.

Barbara opened the gate for him, and said, in a low voice,—

"My mistress will not believe it, but all the things have really been consumed in the house. Only think of all the raw cutlets that she puts on her face at night!"

A few minutes before Cortis reached his hotel, this telegram had come for him from the chairman of his electoral committee,—

"To *Cortis, Hôtel du Panorama, Lugano.*

"Opposition press prints your private letter, and accuses you of belonging to clerical party. Great impression. To-morrow here meeting of electors, one o'clock. Come, or send telegram for publication. Newspapers follow. B."

The next train for Milan started in three quarters of an hour. Cortis hastily despatched a note to his mother, and the following telegram to Signor B. :—

"I arrive to-morrow, 11.30. CORTIS."

Then, in frantic haste, he packed his things, and reached the station just as the passengers were taking their seats.

"*Fertig!*" * cried the guard.

Until that moment Cortis had thought of nothing but how to catch his train. As soon as he took his seat, he saw himself in the hall at the public meeting, in presence of his friends, amazed or angry, possibly, too, of his mocking adversaries; alone, assailed by weapons which he himself had forged, with words that as yet he did not know, but which he had certainly written in all sincerity, but who knows when or where; determined to attempt no evasion, no denial, no retractation; compelled to fight under a new flag, and at a time and in a place not chosen by himself. He saw all this, and at the same moment he felt as though a flood of vital fire had filled his head and heart, and his courage rose higher than ever, and, as he stretched himself upon the red velvet seat, with a certain haughty in-

* In German in the original.—Note by the Translator.

difference, he mentally answered to the guard, "Go a-head! I am ready!"

As the train rushed over the bridge which crosses the road leading to Pazzallo, his thoughts turned for an instant up the hill, but they did not get as far as the little house with the red railings, in which, during the last few hours, he had heard such strange words, and where he had failed to discover the hidden meaning of the accusations that had been made. His thoughts turned back to the railroad which was carrying him on towards his goal.

Meanwhile, the sheet of water to the east, black with the wind, spread itself out gradually, unfolding itself before him till it reached the very foot of that lofty dolomite peak, which rose in front of Cortis in all its full length, towering above the other mountains, giving him an example of enduring boldness.

CHAPTER VIII.

IN THE FIELD.

The following morning, at the penultimate station of his long journey, Cortis found B. and several other friends, who had come to meet him. They rushed anxiously up and down the train, opening doors, and examining the carriages. When at last they discovered Cortis, they all scrambled to shake his hand, and to greet him in low voice, and with every appearance of sympathy.

"Is it very bad?" he inquired, looking round him at their somewhat blank faces.

"As bad as can be," answered B. dejectedly. "I am honest with you, and I tell you clearly that I consider it's all up with your chance."

"Gently, gently," broke in another. "Excuse me, but I don't think everything is lost yet."

Then B., who at first had spoken as though he had no breath in his body, got up and began to storm like a madman.

"It's all up, I tell you! You don't think so? What do you mean with your '*I don't think so?*' Where do you come from? Don't you know, from the Society of Labour and from the newspapers, that it's all up?"

"And from the walls," suggested a third.

"Bravo!" yelled B. "And from the walls. Ten manifestoes of our opponents' to one of ours!"

"Wait, you will see to-day."

"All very well; what do you expect us to see to-day?"

"You shall see what you shall see."

"Ah, yes! you think you are going to upset all those people, do you?"

"Yes."

"No."

Then they began to fight and argue among themselves, as if Cortis had not been present.

"One moment, gentlemen," he said, making his voice heard above the rest. "Is this meeting to take place or not?"

"Yes—of course—certainly," were the answers.

"And I am to take part in it?" he asked.

"That is the very point, you see," cried B., facing him, and leaning his face on his clenched fingers. "That was one difficulty when we invited you to attend, because some said that it was unnecessary, others said they knew enough, others again—"

"But this letter," asked Cortis, "this letter of mine that has been printed?"

"Ah!" exclaimed B., striking his forehead, and then fumbling in every pocket. "What a memory mine is! I came on purpose to show it you. I have it here somewhere."

Out came his letters, papers, notes. B., red as a lobster, looked through them all in haste, throwing them on to the floor of the carriage, or the window-ledges, or the knees of his friends. At last he pulled out a newspaper cutting containing the famous letter addressed to a certain professor at Venice, who had been dead two months. The editor declared that he had received it officially, and published some remarks upon it.

"The letter is a pretext," said B., collecting his scattered letters and papers. "It is a pretext. They don't like you."

"Well," said another, "but if the letter could be shown not to be his?"

"But it is his," muttered another, while Cortis, skipping the editor's comments, lighted upon these terrible passages,—

"If for the present we can do nothing better, *transeat*, we must try to get on as we are; but you know that I am a Catholic, and that I trust in the progressive development of Christian civilisation in which Cavour trusted. For that reason I look forward to the time when a parliamentary party shall be formed to keep before itself this ideal as an element of government. It must needs be that some of the attempts to move public opinion in this direction will fail; you know even better than I, that this has always been the historical preparation for every great and difficult enterprise. Many may fail, but I am convinced that at a certain moment this party, the effect of political necessities, will rise, and that then, if not before, the hero, as your beloved Carlyle would say, will be found to lead it; behind that hero, either in the front rank or in the last, will be found, if he be alive, your affectionate DANIELE CORTIS."

"Of course it is mine!" exclaimed Cortis to the man who had expressed a doubt. "Of course it is mine! Altogether mine!"

"Alas!" said B., "I feared as much."

The rest were silent.

"And what do the electors say?" asked Cortis.

"What do they say?" answered B. "Look at your paper, and you will see what they say."

"The editor is an ass!"

"Ah, my dear fellow, the electorate is not composed of Cavours. They don't understand. They see *Catholic, Christian civilisation, new parliamentary party*—they do not see clearly the distinction that may be drawn between conservative and clerical, and straightway they proclaim you a clerical! They make the greatest fuss over your phrase, 'we must try to get on as we are,' and they declare—forgive me for repeating what I hear—that it s disloyal and dishonest of you, that you only want to be elected by one means or the other, that you are making game of the electorate, and so on. Besides, you must understand that your opponent has been working like the devil, and that for the people whom he has influenced, your letter is a pretext. Those are they who will refuse to listen to you."

"But they must, they shall hear me!" cried Cortis, his eyes flashing. "What in the world can they have understood from that letter? They must hear me!"

"Yes, of course they must," grumbled B., with a sarcastic laugh. "But we shall see whether they will, al the same. We must hope so!"

"I shall appear before them alone, and without invitation, if my friends have not the courage to accompany me," said Cortis. "And if no one asks me to speak, I shall take French leave. And ——?" Here Cortis named a great man, who was one of his strong supporters.

"Ah, my friend," answered B., "this represents his condition," and, raising his right hand, with his fingers apart, he let it swing slowly to and fro from his wrist, as if the muscles of his forearm were useless. "As far as he is concerned," he continued, "we are all in the same boat. Remember that, if you speak to-day, you must make an allusion to that despot who pretends to order rain and fine weather in the whole division."

"Good," said Cortis; "now, I would beg you to let me think a little."

He retreated to a corner of the railway carriage, and read over and over again the act of accusation, then began to reflect, sometimes looking out of the window, and sometimes burying his face in his hands, till at last B. said to him,—

"Here we are. It is now twelve o'clock. My carriage is here, and I will drive you home, and let you get some luncheon while I go out and see how things are. At one

I will come for you, and we will go *coûte que coûte.* Oh, look at that fellow!"

As Cortis was getting out of the train, his opponent was being met on the platform by a crowd of friends, who were all talking and laughing loudly.

"Do you see them? Do you hear them?" asked B., in solemn voice. "They are sure of their victory!"

One of the group noticed Cortis. They all turned and stared at him, as though to see which could be the most insolent. Just as he and his committee were passing through the gates of the station, a few hisses were heard in the background.

"Wait here for me," said Cortis, stopping short.

He turned back quietly, and went straight towards the other candidate, who had one foot on the step of his carriage, and stretched out his hand to him, without noticing the others any more than if they had not existed. His opponent grew crimson, greeted him with evident confusion, and clumsily excused himself for not having seen Cortis sooner.

"Not at all!" answered the latter. "I do not demand any recognition from you. But I, as a gentleman and a friend of gentlemen, wish to go through the ordinary forms of courtesy with my adversary before we cross our swords. Good-bye."

Having said this, he passed haughtily through the group, and rejoined B. and the others, who had watched the scene from a distance.

"What is it; what happened?" they all asked, looking pale and anxious.

"Nothing; let us go away," answered Cortis, taking B.'s arm. "I merely showed him and his friends, with the most exquisite politeness, that they are a parcel of cads. Now they respect me, do you see. And besides, it always does me good to call a man a cad who deserves it"

Twenty minutes later every one in the little town had heard of the scene at the station, of the hissing, and of what Cortis had done. B., who had just deposited him at his house, rushed off to the *café*, and came back at one o'clock to fetch him, breathlessly crying,—

"Quick! come on, good impression; I have arranged with the heads of the party. Your swagger—for that is what your opponents call it, but under their breath—your swagger has made a good impression. A gentleman, they say. Then I lectured some of the miserable beings who don't mean to listen to you. What idiots they are! But I gave it them! I gave it them!"

Cortis interrupted him by saying, with a smile,—

"Thanks. But are you sure that you will be pleased with what I am going to say?"

"I won't have that cad at any rate," screamed B. "Quick, now, come along!"

Outside, the fly-driver who was frequently employed by Countess Tarquinia stopped Cortis. The countess was very anxious to speak to Signor Daniele, and she had ordered him to wait and bring him over to Passo di Rovese immediately after the meeting. Cortis ordered him to be in readiness at half-past two.

"No news?" he asked.

"No, sir."

"They are all well?"

"Yes, sir; I think so."

"And the contessina?"

"The little countess went away last night, sir. I heard that she was going to Rome."

"Hi!" cried B., seeing Cortis standing in a dream, without speaking or moving. "Come along! quick!"

On the steps of the hall where the meeting was to be held, groups of electors were already collected, who opened their ranks as Cortis approached, saluting him with manner expressing both curiosity and coldness;

then forming up behind him, they advanced in silence to the hall. There they found three or four members of the electoral committee talking near a long bench that faced serried rows of empty chairs, which, to Cortis, seemed stiff and unfriendly. When he entered, these men advanced towards him with some shyness and embarrassment.

"You have come from Switzerland?" asked the boldest

"Yes, I have."

"It is a fine country."

"It is indeed."

Then B., with his most smiling and pleasant manner, advanced and said,—

"Our friend Cortis is quite prepared."

"That is not the word," broke in Cortis, while the other repeated, "Well, well," making great gesticulations of agreement, and drawing back so as to make room for the principal actor. "That is not the word. I am most anxious to offer to the electors those explanations to which they are fully entitled; and, as my candidature has already been discussed and talked over in this place, I have considered it my duty, as I must speak somewhere, to speak here."

"Here is our president," answered one of the committee, pointing towards a tall, stoutish man, who came in just at that moment in haste, and out of breath, and who greeted Cortis with much more cordiality than the others had displayed. When they asked him to repeat to the president what he had just said to them, the latter interrupted them, and said,—

"Yes, yes; it's all right. I have settled all that with our friend B. here," and then he dismissed his colleagues to assemble and bring the electors into the hall.

"The four muffs," murmured B. to Cortis, who was studying the roof.

"Look here," said the president, taking Cortis aside, "I should speak in this manner," and he primed him with a little speech that he had prepared, keeping one eye upon his interlocutor and the other upon the people who were crowding in, involuntarily dropping his voice at the appearance of a hostile face.

B. had taken up a position close by, so as to be able to catch all that fell from the president without appearing to listen ; but he also did not lose sight of one of the faces that appeared, studying them, observing them as they took their seats, leaning his head first towards one and then towards another with the manifest desire of overhearing every whisper.

"A lot of people," he said to Cortis, when the president had taken his place, "and some nasty-looking ones among them too! Will the president's speech do?"

The latter rang his bell at this moment, and looked round him with great dignity, and without the faintest idea that many people were laughing at him. He reminded his hearers that on a previous occasion the candidature of Cortis had been supported by a large majority, wherefore the committee had approved his canvass. He added that a recent publication, well-known to all, had produced such varied impressions, that it had been considered necessary to call this meeting. To tell the truth, there had been some discussion as to the advisability of asking the honourable Signor Cortis to address them, as it was known that he was at a distance. It had been proposed to discuss merely whether the candidate should be asked to limit himself to explanations or not. The unexpected arrival of Signor Cortis had removed all these doubts, and the committee felt certain that the electors would rather have before them the public statements of the candidate than an extract from a letter. Then, without opposition, he called upon Signor Cortis to address the meeting.

The president seated himself, looking round smilingly in hope of catching tokens of approbation on the faces of his colleagues, and for a moment nobody spoke, when

Cortis rose and began, in a deliberate voice, to speak thus:—

"Gentlemen, I thank you for, and I congratulate you upon, having been willing to listen to me to-day. I neither complain nor boast because my enemies have done a dishonest action; it was natural for them, and I willingly leave in obscurity those who did it, their deeds, and names. I know that a letter of mine has been published—"

A murmur arose in the hall.

"Yes, gentlemen," continued Cortis, while his friends looked at him with anxious faces, "a letter which, without fearing to lower myself, I acknowledge as mine."

Some one in a corner of the hall cried "Hear, hear," and then all was silent again.

"A letter of mine, susceptible of grave interpretations, and calculated to remove from me the confidence of those who dread to see the introduction into the Chamber of elements hostile to our institutions and liberties, has been published; and one effect of this has been that some of you, gentlemen, whose honest fears I respect, have, as I have just heard from our honourable president, strong objections to listening to me. Well, gentlemen, I congratulate you upon having allowed the more liberal and just side of your natures to prevail, notwithstanding the unworthy interpretation that has been put upon some of my words. I repudiate the charges that have been brought against me of disloyalty, and of wishing to make game of the electorate of this division.

"Yes, I have written privately, and I now repeat publicly, without hesitation, that, if for the moment we cannot change for the better, we must try to get on as we are; and I am sure that, if you read my letter again, you will see at once that no allusion whatever could have been intended to this electorate, but that I alluded to the present condition of our national, political existence:

a condition which, in my opinion, is neither prosperous nor promising, but through which we must pass in order to reach something better, keeping before ourselves a higher ideal."

The same voice again cried "Bravo." There were a few cries of "Silence," and some subdued titterings. All eyes were turned to one corner of the hall.

"I thank my unknown friend," said Cortis, looking in the same direction, and obtaining, fortunately, a friendly laugh from his audience, "I thank my unknown friend who gives me a good example, inasmuch as he expresses the convictions of his heart, and like myself does not mind doing it at the cost of being *Vox clamantis in deserto.*"

Laughter and some quickly-suppressed applause followed. Cortis stopped a moment; when he spoke again, it was in a somewhat lower tone,—

"I come now to this ideal."

He bent his head in thought. No one breathed. Every eye was fixed on him when he raised his head and began again,—

"No, gentlemen, my political ideal will never be that of any party which would desire to subordinate the interests and rights of the State to any authority, however great, however legitimate, but which is founded on another basis, and maintained by other means for other ends. I might wish, in my scheme for political equilibrium and internal pacification, that this party should honestly accept the present state of things, and should try to be useful in the Chamber; but if ever I have the honour of representing you, I will never fight on its side —"

Here and there some applause was heard, not warm nor unanimous; the unknown friend remained silent.

"—Until it has been transformed from an essentially clerical party into an essentially civil party, and has modified entirely its views upon the rights and duties of the State.

"It is evident, gentlemen, that in writing a familiar letter, I could not have made use of more clear and exact words."

At this point a murmur rose in the hall which sounded like "At last!" in tones of not unmixed satisfaction. Cortis went on,—

"No, I do not repudiate anything I have said, but I might have been more precise in the expression of my opinion, and have made it as clear in my letter as I shall try to make it now to you.

"It is you, electors under the old law, who to-day hold in your hands the great power of the State; but there are people who are already preaching a new gospel, and to-morrow you may be called upon, too, to evangelise the populace. It is wrong and foolish to anticipate that these new electors will want to lay their hands upon the existing state of things, and that the country will go to rack and ruin; but it is only foolish not to recognise that there will be taken, not a leap in the dark, but a long step forward on the clear and fatal road of democratic evolution, and that the newly enfranchised multitudes will strive to procure for themselves some direct advantage from their participation in the government, and to promote some legislative action which, though exaggerated and imprudent, will tend exclusively to their own profit. For myself, gentlemen, I feel no empty or childish fear of this. I believe that in this democratic fermentation there is some leaven snatched from Christianity. In my mind's eye I see a bright ideal of a Christian democracy, one also capable of realisation very different from the despotism of selfish majorities only greedy for their own advancement, which now threatens our modern liberties. A real political party cannot be founded on airy ideals. I know well that they will bear no weight. But we must have an ideal; therein lies the strength of those who seek to destroy our institutions; and what ideals have we to oppose to them? One day it is electoral reform, and the abolition of the exchange upon the paper currency; another day it is the equalisation of the land tax, and the maintenance of the 'rentes' at par."

"And isn't that enough?" asked a voice.

"No," retorted Cortis, "it is not enough to keep hearts and minds united, much less will it suffice for an enlarged electoral body in which sentiment and fancy will play an important part And when you talk to me of a new party, whose ideal shall be merely the preservation of the existing social and political ranks, then again I reply that it is not enough, and that such an ideal would be without grandeur, and without life. You cannot uphold our fatherland, gentlemen, as you would an old monument, by girding it with iron railings and supports; our country is a living creature, an organ continually working and developing itself, and which, by the reasonable use and proper exercise of its natural faculties, keeps itself in good health."

At these words, uttered in a passionate voice, loud cheers burst from the audience.

"I desire," continued Cortis quietly, "to see the foundation of a party which will keep before itself the shining ideal that I have described, and which shall expressly consent, in order to produce this result, to the present state of our requirements. I am convinced that, if you wish to pave the way for a sincerely liberal democracy, without the predominance of any class, you must have a political power sufficiently strong to lead the country; and now a fixed idea is necessary, if it ever were, to stand against the rising tide of parliamentary majorities. You must have ministers convinced that the monarchy is not a hazy irresponsibility, that it is not merely a gilded coat-of-arms on the summit of our constitutional mechanism, but that it is the mainspring, if I may say so, of this mechanism; that it is a wheel answerable to God and

History, and which, by a natural law, will soon spoil and rust if it be left unused. Then this mighty power, certain of widespread support in the country, can and should be bold, and, allowing full liberty to all opinions, should take in hand the vexed social questions, and lead the van in every reform with caution, moderation, and firmness.

"There are writers of great talent—"

Here some mutterings rose from the audience. It seemed as though the word "writers" had made them restless, and cast a feeling of weariness over them.

"I do not know," said Cortis, interrupting himself, "if I am trespassing too long upon your patience—"

Some cries of "No," rather courteous than cordial, were his answer.

"I remember," he went on, claiming the attention of his listeners, "that a man of great genius, who had carefully studied politics, once said to me: 'The people are like a child; let them play with the fire, let them burn their fingers, and they will learn. This is the law of nature, and if you try to change it, you will only make things worse.' Well, gentlemen, I am not at all sure that this doctrine is right. I say that, by the law of nature, those with sense, will, and power, ought to band together to prevent the others from setting fire to their common house."

"That's true enough," cried several voices.

"But it is not enough that the party of the future should be of one mind upon these questions of government alone; it must also agree upon the religious and ecclesiastical question."

"Now we are coming to it!" exclaimed his unknown friend in the corner.

Every one repressed him, and Cortis went on in a silence which seemed charged with electricity,—

"I tell you, gentlemen, that no monarchy, no republic, will ever succeed in unravelling the social problems of the future, without the co-operation of religious sentiment, which, in Italy, can only be given by the Catholic Church."

A wave passed over the audience, and nothing could be heard save murmurs, groans, and confused voices.

Cortis, leaning with both hands on the seat in front of him, threw his body forward, as though to receive the shock of an emeny. He waited till the tumult had subsided, and then went on in his firm and measured voice,—

"The curia of Rome, gentleman, and a large portion of the Catholic clergy, have displayed, I regret to say, so blind a hatred to our national movement—such a fatal apprecia- tion of their temporal possessions—that any one who, in Italy, talks of favouring Catholicism, may almost expect to be answered as the missionary in Africa was who preached about God: 'And what if he eats us?' I have frequently asked myself whether the present violent re- action against the Church and her institutions, by bringing back the clergy to poverty and evangelical humility, by forcing them to study, and to lead blameless lives, may not be productive of results very salutary for the true Catholic sentiment. But a prudent statesman ought to discover in such an excessive reaction the danger of those opinions which inculcate respect for law, brotherly love, and a kind of moral subordination of the more favoured classes to those less well off, in which assistance is more vigorous than is quite desirable to repair all the social injustice and misery.

"The party of the future, therefore, must, to a certain extent, agree to the rigid application of our common law to the Church.

"I will not tell you how far I should go on this road. I am already too dear to your venerable clergy; and I have no intention of offering them, in expiation of my political sins, either blessed medals, or lives of the saints, or increased stipends."

An ironical smile twinkled in his eyes as he thus alluded to certain proceedings on the part of his adversary. The hall rang with laughter and cheers.

"But, on the other hand," continued Cortis, raising his forehead and wrinkling his brow, "we must agree with the principle laid down by Count Cavour, in a memorable speech upon the abolition of the Ecclesiastical Court, namely, that the progress of modern society demands the assistance of religion and liberty. We must require that religious instruction shall be given by the clergy, wheresoever and whensoever they please. We need not stupidly imagine that we are sinning against liberty because we refuse to pay professors of atheism out of State funds; we must recognise all religious associations whose objects are not contrary to law; guarantee to all persons, without exception, the full and complete exercise of their religious rites in public and in private; abstain from any legal or forcible interference with the internal affairs of the Church, save the right of guardianship of property. The government must always show, by its behaviour, that it places the highest value upon the spirit of religion."

The phrases relative to instruction and religious associations were the only ones that moved the audience, who allowed the rest of this rugged sentence to pass in silence.

"You murmur, gentlemen," exclaimed Cortis; "but I can picture to myself the very much less friendly reception that I should receive from a meeting of priests, if I ever had the honour (I certainly should have the courage) to tell them what, in my opinion, ought to be the conduct of the priesthood best calculated to secure the advancement of the Catholic religion. Your rare interruptions recall to my mind something that I learned at school. I remember hearing a description given of large banks of living shells, which lie on the sea-shore, and open in the sunshine, sending forth a deep murmur whenever a cloud obscures the sun, and closes them up. Allow me to believe that you have found in my ideas more sun than shadow.

"I must admit to you that I do not consider the time to be quite ripe for the formation of this party of the future, and, therefore, there was not yesterday, nor is there to-day, any reason for including its bases in an electoral programme, especially as foreign complications, combined with our ecclesiastical policy, might compel the State to be temporarily less liberal in its judicial dealings with the Church. I should not, therefore, have mentioned it had it not been brought into prominence by this recent publication, and if your wish had not been to me a law.

"Desirous of obeying you, I did not consider, I disdained to consider, the risk that my too open and plain-spoken declarations might deprive me of the honour of entering parliament as your representative. In that letter of mine, I made an ill-omened quotation; the sentence about the development of Christian civilisation was written by Count Cavour in an address to the electors of Vercelli, who rejected him. It is probable, if I may compare myself with so shining an example, that the same fate is in store to me. While I shall be grateful to those among you who have trusted me, I shall feel no resentment whatever against such as have withdrawn their confidence.

"I hear talk of high influence being brought to bear in my favour; I have never begged for such, nor shall I beg now. If, in this division, you have deities who can move the earth with their nod, I do not wish that it should be said of me, as it was said of a Roman emperor on the point of losing life and power: '*Alieni jam imperii fatigabat deos.*'

"If, at the conclusion of this struggle, I am beaten, I shall not be disgraced; and I shall remember, gentlemen, that in every free country there are representatives unelected, legislators not in parliament; that there are many methods whereby every citizen can fight for what he thinks politically right, and that a dumb black or white ball in the ballot-box is not the only, or even the most powerful, way of securing the supremacy of truth."

The first rows of the audience, immediately below the speaker, applauded; from the others rose a roar of diverse opinions. The members of the committee remained motionless. The president alone seized Cortis by the hand, and said in a low voice, somewhat with the manner of a master pleased with an industrious pupil,—

"Bravo, bravo! Very frank, and very clear. Fine ideas, noble ideas."

Cortis, pale and grave, only answered,—

"Now, it is for you to settle, gentlemen," and left the hall, followed by B. and some few friends.

"Your servant, sir, your servant," said his unknown supporter, pushing a way for himself through the crowd, and seizing his hand just as he was reaching the door. "I congratulate myself upon having heard you," he continued. He was a fine-looking man, with a ruddy countenance and bushy white whiskers. "You are a great man, sir, and you are not a bit of a clerical; you are religious, and so am I. Doctor Franceschi, at your service. And don't be afraid that we shall leave you in the lurch whatever that d—d fool, the *deity of our division*, may say."

The bystanders laughed. Cortis bowed, and passed on with his friends.

"Well," he said as soon as they were outside the hall, "I am not a bit pleased. What do you think?"

"You humbug!" said B., seizing him. "I must embrace you."

They all embraced him at once, suffocating him with fulsome adjectives.

"The part that pleased me most was that about the shells," said one; "it was magnificent."

"And I liked what you said about our country," said

another, 'when you compared it to a slowly developing monument! Nobody can deny hat that is a splendid idea—a true idea, a novel idea!"

"Yes; but that bit about the shells was so good, because it was like saying to your audience: if you grumble, you are a pack of oysters."

"And the medals?" put in a third. "Where do you place the medals and the lives of the saints?"

"Yes, yes," said B. "The oysters and the medals were both good, but the great point of this speech lies in the ideas expressed in it. The ideas are new and burning—worthy of Bismarck! Force and progress! Throne, altar, gallows, and forward!"

"No, no, no," cried Cortis; "what the devil do you mean?"

"Oh, no, signor," observed the man who had talked about the oysters, while B. muttered to himself, "We understand each other, we understand each other!" "Why, Signor Cortis wishes to abase the throne, to drag it down from its lofty place among the clouds: to drag it down from the clouds, he said, and to make the king responsible just as the ministers are; that seems quite fair too!"

"Bless my soul!" exclaimed Cortis, "did I express myself so badly as that?"

All the others rose against such a disgraceful critic. They would have torn him to pieces almost.

"Well, gentlemen," observed B. presently, "we ought to be going in again. Don't you think so?"

In the hall a great uproar was going on, notwithstanding the frequent and angry ringing of the president's bell. B. promised Cortis that he would sent him word to Villascura that evening of the result of the deliberations of the meeting.

"What do you think they will settle?" asked Cortis. "To me they seemed so cold as almost to take away my breath."

"Yes," answered B., "they were cold, but less so than I feared they would be. Besides, many of them were puzzled at the beginning, and never could pick up the thread again. You were rather above them. Do you know what I am afraid of? Of that closing sentence of yours about legislators outside parliament. People might say that the electorate — I don't know if I make my meaning clear."

"Above them, no," said another; "it was not elevated, even in idea. I will explain myself: elevated it was, but we could understand it perfectly. Perhaps, though, you might have put in a word about our external policy, about the army and navy."

"Are you never coming?" groaned B., raising his eyes to heaven. "Do come along; we must go back; do make haste!"

Cortis descended the steps alone. At the bottom he was met by Signor Checcho Zirisèla, who said,—

"Your servant, I am sorry I cannot stop now; an absolute king, if you like, but I am satisfied to play at cards with the priests, and then to have done with them. You know I am speaking for myself. Priests in an alehouse are all very well, but not in church—your servant."

"Cortis!" cried B., from the top of the steps, "when shall we see you here again?"

"I don't know. It depends upon what my aunt wants."

"Oh, send her to glory! We haven't time for aunts now"

The fly-driver who was waiting in the courtyard went to meet Cortis, hat in hand.

"Put to," said the latter; "where are your horses?"

"At the 'Golden Shield.'"

"I will be there immediately."

Cortis walked to the *café*. The corners of the streets, deserted at that, the hottest hour of the day, were covered with electoral addresses. His own were few in number, and were for the most part concealed by the flaring posters of his opponent, which nearly all began thus: "Do not elect enemies of your country." Near the door of the *café* there was scribbled on the wall: "Down with the people of Friuli!"

Cortis entered somewhat excited. A group of young men were discussing the meeting, and one proposed to go and wait for the "little Saint Paul" Cortis at the door of the hall, in order to hiss him. The rest agreed. Cortis meanwhile sipped his coffee in silence.

"And we will hiss B., too," said one of the group.

Cortis stood up, very pale.

"You will do nothing of the kind," he said.

The other looked at him in amazement, and answered in an uncertain voice.

"Won't we? Who are you to dictate to us?"

"I am a man," thundered Cortis, "who, if I say *no* to you, and to a hundred like you, do not expect to get *yes* for an answer, unless you are prepared to feel your face—"

He did not finish his sentence, but threw down, in order to make a way for himself, tables, chairs, and all that was on them, and finally stopped in front of his adversary, with his arms crossed on his breast. The proprietress shrieked, the waiters hurried up; the rest of the party were so taken by surprise that they did not know whether they stood on their heads or their heels. Cortis, seeing that the other neither moved nor spoke, threw his card to one of the waiters who was picking up the broken pieces.

"I will pay for everything," he said, "including a glass of rum that you had better give to that gentleman."

And he left the *café*.

A quarter of an hour later he was in the carriage, on his way to Villascura, and thinking of Elena. He felt ill at ease, and disturbed: disgusted with himself, with politics, with his obstinate enemies and his stupid friends, with the anger he showed to some, and the toleration he showed to the others. Italy! Yes, but if he did not succeed to-day, he would to-morrow. It was his destiny, and his determination; but what would he not give for one day of love! To forget everything for one day, to contemn the world, and to unite her the most beautiful to himself the most powerful! Visions of intense happiness passed before him. From the road which, passing straight through the plane trees, on the border of an immense plateau watered by the blue streams from the Alps, the eyes of Cortis greedily sought the shadowy clouds which hung on the edge of the mountains. He could see Elena and himself hidden in a house amongst those deserted wilds. Elena did not look melancholy as she often did, she was so happy in his love. Now he felt her arms, fresh and gentle as those streams, encircling him; now he sought her in the forest, and she came out to meet him, laying her head on his breast, and saying to him: "Art thou happy? I am!"

Cortis leaned back in a corner of the carriage, and looked at the distant horizon in which she had vanished.

CHAPTER IX.

VOICES IN THE DARK.

Countess Tarquinia was much disturbed. As soon as Elena was gone, she wished to have a conference with her brother-in-law; but how was it possible in the middle of all this bustle? And, besides, Count Lao had vanished suddenly. At midnight, when the band had taken itself off, and the lights were all out, the countess remained alone, not daring to go and attack him in his own room. She went to him in the morning, and found him in bed with a headache, black, and so cross that she could do nothing with him. He cursed the noise and the illuminations; he knew nothing, had heard nothing, had given nóthing, had taken part in nothing.

"So," said the countess, dismayed, "they went off without either money, or letter, or promise?"

Count Lao, notwithstanding the pain in his head, raised himself to a sitting posture in bed, and cried,—

"Yes; and I should not care if they had gone to hell! And now don't stay here to bore me any longer! Get out of my sight!"

The countess ran away, banging the door behind her in her wrath.

"What an old bear!" she said.

So Elena had deceived her! And she had deceived her husband too! And certainly she had come to some arrangement with her uncle. Now she understood it all. It was a stratagem of Lao's to save his money, and of

Elena's to prevent a family scene. She ought to have been told about it! But where did Elena get her zeal from? She who had hitherto always disregarded questions of money, and who had never taken the smallest pains to avoid family quarrels! She must have had some secret reason for her conduct. And what was it? It was enough to drive one mad! And now what would that beast of a son-in-law of hers do? He was capable of anything! She had known nothing about it. All this disturbance of things and people had left her no time for anything else. And now she was alone, for Grigiolo and Malcanton were gone alone with that old toad of a brother-in-law of hers, without any one to help or advise her! What in the world had become of that Cortis! He would be better than nobody. How ill she felt! And the garden and house annoyed her because of their untidiness; there was nothing left but disgusting dregs, out of which all the pleasure had been squeezed! The beds of mignonette and vanilla round the house were all trampled; the fir trees and the meadow were littered with half-burnt papers; even the billiard-room was all daubed with gum from the horrible balloons that Grigiolo had made there! And how every room in the house reeked of stale cigars!

At eleven o'clock the driver came to the door, according to orders. The countess had forgotten all about it. She had other things to think of besides paying visits! She was just going to dismiss him, when she heard shouts of "Your servant! your servant," and in the field she saw little black Don Bartolo, in his three-cornered hat, and with his bamboo cane. He had come to return the decorations from the church of St Peter, and to drink a glass of white wine. The countess asked him at once if he knew anything of Cortis. To be sure he did. Doctor Picuti had just returned from the chief town of the division with all the last political news. Advertisements of a public meeting to be held that day were out, and Cortis was expected to be present, and Signor Zirisèla had gone into town with the idea of hearing him.

"I believe," added the priest, "that he has telegraphed to his bailiff from Milan, and that they expect him home to-morrow."

It was then that it occurred to Countess Tarquinia to send the fly to meet him. She had great faith in Daniele Cortis. He would tell her what to do, and would give her good advice; while that selfish wretch Lao could think of nothing but his aches and pains.

"Of course, countess, you know where that stay-at-home, Signor Daniele, has been to?" suddenly asked Don Bartolo.

"I do not," answered she drily.

"How strangely things are divided in this world!" exclaimed the priest, rising. "Why, here is a real countess who does not know something that the poor housekeeper of the priest knows."

"Well, where has he been?"

"Now, now; of course you know; you are only laughing at me, countess. Do you not, really? He has been to Lugáno. And do you know what he has found there? Why, no less a person than his sainted mother, whom they have always tried to make us believe was dead, and who now turns out to be alive, the great—"

The countess did not show much surprise. She had always doubted her death; and as she very cordially hated everything to do with her sister-in-law, she rather preferred that Cortis should have said nothing to her.

"How did it become known?" she asked.

"It was known that he was gone to Lugano, because his servants at Villascura had orders to forward letters or telegrams there. It was the parish priest who knew about his mother. It appears that she writes to him sometimes."

"What about?"

"How should I know? To show that she still has good manners, perhaps—pray don't go away!"

The usual clinking of glass was heard as the tray was brought. The countess, having sent away the keys of the chapel, left Don Bartolo to enjoy a pleasant glass of white wine, on the balcony, in the cool breeze.

"I must get ready," said he, "and then I shall be off immediately."

She went up to Elena's room, remembering that she had promised to restore to Cortis a book that had been left on the table. She entered the empty room, and was somewhat moved to see how coldly tidy everything looked, and how sadly Elena's beloved roses were hanging their heads at her window. The book was there on the table. The countess remembered having seen it several times in her daughter's hands. She looked at the title-page—*Châteaubriand — Mémoires d'Outretombe.* She did not know it. It was probably some sad, deep book. Elena preferred that kind of reading. Daniele Cortis had written his own name on the first page. The countess looked at it for some time, and then said to herself, with a sigh: "He wanted Elena!"

But, in this matter, she really was not to blame. When Daniele first began, perhaps, to think about it, Elena was a girl who had grown up prematurely, and perfectly unattractive to most young men. And then he had gone away, and the other one had made his appearance; and it seemed a good marriage, and one that promised well.

She opened the table-drawer. It contained nothing but an old torn visiting card of Elena's. But it bore on it, besides her name, a few words scrawled in pencil, which had been obliterated, and were now illegible.

The countess instinctively understood that the secret reasons that governed Elena's conduct could not be discovered by her in any manner, save perhaps through that obliterated writing, whence a voice seemed to reach her.

Towards four o'clock horses and wheels drove noisily up to the portico. The countess rushed out to receive Cortis, who jumped out. She seized both his hands. How grateful she was to him. With what warmth she received him.

"Poor beasts," grumbled the driver, looking at his horses.

"Well," said Cortis anxiously, "are you alone?"

"Very much so, my dear boy."

Scarcely had they entered the house when the countess began to weep. Cortis did not know what to think.

"My dear aunt," he said, "tell me what is the matter."

The aunt hesitated before replying. Presently a bell was heard ringing two or three times.

"Nothing," she said; "it's nothing; it's only my weakness. But now I feel convinced that there is something very wrong, Daniele, and I did not know when I should see you here, and be able to talk to you, and hear what you would say. Do you remember the evening of the storm, when you were coming from Lao's room, and met me just by the door of the hall? Do you remember that there were tears in my eyes?"

Then she began to relate many things to Cortis of which he already knew a large part; how embarrassed for money her son-in-law was, his demands, the difficult family questions that had been raised thereby, Lao's inflexibility, her own sufferings.

"Signora," said her maid, coming in at this moment, "the count heard the carriage, and desired to know who had arrived, and now he begs that Signor Daniele will go to him at once."

"Good gracious!" exclaimed the countess, displeased, "I never get a chance of two words with you. He has got a bad headache, I warn you. Signor Daniele will come in a minute. Wait a little."

She wished to finish her story, and she did finish it in

furious haste. Neither Cortis nor she noticed that all the time the bell was ringing more violently than ever, and that her maid had come back and was waiting on the threshold.

"Signor Daniele," she said at last, timidly.

"Yes, yes, go to him, in Heaven's name!" ejaculated the countess, "only make haste and come down again, because I want you."

Before Cortis had reached the staircase, the door of the verandah was pushed violently open, and Saturn dashed in, barking and leaping for joy. Behind Saturn came the bailiff of Villascura and two other persons. The bailiff had heard from Don Bartolo that Cortis was expected at Villa Carrè, and so he had come for his orders, and also to bring with him two gentlemen who were the secretaries of the communes of A. and B., and who were most anxious to talk to him. Cortis shook hands with them, and, begging them to wait a few minutes, went to Count Lao's room.

On the stairs he was joined by the maid, who said,—

"Signor Daniele." He turned round. "May I speak to you about my young mistress?" she continued. "I haven't spoken to the countess, because—poor thing!"

"What is it?"

"Yesterday I was helping her to pack her trunks. 'Bettina,' she said, 'I fear we shall never meet again.' 'Whatever do you mean, signora?' said I. 'Why should we not meet again? I intend to live for several years yet,' I said. 'That may be,' says she; 'but I, Bettina, shall not come back. I am going far away,' says she. 'But you will come back?' I said. 'Why shouldn't you come back?' 'I don't know,' says she. Do you think now, Signor Daniele, that the contessina would have said all this without good reason? Heaven knows what she may have got into her head, poor dear! Only think! A minute later she takes up a book, stands looking at it for a quarter of an hour, trembling like a leaf all the time, puts it down at the bottom of a trunk, and then, when the trunk is quite full, nothing will satisfy her but she must open it, take out everything till she comes to her book, then she writes a note and puts it into the book. Then she leaves the room, and comes back suddenly in a great hurry, tears up her note, and writes another instead."

Daniele made no reply, but entered Lao's room. Darkness, heat, and the odour of camphor stopped him at the door.

"Forgive me, my dear Daniele," said the count's voice; "light a match. The candle is on the floor, behind the bed."

"How are you?" asked Cortis, gently.

"Bad, but no matter. And how—"

At that moment Cortis struck a match, which flamed.

"Oh, I see," murmured Lao. "I could have told you so beforehand. That woman could only change for the worse."

"I will tell you about that presently," answered Cortis.

"Good. And the election?"

"Bad, too."

Cortis lighted the candle, and could at last distinguish Lao, who, lying on his bed, pale, with his head tied up, and his eyes half-closed, was saying in a low voice, "Pigs!"

Cortis pressed his hand.

"I will leave you quiet," he said.

Lao detained him, and asked if he had told him of the upset of the previous day.

"I advise you," he said, "to do nothing without first asking me. Good-bye. What time is it?"

"Ten minutes to five."

"Give me my pills. There they are on the table."

He took a pill of valerian and quinine, and, letting his

head fall again on to the pillow, muttered, as Cortis was leaving the room: "Pigs!"

Cortis went down hastily to the secretaries, who were waiting. They brought good news from the mountains. Up there, people did not care a bit for what the town thought. On the contrary, there was a great jealousy existing between the mountain and the plain—a keen antagonism. All the same, it would be well if Cortis would go up there the next day, just to show himself. He promised.

All this time Countess Tarquinia was coming and going, throwing impatient glances at Cortis and his political friends.

"At last!" she said, when the latter were gone. She gave the *Châteaubriand* to Cortis, who did not remember having lent the book to Elena, and opened it with curiosity. He found one of his cousin's cards inside, bearing the words: "With many thanks and greetings."

"By-the-bye," said the countess, "I will go and fetch you another card that was on her table."

Now Cortis began to understand the maid's story. That was the book which Elena had at first packed up with so much emotion; with an emotion that was so jealously concealed in her last note, after the first rush of repentance. Perhaps it appeared too plainly in her first letter, and she did not wish to betray herself.

The countess returned with the note. It was impossible to make anything out of it. Cortis tried in vain, and handed it back to the countess with apparent indifference, and without a word.

"I wrote to her this morning," said the countess; "but I can't help wondering what has happened, or what will happen when her husband learns that he has been deceived. A wretch like that!"

The countess talked, groaned, wept and talked again,

mixing up in her lamentations the past, the present, and the future. Cortis answered nothing.

"If I were a man," she said at last, "I think I should have gone after her. Do you think I can ask any one, Daniele, to do me this favour?"

Cortis had not heard the question, and had to ask her to repeat it. The countess bewailed his inattention, and accused him of having no thought for anything but his election.

But still he did not see why he should run after the Di Santa Giulias. And besides, for three days, without counting the all-important Sunday, he could not leave home.

They dined together in the cool north room which looks to the firs of the garden and the bare rocks of Monte Barco.

"And I must stay here in this melancholy plight," said the countess. "Who knows when I shall be able to drag him up to town?"

Then neither spoke again till the end of dinner. When the servant left them to fetch the coffee, the countess clasped her hands and said,—

"At least, write to her."

He bowed in token of assent.

"I will write to-night," he said suddenly, like one awaking from a dream.

The countess thanked him heartily. It never occurred to her that there could be any risk in encouraging a correspondence between her daughter and Cortis. She had such perfect confidence in both of them, and saw that they were so different from the frivolous and corrupt people amongst whom she had learned what love was. They were only capable of an airy sentiment at best, which seemed to her somewhat ridiculous.

"Scold her!" she said; "write that no scene with her husband could have been more displeasing to me than what has happened. Say that she ought to have spoken clearly and distinctly to her uncle, and to have asked him to make the sacrifice. She has never spoken to him at all, you know. Say (I have said it to her once, but you can repeat it) that she shall have the money somehow or other, and that she may tell her husband so at once."

The servant reappeared with the coffee, and a letter for Cortis from B., which had been brought by a special messenger. He wrote :—

"A line in haste, from the benches of the electoral meeting. Excited discussion followed your speech. Your opponents accuse you of clericalism and masked absolutism, or at any rate of belonging to no party, because those that exist do not suit you, and your own is not yet formed. The ballot showed forty-six votes in your favour and fifty-eight against. Great confusion. Every one will vote according to his pleasure. Your friends will fight to the last, and even longer for you. News from the mountains assure that a visit from you will be attended by great results. B."

"Elections?" asked the countess when Cortis had finished reading; and without waiting for an answer she went on: "To-morrow you must give up the whole day to me. Either my brother-in-law must be persuaded to give this money, or else I must find it somehow. In any case, you must help me."

Cortis replied that it was out of the question. He had to start at dawn for the mountains, and he could not be sure of reaching home again in the evening. The countess had a fit of weeping. He remained firm and cold as ice.

Seeing that he could win, he felt it his duty to fight. Every sentiment, even that of love, disappeared, went down without a struggle, in presence of the clear and distinct vision of duty. He rose, and promising to write to Elena that night, he went to Villascura.

As he passed the little rose-covered house in which was Elena's studio, he thought of an evening twelve years ago, on which Elena, coming from the meadow to her room, with a red flower in her hair, and flaming cheeks, had said: "Oh, Daniele, how I have run," and then she ran on again, sending out a silvery laugh into the air. Now the meadow was deserted, the studio closed, and she far away. And she loved him, and suffered, and was miserable. Cortis picked a rose growing near the door of the studio. "Elena," said he, "I beg thee of God."

And after that he thought no more about her, and began to talk to Pitantoi, whom he met carrying some cray-fish up to the house. Only late that evening he returned to the thought.

After he had written a dozen notes in his own room, with Saturn at his feet, he rang for his servant, and ordered that they should be despatched the first thing in the morning. Then, having dismissed him, he took a large sheet of paper and began to write hurriedly:—

"VILLASCURA, 30*th June* 1881.

"ELENA,—I expected to find you, your voice, your face, your heart; I have found your thanks and your greetings. What had you written in the note that your mother found in your room? What was it, Elena, that you wished to destroy and obliterate? I, who am writing in this great empty barn of Villascura, with my head tired, and my heart full of bitterness, feel, notwithstanding your treasured thanks and greetings, that your soul is here, near me.

"It would have been better had my mother been really dead. I need say no more to you. It will be difficult for me to see her again yet awhile. I will provide for her suitably, but from a distance. Do you know what remains in my heart? The memory of my father, which is more bright and clear than ever.

"I came away post-haste from Lugano on account of my election, which is going on wheels. I am sorry for my poor friends whose livers will suffer, that is to say, those who have any! I came direct from Lugano to ——. At the station they hissed me, but then I made a speech to the electors, and later on I offered, at the *café*, an indefinite number of thrashings to any body who cared to apply for one; so that I don't think I am much in debt to my good neighbours.

"My speech, very Catholic, but always from the point of view of the State, went fairly well. You know that I am not an orator yet (shall I ever be!); besides, just before I spoke, they told me that you had gone away, and also the atmosphere was charged with idiotic fluid. On the other hand, my proffered thrashing, less Catholic, answered very well, and I am not likely to be led into the temptation of following it up by a sword-thrust. I only intended to give a lesson, or an example, whichever you like, of brotherly love; and I think that I did well both with hand and mind. Finally, our old friend, Schiro, sent by your mother, drove me out to Villa Carrè, cursing the blazing sun all the time; and I dreamed violently of a certain lady who is cold as ice. We stopped a moment near Rocchette, under the fortress that you know so well; and thence I made a sentimental journey up to that level bit of ground where the said lady once picked some colchicum in autumn, which I begged of her, but which she hid in her bosom, giving me instead only a stony silence. At Villa Carrè I found my aunt very unhappy, and your uncle delightfully rabid. I could only give him a hand and a quinine pill, and we did not talk about you, although his head and my heart were aching on your account. Your mother talked a great deal about you instead.

"What have you been doing, Elena? I cannot pretend to have thoroughly understood from Aunt Tarquinia, and I don't think she was very clear about it herself; but from what I could gather, it looks to me very like a deep and subtle plot laid by you against the peace of Villa Carrè, for the sake of one day's peace, and torture ever after. Your mother is trembling for you, and would make any sacrifice to confine the storm which she fears will burst upon you. For my own part, I know you better than your mother does, and I am not afraid for you. Another feeling rises in my heart; a contempt which I cannot express. In any case, reassure this poor woman, towards whom you may be, sometimes, ever so slightly unjust.

"Good God! Elena, why did I not find you here? Why did you scruple to leave a better word for me?

"I picked a rose this evening at the door of your studio. Its delicate beauty, lying as it is on a barbarous volume of Hansard, is dying with a sweet gravity that somewhat recalls you to me at certain moments. I thought, as I looked at your studio, of the past, and of what might have been. We will live among the roses, Elena. Is it never the lot of souls like ours? We are made to meet war and tempest, we are weapons in an unknown hand which never rests, and never lets us rest; and how firmly it grasps us.

"To-morrow morning I am going to carry my gospel into the mountains. I shall preach at —— and ——. I know that this will not please you, my haughty lady; but there is no politician and no patriot who has not felt it necessary in certain times and places to depose his weak pride. I am as haughty as you, and if the world could only read my feelings when I am asking for votes, *it would indeed praise me.* But if the electors had left me at Villascura, as after all they very likely will do, I certainly should not have troubled to run after them. I calculate that I have in me still thirty-five years of political life; if I am to waste two of them at the doors of the Chamber, it will not ruin me. Nevertheless I will not hide from you, as I do from the rest of the world, that I feel a certain agitation, an excitement, which will prevent me from sleeping much till after Sunday.

"Do you know that the evening before I went away, you said, 'Write to me'? This is the second time I have written, and if the Holy Inquisition itself were to see my letters, it could find no fault: it would not find one of the words that I may have whispered to that dying rose, who won't repeat them. So now, answer me. If you do not do so at once, and fully, I shall come to you, wherever you may be, and demand an explanation.

"Now I am going to cool myself in the lake in the garden. It is half-past eleven, there is no moon; it would be hard to distinguish between a fish and a candidate; but make your mind easy, politicians never sink.

"Good-bye, Elena. If things go badly with me on Sunday, I shall bury myself for a month in my garden, with Shakespeare and you. DANIELE."

He went out with Saturn, and disappeared in the thick shadows of the limes growing by a path leading to the lake, an oval sheet of water, bordered by dark foliage, and shaded by the overhanging peak of Passo Grande. A few minutes later, Saturn was left alone on the bank, and was mournfully wagging his tail, while violent splashings were heard from the middle of the dark, motionless water.

CHAPTER X.

THE BARON'S AFFAIRS.

THE Di Santa Giulias had been two days in Rome, and the baron had not as yet addressed a word to his wife. They had two bedrooms and a sitting-room at the Hotel Bristol, having given up their usual dwelling in the Via Quattro Fontane a month previously when they went into Veneto. The senator had chosen this hotel in the Piazza Barberini so as not to be too far away from his usual haunts; although in July, at certain hours of the day, the piazza was baking. It is true that the baron suffered but little from this. He never got up until after two o'clock, when he went out, not returning until daylight. Elena never saw him. The first day the chambermaid told her that the baron had gone out, and would not be in to dinner. The second day she happened to be in the sitting-room when her husband passed through, looking cross and worried. Neither of them spoke a word; she heard him come in at four in the morning. Henceforward it became a daily occurrence.

It was better for Elena that it should be thus; it was better for her not to see him, to know that he was out. It mattered little where he spent his time, whether at the senate, or at the club, or in some place where the play was higher and more secret than at the club. She had heard rumours some time before that there was such a place in the immediate neighbourhood of the Piazza Barberini. Perhaps her husband spent his nights there.

This thought occurred to her the first time that she was disturbed by his return. It did not make her unhappy; she was perfectly indifferent.

Neither did she worry herself about Cefalù; she waited apathetically for the sea and solitude. She might perhaps become fond of them, but she cared little even about that.

Since the first days of her married life she had never felt such a profound hopelessness. Her virtuous sacrifice, her plan made, and already in part carried out, of removing herself as far as possible from the heart and sight of Cortis, had not at all raised in her that secure consciousness of having done right which exalts the mind. On the contrary, she felt keenly the pain that her cold note must have inflicted upon Cortis; she hated herself at times for having been more hard than was necessary; for never having made any allusion to the letter she had received from Lugano. And immediately afterwards she scolded herself for these uprisings of feeling and these falterings of will.

As soon as she reached Rome, she wrote a fairly affectionate letter to her mother. She answered her uncle Lao's letter the following day, thanking him, but not accepting the proffered money. She joked about the sermon that her crabbed old uncle had preached to her, to the sound of his polka, about this wretched money; she joked about the prodigality of the preacher. She went on to speak of the heat of Rome, where she found no one she knew, and said that she sighed for the sea, and preferred Sicily to the horrible watering-places of the continent. She ended her letter by announcing her intention of going up to the Church of the Capucins, where she would get a breath of air, and where she could pray for all rheumatic uncles.

As she wrote she felt bitterly amazed at herself, and a good deal humiliated at finding that she could act so cleverly. Henceforth everything seemed to her a comedy.

everything seemed false, all human faces, words and actions. And the "I will" spoken at the altar, might she not consider that too as an answer given in a play?

At this idea her blood boiled. Never, never! No sentiment, not even that of religion, spoke so loudly in her as her proud fidelity. Moreover, she did not believe in her religion: her mother had always gone to mass too much, and her uncle too little. She only preserved a sad, severe faith in God, a faith which forbade her, as weak and unworthy, any expectation of reward or of personal happiness either here or hereafter. And at this time, even this, her last light, was burning very dimly. Up there, in the Capucin church, when she wanted to pray with fervour, and to beg help from God against herself, a sinister impression, carried away by her years previously from that same church, suddenly recurred to her. A lay-brother had shown her the horrible mortuary chapel without causing her much disgust; afterwards, in the church, he had said to her quietly, with his expressionless face: "Under this stone is buried Cardinal Barberini, founder of the church. See, signora, the inscription: *hic jacet pulvis, cinis et nihil*—that means dust, ashes, and nothing!"

Pulvis, cinis et nihil. Elena had looked at the words cut into the stone with wonder and terror, as if they had risen from the kingdom of the dead to explain to her the sad mystery of human life, *pulvis et nihil*, to the utter exclusion of the spirit; and the man with the expressionless face looked to her like the priest of some tragic religion of death and nothingness. At Rome she was often assailed by those pangs of hopeless scepticism; she found it in the ruins of a dead faith which were scattered around her, in the worn-out pomp of a sickly faith, in the campagna, which girt her round with its silence and desertion.

The evening after her arrival she drove to the lending-library to get the *Memoirs d'Outretombe*, and there she met Senator Clenezzi from Bergamo, a lively little old man, who had always been at her feet on account of her beauty, her cleverness, and also because, *rara avis*, she never worried him with tickets for charity concerts or other good works. He did not know that Elena was in Rome. He kissed her hand with unusual tenderness, and kept repeating: "Dear Donna Elena, dear Donna Elena!" till at last the librarian, waiting with the *Châteaubriand* in hand, laughed. Before getting into her carriage, Elena told him that she expected to remain a few days longer in Rome before going to some baths, and that she hoped to see him again.

"At the Quattro Fontane?" asked Clenezzi.

"No, at the Bristol."

"At what time shall I not find your husband?"

Elena smiled.

"I never see him," she answered. "Come when you like. Why are you afraid to meet my husband? Have you quarrelled?"

"It is not that," answered the little old man.

"Well, then?"

He helped her into her carriage.

"Am I so old as all that?" he said. "He may stab me, but all the same I will come."

"Do," answered Elena, smiling. "And if you know any more friends of ours in Rome, bring them with you. I am always alone; come soon if you want to find me."

"That poor thing knows nothing," said Clenezzi to himself, returning into the shop as the carriage drove off in the direction of the Piazza Colonna.

The next day he went to the Hotel Bristol. Elena received him with considerable excitement, talking to him of this, that and the other, with a feverish gaiety that caused him some embarrassment. He answered in monosyllables, fidgeted on his chair, looking uncomfortable, and yet unable to go away, till Elena said to him,—

"What is the matter with you, Clenezzi? You are like 'une âme en peine.' Tell me, have you to make a speech in the senate?"

"Bless my heart!" exclaimed the startled senator; "no, no, not in the senate."

Elena thought for a moment.

"Ah!" she said, lowering her voice to a tone of freezing indifference, "have you anything to say to me? Is it something which concerns my husband?"

The man's embarrassment left him all at once, leaving in its place an anxious look and a nervous countenance.

"So you know?" he asked.

Elena shook her head, shrugging her shoulders, and raising her eyebrows, and in a scarcely audible voice answered,—

"I know nothing."

Clenezzi, stupefied, remained with his mouth open, not knowing whether to continue or to hold his tongue. Elena's lips moved again, and she whispered,—

"Tell me."

The senator fancied her indifferent. He grew very red, and protested that he had no desire to touch upon certain matters, that he had only been induced to do so by a feeling of devotion, but that, if it did not interest Donna Elena, he had no wish—

"Clenezzi," she said, interrupting him in a tone of mournful reproof, as she stretched out her hand.

She was accustomed to these outbursts from her old friend, who, notwithstanding his seventy years, had all the fire of a boy of twenty.

"Forgive me," he said, greedily kissing the white tapering fingers. "I am wrong. I come from Bergamo, I was born on the Brembo, and I am violent."

"No, no!" exclaimed Elena, "but listen. Supposing

you had children! Now tell me everything. It is my duty to do all that I can for my husband, and I will do it."

Then the senator asked her whether she had never suspected anything wrong in the state of her husband's affairs. Yes, her suspicions might have been roused long ago, if she had noticed certain ugly people who used to come and inquire for the baron, certain letters that irritated him, the fuss he made over every domestic expense. She knew also that he gambled; she had learned that from the first anonymous letters that had come both to her and to her uncle; besides, an officious woman friend had whispered it to her at Rome. In May, before going to Passo di Rovese, her husband had begged her to use her influence with the Carrès to get him a certain sum of money.

At this point Elena stopped. It appeared impossible to Clenezzi that the baron should have entirely concealed from his wife all the threatened misfortunes that were hanging over his head. But still it was the fact. Donna Elena knew nothing, and turned towards him the indifferent face that she had at first displayed. Then he told her roughly that her husband's honour and liberty were at stake.

Elena shook her head.

"I don't believe it!" she said.

She knew that she had a rude, violent and vicious man for a husband. She did not believe him capable of a dishonest action.

"Ah, Donna Elena!" exclaimed Clenezzi, with a look that expressed a hundred things.

And then he told her that, two months previously, the lawyer Boglietti, commissioned by a Sicilian loan society, had been to the president of the senate bearing a most serious accusation against Senator Di Santa Giulia. The society had charged him, as their chairman, to obtain a sum owing to them by a banking-house in Rome, and to deposit it with the Minister of Finance as security for certain borrowed money.

Di Santa Giulia had performed the first part of the commission, but not the second. The board of directors having discovered this fact, had immediately instituted inquiries as to the manner in which their commission had been carried out. Here there was a dark spot. It appeared that Di Santa Giulia had alleged some pretext or another, and by means of promises had persuaded the board, of which several of his supporters were members, to proceed no farther. But the matter had got abroad, and the board had been compelled, at the end of May, to call upon Di Santa Giulia to restore the money, and to make good their losses by the 18th of June, threatening him with criminal proceedings for misappropriation of funds in case of refusal. The baron had begged for a delay, promising to repay one-half of the sum on the 30th of September of that year, and the remainder on the 31st of March 1882. He trusted that his friends on the board would be able to bring about a settlement upon these terms. But instead, Boglietti had been instructed to make one more attempt at a friendly solution, demanding the immediate payment of one-third of the sum, and agreeing that the remaining debt should be paid in two equal portions, just the proposal of the baron. Failing this, he was to move for a writ against him. The lawyer had thought it best to go and lay the whole case before the president of the senate, hoping that he might find a means of avoiding such a scandal, and of forcing the baron to do his duty. The president telegraphed on the 29th of June to Passo di Rovese, recalling Di Santa Giulia to Rome. On the 1st of July, at four in the afternoon, a few hours before the meeting of Elena and Clenezzi at the library, a member of the president's office had received a promise from the baron that the required payment should be made before the 7th, failing which his name was to be struck off the list of senators of the kingdom.

Now there was not the slightest probability that the baron would be able to find the money. It was said that he was over head and ears in debt. Would his wife's family come to the rescue?

"In such a case as this," Clenezzi concluded hastily, "no one can help but relations."

"I believe," Elena began, "that all my money has long since been dissipated. And, besides, do you suppose that my family has never done anything?"

"I understand; but—"

Elena thought for a moment.

"What is the amount?" she asked.

"From twelve to fifteen thousand lire. If you can raise that sum, your husband must never see it. It must be in Boglietti's hands before Thursday."

"Ah! dear Clenezzi," sighed Elena, "if money could do everything! Supposing that we can find this money, may I send it to you? Will you look after it? If it had to be drawn out of the National Bank, would you see to it for me?"

The senator, who for love of Elena and for the pleasure of saving his own money, would have walked into the fire, placed himself entirely at her disposal. He looked at the clock. It happened that on that very day the plan for electoral reform was to be laid before the senate, and a debate was expected on the composition of the Central Office. He must get to the house.

"We must hope," he said, rising.

"What for?" asked Elena, with a smile so bitter, and a look so sad, that it brought tears to the eyes of the poor senator.

"Forgive me!" he exclaimed. "I am a poor old man, a poor old fool, but if you were my daughter, by our Lady! I would carry you off into my own country as sure as God is above us; and if that ugly fellow came to take you away, he should see what we are made of in Brembo!"

"No, no," she said, in an offended tone, "you don't know me."

"And me?" retorted the senator, "do you know me? I should like to see him come."

Elena seemed afraid to discuss this question, for she hastily replied,—

"Go to the senate, go to the senate," and rang the bell.

She remained alone, standing in the middle of the room, gazing fixedly at the triton in the fountain on the piazza. A waiter opened the door and asked: "Did you ring?" but receiving no answer, he repeated: "Did the signora baronessa ring?"

"Ah!" said Elena looking at him, and just realising that he was there, and then she added: "Nothing."

Scarcely had the waiter retired when she remembered that she had rung and what she wanted, and going to the door, called after him: "A cab," and then returned to the contemplation of the fountain. Within her mind all was confusion. With her other feelings for her husband there was now mingled, for the first time, one of horror. He was laden with other people's money. And then it appeared to her that all this tumult quieted down; her fancies and thoughts subsided as though some invisible door had been opened for them in the depths of her mind. All was blank and dark; and as her eyes unconsciously gazed at the fountain, so there came unconsciously into her mouth a few words recently read in the *Mémoires d'Outretombe*, the words of poor Madame de Beaumont at Tivoli: "Il faut laisser tomber les flots."

However, this deadly calmness could not last long. As soon as the waiter came back to tell her that the cab was ready, she got up, determined to think of nothing but her duty. She drove at once to the telegraph office, and despatched a message to her Uncle Lao, accepting the money she had previously refused, begging that it might be sent to her, and promising explanations by post. On her return to the hotel, with a feeling of bitter satisfaction, she thought over the excitement that would be caused at Villa Carrè by her telegram, the fury of her uncle, and the lamentations of her mother. There came into her mind, who knows why, a recollection of the roses which were peeping into her empty room. The previous morning she had received from her mother a letter full of affection, of fears, of reproof. What would she say now? At the corner of the streets of the Due Macelli and the Tritone, she thought she saw her husband turning hastily down a back street to the left. A wave of anger swept over her. Could that gambling-house be down there? Her first impulse was to stop the cab, and rejoin him. Her contempt overcame it; she let him go. For some time past she had known him to be coarse, violent, and vicious; but she had always attributed to him a certain rough honesty, the brutal frankness of the barbarian; also of the heart. But now no more; now that money that did not belong to him rendered him unclean in her eyes. She let him go.

At the hotel she found Cortis's letter. When she left that dry note for him at Passo di Rovese, her design had been to irritate him, and to prevent him from writing to her, at least for some time. She hoped for much from distance and silence; not for herself, but for him. She experienced an invincible feeling of pleasure when she saw that her plan had failed; and as she opened the letter she did not know whether she felt afraid of, or anxious for, passionate words. She devoured it, first of all, from beginning to end, slurring over the little expressions of affection as though they burned her; especially over the sentence, "it would not find in my letter one of the words that I may have whispered to the dying rose, which will not repeat them." She thought that Cortis ought not to have written thus; and on reaching the end, she turned hurriedly back to the first page, whereon he spoke of his mother. She read once more those disconsolate lines, and experienced a profound sorrow. At that moment she felt neither her own troubles nor the sweetness of knowing herself loved. All her heart had gone out to him. She suffered with him, she shared his disenchantment, his bitter loneliness. She realised all this so deeply as to fear lest she no longer belonged to herself, but had become part of him. And his election? Daniele only spoke of it jokingly, but here, as in other parts of his letter, his gaiety betrayed the real disturbance of his mind. A rush of indignation against the stupid electors made the hands and silent lips of Elena tremble; the man whom she loved could not please the crowd. Nevertheless she felt no shadow of a doubt as to his ultimate success. The future of Cortis was certainly not in the hands of a few idiots. And there was some comfort to be extracted from his letter. She felt that his moral strength was greater than his love, that his great soul might suffer by a woman's abandonment, but that it would not crush him, nor make him swerve from the path he had marked out. Thus, and thus only, did Elena love him! As for herself, whatever fate might await her, whatever misfortune might come upon her, it should not be allowed to signify either to herself, nor to the world, nor to God.

A fleeting vision rose before her, and showed her the placid lake at Villa Cortis, with Daniele seated on the brink. She was seated beside him, having fled from Rome and her unworthy husband. The shadows of the garden, the lake, and their own hearts, were all at peace to their inmost recesses. She chased away the picture with a sudden frown. It could never be! Cortis must not love her. Even if she sacrificed herself, she could offer him nothing but a feverish present and an overcast future; even by allowing him to love her thus ideally, she saddened his life. He was alone in the world, and on the path he had chosen for himself, fatigues, pains, and weariness were lying in wait for him. Why had he no family to be a rest and a comfort to him? She must make him forget her. She thought of the little meadow near the fir trees, where Cortis had left her; she thought of that colchicum blossom, that flower with its powerful juice, which she had insisted upon keeping for herself. She smiled and wept.

Her husband did not reappear during the whole day. Elena ought to have gone to some friends in the Via Urbana, who were kind enough to take charge of her plate, but she did not feel in the humour to see people, or to put on a mask of gaiety. She read over and over again in the *Mémoires* all the passages of which Cortis had told her, but, above all, the letters of Madame de Caud, and she turned now and again to the passage which speaks of unintentionally dashing against the destiny of another. She eat no dinner. In the evening, as her head and her eyes ached with the constant reading, feeling herself suffocated in her little room, she ordered a cab, and had herself driven beyond the Porta Pia. The last lights of the sunset tinged with purple the Sabine hills, the air was pleasant; Elena could not but weep. But the melancholy of the hour, the solitude, and, away towards Ponte Numentano, the ruins scattered about, seemed all to find voices of sympathy with her, and her tears were less bitter in consequence. As they went down towards Ponte Numentano, the driver let his horses walk. An old woman begged of the beautiful lady, and on receiving her alms, she noticed that the giver's eyes were full of tears.

"My daughter, God will give you peace," she said.

At the same moment, Elena experienced a violent fit of shivering; her thoughts turned to the fever, to a possible and desirable peace, and to the words on the marble tomb in the Capucin church: "Pulvis, cinis et nihil." As she descended towards Rome, she saw before her the moon setting behind the cypresses in the Villa Albani, and as she drove past the gardens, the air was heavy with the scent of magnolias. Near Porta Pia she met a young man and woman riding. How handsome they looked on their fiery horses. To her, the evening voices spoke only of sadness, but how sweetly must they speak of love to others!

At ten in the evening she received a telegram from Lao, which began by promising her the money within three days, through the National Bank. It went on: "At to-day's ballot, Cortis had 342 votes X 338. Cortis elected."

Elena felt a keen sensation of joy in her heart, and her face flushed with pleasure. She put her hands to her cheeks, they were burning; to her temples, they were throbbing. Cortis elected! He had conquered, he had won the first step, he must be happy. He would come to Rome, he would have to live there for many months, and she might be there too. No, no, good God! keep away that thought. She was going to Cefalù, to remain there for ever, never to see him again, and, above all, never to be seen by him, and to betray herself. Oh, heavens! might she not send him one word? What would he think of such a silence? Certainly he would guess its true cause. Would not that be worse? He would want one line, one word; and she would only answer him very coldly, very distantly, so as to keep him off. She began to write this cold and severe letter with fever in her heart and in her head.

"Rome, *2d July* 1881.

"Dear Cousin,—They tell me you are elected. I am sincerely glad to know that you have taken this step on your road, which I trust may be happy and distinguished.

"I have just received your letter, and have been much pained by what you wrote to me from Lugano. I would I could hasten by my prayers the moment—"

Here two tears fell on to her paper, but she continued to write, setting her lips tightly.

"—In which a pure and faithful woman might comfort you, and warm your deserted hearth.

"I think, and have always thought of you with friendliness, but there cannot be in my heart, and I will not allow in yours, any other feeling. I am therefore compelled to say to you that several sentences in your note from Lugano, and in your letter of to-day, have offended me. I hope you will not find it very difficult to alter both your mind and your language; otherwise I should prefer not to have to see you again."

Elena ceased. The labour of writing these cruel words had been too great; fancy, stimulated by passion and fever, suggested others of a very different nature. She did not know how to go on. And as she was thinking, with her eyes fixed on the white paper, as thought after thought passed through her mind, her hand unconsciously wrote: "In winter, in summer, from heart and—"

She started, saw it, and tore up the sheet. She was suffering, she was mortally tired, but the thought of finding that letter there on the table the next morning frightened her. She took another sheet of paper, and copied the first letter down to the word "again," and then continued:—

"You will forgive me for writing so briefly. As I am in Rome for so few days, I have very much to do, and the evening always finds me very tired. Please tell mamma and my uncle that I am very well, and enjoying myself. Rome always fascinates me!

"Good-bye, and once more a thousand congratulations from your affectionate cousin, ELENA DI S. G."

She fastened the letter, and sent it without delay to the post. No sooner had the waiter gone, than she regretted not having said to Cortis that she was sorry for the pain she was causing him; but then she told herself that he, with his temper, would be irritated and not pained by her letter. It was better so! Because certainly the love that Cortis bore her in nowise resembled her own inextinguishable passion. He would fly into a rage, and would not write to her again; it would be easy, during his contemptuous silence, to draw herself little by little out of his heart. But what if he should suddenly come to Rome? What if she were to find herself obliged to see him?

Elena passed the night in weary restlessness, troubled by a succession of dreams. She fell asleep at dawn, and fancied herself, sitting by the lake at Villascura, alone, a volume of Shakespeare in her hand, her eyes fixed on the motionless water, and engraved on her heart the melancholy words of Portia in the "Merchant of Venice": "My little body is aweary of this great world."

At six o'clock she heard a violent knocking at her door, and, as she did not answer at once, it was opened with pushes, kicks and blows, and somebody came storming into her room.

"God bless my soul! what an oven!"

Elena raised her head from the pillow, and saw her husband throwing her windows open.

"This room is stifling!" he growled, leaning over the bed. "How are you?"

Elena answered him shortly. That was a nice way indeed of entering her room! The baron's hair was dishevelled, his necktie awry, his eyes shining. In his grumbling there was a sort of good temper like that of a wild beast in a pleasant mood.

"Are you angry?" he asked. "It is three days since we last saw each other." And stretching his hand over the bed, he seized her foot.

Elena started, and withdrew it at once.

"Leave me alone!" she said.

"That's nice, too!" exclaimed the baron. "You should say, my dear husband, how good of you to come and see me after the trick I have played you."

Elena did not condescend to answer.

He pulled an arm-chair up to the bedside, and threw himself into it, with his legs apart.

"I am good!" he said. "I am very good! Why do I speak like this?" he continued. "Why do I look like a good-natured devil, but because I have in me the fire of the south. You cold-blooded northern creatures regard me as a Bacchus, and perhaps something worse! Look here, you who are the angel of Paradise, whose finger no one is worthy to touch, you have deceived me, you have tried to take my life, my pretty charmer!"

"Your life!" exclaimed Elena.

"Yes, my life, my life. Those fifteen thousand lire represented my honour, and I would have you know that, although I may be a most cruel tyrant, I would not keep my life a moment if by losing it I could save my honour! Now you have done all in your power to prevent me from getting that money, do you see? I have had to spend three nights in the devil's company in order to get it. And now here I am, peaceful as a lamb!"

He stood up, and leaned over her with a smile.

"And I am very fond of you, my little heart."

She pushed him away.

"Are you afraid of Cefalù? Then you sha'n't go there. I forgive you, but I'll never forgive your people. Who knows where we won't go to. I have heaps of money, you know. But you must be kind to your husband, my pretty lady!"

He had not touched a drop of wine, but the excitement of gambling, the long nights that he had been sitting up, and love, so to speak, made his eyes glitter as though he were drunk.

"Have you been playing?" asked Elena.

"For three nights. I have won twenty-six thousand five hundred lire. Now that I am in luck, I should like to go to Aix."

"No, no. Will you not go direct to Boglietti, the lawyer?"

"Curse him!" yelled the baron. "What do you know about it? Has he been here, the scoundrel? The blackguard! Yes, I will go to him, and pay him at once, and I will give him the September payment at the same time, and I know he won't be pleased with that. So he has been here, has he, the dog? I'll break his head for him!"

"No," said Elena, "he has not been here."

"Then how do you know anything about him?"

"Never mind."

"Well, I won't ask you. I am in such a good humour this morning. Tell the truth now, am I not a good devil—a cloud that thunders but never hails? I like to play a little; it's my only vice. I can't tell you what good thoughts come to me now and then. Why, I would embrace your mother and your uncle now if I were to meet them. But you must be kind to me, my beauty."

He bent forward suddenly to give her a kiss, but she, turning sharply round, received it only on her hair.

"Go away," she said; "close the shutters, and leave me in peace."

"What is the matter?" grumbled her husband impatiently

"I have the fever."

He thought she was not speaking the truth, a flash of anger came into his eyes as he felt her pulse.

His face changed, however, and he finished by letting her white inert hand fall back on to the bed, saying,—

"You have done this to plague me! I had invited some people to dinner to-day."

"Never mind. It is Roman fever. It will be gone by this evening."

"Roman fever?" exclaimed the baron, frowning. "I will send for a doctor."

"It is not necessary. I know what will cure me immediately."

"What?"

Elena turned her face towards him.

"Sicily," she said.

CHAPTER XI.

FROM CEFALÙ TO ROME.

" *To the Baroness*
Elena di Santa Giulia, at Cefalù.

" ROME. *19th January* 1882.

" ELENA.—Only one word.

" You went to Sicily last July, ill with fever, and you have not sent one line to your mother, who only learned it by accident a few days ago from Senator Clenezzi. You said that you would return to Veneto in the early days of October, and then you made a pretext for putting it off until last month. At the end of October you wrote that the opening of parliament would take place so shortly that it was not worth your while to make so long a journey in order to have to retrace your steps to Rome almost immediately. Parliament was opened; you said that you wished to see something of a Sicilian winter, and that you would come back immediately after the Christmas holidays. Now your husband is here alone. He never answers any letters from Casa Carrè, and it is impossible to get any precise information about you from him. Aunt Tarquinia would start for Sicily if she could. Unfortunately, Lao is in bed with arthritis, as you know, and she cannot leave him, unless it be absolutely necessary. In conclusion, my aunt writes to me this morning, begging me to take the journey and to go and see you.

"Remembering your last letter, and being, alas! unlike you in some things, and unable to change my feelings and language as rapidly as an actress changes her parts and her dresses, I shall answer that I am extremely busy, and that I cannot possibly leave Rome. Good-bye.—Your affectionate cousin, D. CORTIS."

"*To the Most Illustrious Deputy,*
Daniele Cortis, at Rome.

"CEFALÙ 23*d January* 1882.

"MOST ILLUSTRIOUS SIR,—I have had the honour of being charged by the most illustrious baroness Di Santa Giulia to answer your letter of the 19th instant.

"The noble lady is in bed, under my care ; she is suffering from slight rheumatic fever, and therefore is unable to write herself. She wishes me to say that, except for this accidental and unimportant indisposition, her health is good, and that it would be most displeasing to her should you undertake so long a journey. I am to add that the news of her slight indisposition has been all ready conveyed to his excellency the baron, and to the baroness's family.

"The baroness desires me to present to you her respects. —Awaiting your orders, I have the honour to be, your most humble and obedient servant,

"DOCTOR ANTONINO NISCEMI."

"*To the Same (Confidential).*

"By the express desire of the baroness, I was obliged to write as she wished, and she read the letter when it was finished. Now my conscience orders me to write these lines, on a separate sheet, for your better information.

"The baroness, in addition to an anœmic condition, is at present suffering, not from rheumatic fever, but from a slight gastric attack, together with congestion of the liver, the probable remains of an attack of miasmatic fever. In itself the illness would not be serious, but I am anxious about the general anœmic state, and the extreme moral depression of the patient. A few days ago I began the use of some mineral waters of ours from Termini. I have seen miracles done by them. We must hope.

"I do not ask you to come, because the baroness seems to me most uneasy at the idea of your taking this journey, on account of your health, and she is quite determined to prevent it, and I cannot advise you to go against her wishes. I must tell you of one circumstance, however. At my visit of yesterday, I was fairly satisfied with the look and condition of the invalid. Your letter was brought to her just as I came in; and she had not yet opened, nor would she open it, notwithstanding my entreaties, while I was present. It appears that she read it as soon as she was alone, that she then passed several hours in a state of great agitation, and had a very bad night, with great pain in the right side, and violent fits of coughing.

"I do not know the contents of your letter. I only know that you are a near relation of this incomparable lady, who seems to have an exalted and well-merited opinion of you, most illustrious sir. I would therefore beg of you, in my capacity as doctor, to write to her, because she has much need of moral help and amusement, but to avoid saying anything that might upset or worry her.

"You will forgive me, sir, if a feeling of duty, and of respectful attachment to the baroness, have made me write thus earnestly.—And believe me, with profound respect, your obedient, humble servant, DOCTOR A. N."

"*To the Baroness*
Elena di Santa Giulia, at Cefalù.

"ROME, *27th January* 1882.

"I did not expect the obsequiously worded certificate of

your excellent Doctor Niscemi. Rheumatism? It is a slight thing, but, nevertheless, I seem to have entered your sick-room very roughly. Forgive me, dear Elena. Well, I will not come to Cefalù, but, instead, I will try to give you all the gossip of Rome. And I will try to be rather pleasanter than I was last time.

"What would you have? I am up to my neck in politics, and they are spoiling my manners and my style. I was better on that June night, in the lake in my garden. The first plunge into the parliamentary ocean freezes one to the very heart. Amongst my new colleagues I see some who are numbed with the cold, bewildered, ill with weariness and home sickness. They think: Are the heart and the wisdom of Italy here. Last December a minister said that, by comparing our politics with those of Spain, Bismarck did us honour, and we, vain, querulous shadows, puffed up with self-satisfaction, were silent.

"Meanwhile, I am studying; I am studying men and things, for the future. The present is not good for anything. I have spoken twice, very briefly, upon perfectly uninteresting subjects, just to tune the instrument, and find the keynote. Last time there was a lady in the president's gallery very like you. The subject was the agricultural vote, and I spoke on the woods and forests. I fear that, in honour of the said lady, I was more flowery and shadowy even than my forests.

"I ride every morning, notwithstanding politics. Colonel B., now in command of the Staff-College, has lent me a beautiful little Irish bay mare, that jumps like a cat. This morning I went for a gallop beyond Porta Maggiore, along the Via Prenestina, in search of the Temple of Quiet—used there not to be a Temple of Quiet somewhere there? But it is written that I shall never find it! The sky was clear, it was hot, the earth was dusty and green; the mountains were sprinkled with snow. I passed between the great pine tree and the rocks under which we used to sit—do you remember?—amongst the poppies, while we watched the great sea of the campagna, with its tombs and spectres of aqueducts. My mare stopped suddenly about a mile farther on, just by the Via Labicana, near to a square tomb. Perhaps she thought that was the Temple of Quiet, for she is intelligent; or, perhaps, in the silence, she heard the whistle of the Naples train. I heard it too, and I thought of Sicily and you, but, penetrated by the peacefulness and solitude, my thoughts took a new direction.

"Rome, city of the soul: who called it that? I did not remember that I had a body, much less a horse, between my legs. Is my brain giving away, or am I suffering from miasmatic mysticism? I do not think it is likely; but it is a bad sign. Imagine that sometimes I think that I should like to go and live in the palace of Septimius Severus, with Thomas à Kempis and the ravens.

"Perhaps I am talking too much, and you are getting tired. I must remember Doctor Niscemi, and this letter shall be continued in a future number. The recommendation comes a little late, perhaps, but still I will not reject it, though I will write to you again soon. Good-bye, dear Elena. Salute your good doctor for me, and accept a cordial hand-shake from your affectionate cousin,

"CORTIS."

"*To Doctor Antonino Niscemi, at Cefalù,*

"ROME, *27th January* 1882.

"SIR,—I am extremely grateful to you for your letter marked confidential, and I beg you to furnish me with frequent and exact accounts of the state of the invalid. Should she become worse, or even if she do not show an immediate improvement, I should strongly advise your writing directly and secretly to Countess Tarquinia Carrè. In case you feel that personal motives might make it difficult for you to do this, I would willingly undertake to arrange that the countess should come to Cefalù without compromising you.

"I have written to-day to my cousin, carefully following your advice. I will write to her again shortly; but I first wish to discover the effect of this second letter. I have the greatest esteem for my cousin, and we have always been the best of friends, but we do not always exactly agree in our opinions; and then, perhaps, I am inclined to speak out my mind a little too clearly.—Believe me to be your obedient servant,

"DANIELE CORTIS."

"*To the Most Illustrious Deputy,*
Signor Daniele Cortis, at Rome.

"CEFALÙ, *31st January* 1882.

"MOST ILLUSTRIOUS SIGNOR,—The baroness received your last letter on Tuesday, the day before yesterday. I was not with her at the time, and she has, as yet, said nothing to me on the subject. I knew it from her maid, who told me that, though her mistress had said nothing, her eyes expressed great satisfaction.

"For my own part, I am much pleased with my new cure. I have noticed a marked improvement during the last two days. Yesterday the baroness, who generally goes straight from her bed to a sofa, was able to walk about the house a little, and she acknowledged to me that she could eat her food with less repugnance. This morning I found her in tears. She told me, smiling as she wept, that she was overjoyed at feeling so much better, and that she could not help crying. This is merely the result of weakness, which is still great, and her diet has still to be kept to milk and vegetables; but if once we can bring her to stand iron and meat, I hope for a speedy recovery.—With profound respect, I am your most humble and obedient,

"DOCTOR A. NISCEMI."

"*To the Baroness*
Elena Di Santa Giulia, at Cefalù.

"ROME, *4th February* 1882.

"DEAR ELENA,—You neither write to me yourself, nor do you make any one write for you. My conscience tells me that I should have done right in satisfying your mother without further ado. Is the rheumatism not gone yet? And is poor Doctor Niscemi at the end of his science? I have never been clever at finding the equation of two unknown quantities.

"The other day I wrote to you from the Chamber; to-day I write from my rooms in the Via Principe Amedeo, with my windows open to a warm Petrarchesque sun, and to a reviving spring, and also to all the trumpets and whistles of all the trams and railways that Lucifer has put into the world. Had things been like this a hundred years ago, I fancy that Alfieri could not have written the *Merope* as he wrote it, according to an inscription on a stone within a few yards of my house; and I should never have raised a laugh, as I did in the theatre at college, by declaiming like a madman,—

"'Alas, how great an undertaking it is to support thee, O throne!'

"The noise is a drawback, but I have a good view of the slope of Viminale, a picturesque medley of tiled roofs; on the other side of the street, almost underneath my windows, I have a beautiful green carpet of acacias and roses, brightened up by fountains, and to the left, through the telescope made for me by the shady road, I get a peep of the blue sky and the Albanian mountains. I am some way from the Chamber, but I could not live in that neighbourhood; and until Septimius Severus will let me a room in his house, I must abide by commonplace Rome.

"Speaking of the Chamber, I forgot to tell you the other day that I have spoken in favour of the monks, and of the Franciscan monks into the bargain. Oh! I can hear you say. But I say yes, madam, and what is more, I spoke very well, although my words fell by the wayside and among thorns. Imagine that it has been suggested to the minister to increase the subsidies to our lay schools in the East, and to diminish those given to schools kept by religious bodies. The minister answered very feebly, not convinced in his own heart, but bowing before so much wisdom. *C'est bête mais c'est comme ça.* Only one member of the Left dared to say that although we were living in the light of philosophy and science, those poor Asiatics were still in the shadow of religion, and that, if we wished to rescue them from it, we must do it by the means proposed, as France had done! At present one can say nothing more popular than: 'See what they have done in France! See how they manage these things in England!' I despair of ever hearing other countries say: 'See how they do these things in Italy!' However, this time the gentleman in question just gave me my opportunity, and I spoke in the name of a great political interest, and on behalf of those poor noble people who are slaving for an idea, who seek neither fame, honour, nor wealth, and whom these over-fed free-thinking members of the Budget Commission wish to leave in the lurch. I did not quite call them these names in the chamber, you know; there, I rather offered incense to them. After speaking of our country's interests, I begged them, of their great wisdom, to consider whether that splendid civilisation which now produces, independently of religion, such shining parliamentary lights, had no longer need to lean upon the Gospel; in such a case it would be only fair to restore it to the East, which lent it to us, and to aid the monks to maintain it out there. My speech produced no particular effect, either warm or cold. Many congratulated me, and said I was right, but not until after the sitting, and outside the chamber. But I was certainly better listened to than I had been on either of the two previous occasions.

"A few days ago a lady tried to persuade me to go with her and some other people to an audience of the Pope. I declined, as I could not go with my name and position as member of parliament. I am satisfied to go and visit, whenever I can, that lowly pontiff who is saying the *De Profundis* in the Confession of St Peter, and who always gives one plenty to think about.

"I have need of God, dear Elena. I feel that henceforward my life ought to be made to conform rigorously to the opinions which I laid before the electors, and for which I will fight. It is a political duty as well; one must raise one's own banner and fight under it; one must stand firm.

"By which I mean, dear, that my passions will be no danger to any one. The one which I fear the most is my temper. I shall try to walk along my own path in the future, and not to box the ears of any one who does not deserve it. Pray for me as regards this particular danger, for here I am tempted at every moment, there are so many vulgar, untrustworthy and boorish people about. I have not very much time to pray for myself! All the same, I am not what Aunt Tarquinia would call an 'infidel.' Last Sunday I went to mass at St Peter's, and I heard the most wonderful music. I could not discover whose it was. I am an outer barbarian as regards music, but that made a great impression upon me! It sounded to me like a sinister prophecy, a voice broken with weeping. When I came out of church the sky over the Vatican was black, a ray of sunlight gilded the fountain on the left, the colonnade, and the palace; there was not a creature in the piazza. What presentiments did I not feel of ruin and storm! '*Tout cela passera comme une voix chantante.*' In how many years? Or in how many centuries? It is more than probable that our grandchildren or our great-grandchildren will see that day. A poet who is a friend of mine said to me the other day that the undecipherable characters engraved upon all the obelisks frightened him, and that they seemed to him to be so many repetitions of '*Mene, Mene, Tekel, Upharsin,*' written over the eternal city. I cannot read these obelisks, but I can read, and to a certain extent understand, men and things past and present, and I see the beginning of a speech that, after heaven knows how many commas and full stops, must end badly. But I don't lose heart on this account. Would it seem to you a little thing if I could succeed in saving a generation or two? The blindness of certain people annoys me. It annoys me, for instance, to hear the deputy L., a very clever, gentlemanlike man, say that if we want to improve the conditions of the working classes, we must not preach to them charity and a future state, but what are and what are not profitable investments. As if the age were not suffering from selfishness in its very vitals. All the same, I envy the man who will see not only the ruins of St Peter's and the Vatican, but who will also see those sublime pontiffs of the last days, that is to say, if they are like what I hope and imagine that they will be.

"My mother is still at Lugano, and wishes to come to Rome. I have paid her debts, and made her a monthly allowance sufficient for her, but on condition that she should live how and where I will. Certainly not in Rome, at least not as long as I am here.

"I am soon going to Villascura, where I shall probably spend in the snow the few days' holiday that we have in carnival time. But I shall first of all go and see your mother and uncle, of whom they write that he is still in the same state. Do you know who often talks to me about you? That good Clenezzi, whom I meet at the D.'s sometimes in the evening. I can never meet him, not even in the street, without his saying to me, in that curious idiom that he always employs when he wishes to be confidential, and which is one-quarter Italian and three-quarters Bergamesque: 'And she? Have you news of her?'*

" He is a dear, good man, the pearl of the senate. Good-bye, Elena. You see I have not forgotten my promise of chattering to you. Now send me some news of yourself. I warmly clasp your hand.—Your affectionate cousin,

" Cortis."

" *To the Most Illustrious Deputy,*
Signor Daniele Cortis, at Rome.

" Cefalù, *8th February* 1882.

" Most Illustrious Signor Deputy,—The cure of the baroness is going on very favourably, thanks to our Bivuto waters. But now, to prevent a relapse, we ought to have some medicines which the wretched doctor here does not keep, and which the contemptible chemist cannot procure. The air of my beloved Cefalù is no longer suited to the baroness. I have already written to this effect to his excellency the baron ; but as you, sir, know so many things and people, I take the liberty of writing it to you as well. My reasoning, if you will kindly think it over, may be a little entangled, but it is nevertheless sound.

" I do not think that the baroness has good mental surroundings. It now appears that the countess, her mother, as you, signor deputy cannot leave Rome, means to come in person and carry off her daughter. Baroness Elena was beside herself with joy when she received this news ; then immediately afterwards she told me that she never wished to leave Cefalù again, and she went out on to the balcony, ostensibly to look at the sunset, but in reality to weep, according to her habit. I can't make it out. Does she dread having to remain for ever at Cefalù,

* The words of Clenezzi's Bergamo patois are: *E ixè? Ha notissie.*

or does she really wish it? If only she would declare herself one way or the other. But she leads here the most miserable life in the world. She sees no one but my wife, who, poor dear, stands in great awe of her, and who is an excellent companion for me, but not for the signora baronessa. She cannot go in a boat, because it frightens her at once; she has no horses, and she can walk but very little as yet. She spends the whole day in playing a certain barbarous music, dull enough to make the whole of Sicily yawn, and she gets so much upset by it that it makes me wretched to see her. I come and cheer her up a little, when suddenly a wretched boy passes under the windows (this happened yesterday) singing,—

"'Wind of the sea, tell me how he is,'

and that makes milady worse than ever. It is true tha this abominable catcher of sardines had an accursed voice like a violoncello, wonderfully sweet, and that his music was not German.

"I therefore beg you, sir, to use your influence to remove the baroness from here. Let her go far away, and live cheerfully among cheerful people, and let her play the blessed music of Cimarosa.—With profound respect, your obedient and devoted

"DOCTOR A. NISCEMI."

"*To the Honourable Daniele Cortis,*
Parliamentary Deputy, at Rome.

"CEFALÙ, *14th February* 1882.

"Am I doing right in sending you this letter? Am I doing wrong? I know not. Forgive this incoherent exordium. I have been more ill than you think. Now I am getting better. God knows why, but I am no longer Elena. I have no longer that firm will of mine. I am a leaf that trembles at every breath; even my intelligence is confused, my heart is very weak, I cry at nothing, a trifle irritates me, I am too much of a child, I am too much of a woman.

"I have received a letter which has upset me very much indeed. It was from your mother, imploring me to mediate between her and you. She wishes to live with you. She says *to die* near you, but perhaps she deceives herself; one cannot die when everything promises and invites one to speedy death! But why do I speak of myself again? Have you spoken to her about me? My first instinct was to reply: 'I am already dead, turn to some one else. I wish you every success.' Then said I to myself: 'Daniele has written me two long, interesting letters; I will thank him for them, and will then mention this to him.' Poor woman, there is so much earnestness in her prayers! Her letter also contains several mysterious hints and dark allusions which I fail to understand. It seems that some member of my family has done her a great injury. Who can it be? But it is not this which disturbs me; you cannot think how indifferent I have become to certain things now that all my nerves are unstrung. It is on her account that I am distressed; I think you are too severe, I fear that you are unjust! You have found a bad woman, but is she not also an unhappy one? And who knows how great a part nature, men, and circumstances, may not have played in her sins? Let her come and live in Rome, where she can sometimes speak to you, and where she can at least see you. Allow her to come and settle in the same town as you, so that she may be certain that were she to die you could be at her bedside in an instant to listen to her last words. Who can tell what may not spring from a heart which is on the point of breaking? It must be a very blissful moment in which one feels that the end is near and that one can speak out everything. I am positive that your mother cannot have had many such moments of happiness; grant her this one. Do I tell you to take her into your house? No, never. The woman whom I wish to see living in your house must be absolutely pure and upright; but have pity on this other one! Daniele, I am certain that God chastises haughty virtue which revolts at the idea of contact with a poor, weak, tempted, fallen creature. Be strong; and, as you are strong, be merciful!

"My head is beginning to tire, and Doctor Niscemi would scold me if he knew that I had written so long a letter. To-morrow he means to carry me off to Cerda, and thence to Termini, to pay a visit of thanksgiving to certain waters which he fancies he has induced me to take. Poor man! If only he knew how little I have obeyed him! I shall look out for a letter from you containing a favourable answer. Let even me do a little good in this world.—And believe me, your most affectionate cousin, ELENA DI S. G."

"*To the Baroness*
Elena Di Santa Giulia, at Cefalù.

"ROME, 18*th February* 1882.

"Poor Elena, it was like her to come and worry and sadden you, alone, ill, out of the world! I was furious when I heard of it. Even you!

"Yes, I mentioned you to my mother last June, at Lugano, and I will tell you how. She made me a sybilline speech to dissuade me from having anything further to do with the Di Santa Giulia family. I imagined she had heard some stupid calumny, for she had secret correspondents at Villascura. I protested, and in my protestations mentioned your name. Thereupon my mother declared that she intended no allusion to you, though she did to your husband. She would not explain herself any further; she promised to speak to me again about it. But meanwhile I was compelled to quit Lugano hurriedly, and without seeing her again. Neither she nor I, in our letters, have mentioned the subject. I will even acknowledge that I have not given it another thought. There is so much gilding, and such a false ring in every word that that woman utters, that it would never pass as good coin. Probably she meant to tell me that which immediately crossed my mind; my disdain made her change her idea, and she got out of her difficulty by the first untruth that came into her head.

"You write to me on her behalf, Elena; you think me severe, unjust; you implore my pity. Have you any more charges? It was unnecessary to call me unjust; you do not know either her or the facts of the case. It seemed to me better that she should remain where she is, out of the world, and under the care of a trustworthy person. But she shall come to Rome, and she shall come into my house, for I cannot leave her, constituted as she is, all alone, to come and go as she pleases, and to make what friendships suit her. Do not think of me, dear Elena, nor of the ideal wife you desire for me. I do not love, I shall never love; I have no time for it, there is no room in my heart for such a bitter vanity; and a family would only be a hindrance to me. I already live in the bosom of the beloved family of my ideas. Do you know what your mother used to say? 'It is all very well to talk, but when Daniele marries, he will take an idea to wife.' Now, I have married several, I love them, they are mine, and, God willing, we will raise a fine progeny in the world. I said this last night to M., as we were walking by moonlight, out by the butts at Trinità dei Monti. Notwithstanding the quilting of tow, which he calls statistics, and the gout, which he calls neuralgia, M. is desperately in love, and took me into his confidence. Then he asked me mine in return. I pointed to the moon. 'Henceforward,' I said, 'I understand no one who does not love as Caligula did. *Plenam fulgentemque lunam invitabat assidue in amplexus.*' Here is another bit of Latin for you to translate.

"Ah, dear Elena, how often, as I thought over my ideals, have I not compared myself to a blockhead contemplating the moon, with a ladder in his hand! Fortunately my doubts pass, and my confidence in myself is prepared to face much severer trials than any it has yet had to bear. But how thankless it is to try to do anything with this flaccid Italian good sense, which rashly demands to know what is the estimated balance, and yet dreads to be thought unpractical, and above all, to lose its dinner hour and the possibility of a peaceful digestion! At heart we are a nation of herbalists. To mature our ideas, we must put them in the sun. In the Chamber there is too little sun. We require a newspaper. It is absolutely necessary for me to have a newspaper, and you cannot imagine how difficult it is to start one, although many people, even among my colleagues in parliament, agree with me in word. When it comes to deeds, then the difficulties appear. The country is not prepared, the moment is not favourable; my scheme of internal policy cannot be carried out unless I have Trent and Istria in my pocket, and it is not worth discussing. You will tell me that, as regards the country, we must prepare it, that one must be in one's place at the right moment, and that if everything depends upon a great success in our external policy, and on the minister who obtains it, we must begin to fight without delay. And what answer should I make to you? Nothing very clear, but one herbalist won't take any trouble, another won't risk his money, a third is afraid of what his friends will say; a fourth, of his constituents; a fifth, and, indeed, a whole crowd of druggists, fear to be taken for clericalists. I shall succeed in spite of all, but it requires energy, and a certain amount of perseverance. Now let us leave these perplexities.

"You tell me that you have been more ill than I think. And why stain the conscience of the too tractable Doctor

Antonino? I can quite understand your having concealed the whole truth from your mother; but why from me? And how can I now believe you when you say you are 'getting better'?

"Clenezzi sends his best remembrances. I discovered last night that he loves music even better than he does the wine of Albano, and a particular dish called 'casonsei,' which is peculiar to Bergamo, and of which he partakes once a week at Trastevere, at an inn kept by a compatriot of his. Last night at the P.'s house we had a regular concert of ancient music, and Donna Laura sang one of Pergolese's songs, which actually brought tears to the eyes of our good old friend. I joked him a little about it, telling him that I should write to you and tell you. 'By all means,' he answered; 'and send her at the same time the melody, or, at least, the words by Metastasio, which alone are worth all the modern stuff.' Here are the words as I copied them from Donna Laura's music:—

"'Should they seek to discover
Where, now, is your friend,
Your unhappy lover,
Say "Death was his end."
Ah, no! do not give her
Such sorrow for me;
"He wept when he left me,"
Your answer shall be.'

"As I walked home I remembered an anecdote which Braga, the famous violoncellist, once told me, and which I do not think I have ever seen in any book. 'The Olympiad,' the opera in which this song occurs, was first given at the Argentina, and cruelly hissed. Poor Pergolese, wounded to death, leaned forward in his stall, covering his face with his hands. The theatre emptied gradually, and he still remained there, prostrated, when the hand of an invisible person appeared out of one of the boxes, threw some flowers over him, and disappeared.

"Happy he! for no greater reward can be given to us in our miserable life than to receive flowers from an invisible person. Do you think, Elena, that she and Pergolese are together now? I confess that I asked myself this question on my way home, but since then the ballot has been voted, and I have thought no more about it.

"The Chamber has adjourned till the 2d of March. I start to-morrow, spending Monday, and possibly Shrove-Tuesday, at the Villa Carrè. Thence I shall go to Villascura. I shall have worries even there. Protests are being circulated, and signatures collected against my speeches and the votes I have given.

"They may hiss me; what matters it? No hand will throw flowers over me; so be it! Had I a coat-of-arms, I should choose this motto: 'Against the many.' Good-bye, dear Elena. Do you think that she and Pergolese are together now? DANIELE."

"*To Senator*
G. B. Clenezzi, at Rome.

"CEFALÙ, *4th March* 1882.

"DEAR CLENEZZI,—I know that you have always been a true and faithful friend to me; I know that you remember me still after these ages; therefore, I thank you for having sent me, a few days since, some verses which touched me, as they did you, even without Pergolese's music, and Donna Laura's voice. But for my part, dear Clenezzi, poetry is dead in me, or at least it left me in tears, as those verses say, which I have exchanged for ugly prose. I prefer prose now, however sad, however hard it may be. I am like a person who, having lost all that was most dear, throws himself into the driest business and flees music.

"You know that the last payment agreed upon between

my husband and Boglietti, under penalty of a criminal prosecution, ought to be made on 31st March. I believe that we are in great difficulties, and that there is no prospect of my husband finding the money. I will speak quite plainly to you, it costs me nothing to speak out. A slight illness, from which I am recovering, seems to have deprived me of all sensibility. Certain follies make me weep, certain ruins leave me indifferent.

"When my husband went to Rome last November, there remained scarcely any trace of the fortune that he received, as you know, in the summer. The payment he had to make in September, and probably other debts, had swallowed it all up. It is on this account that I am staying here, being anxious to avoid every unnecessary expense. When my husband went away, he left me very little money. No sooner was he gone, than I discovered that he had left a number of wretched little debts here to workmen, small tradespeople, and so on, which made me blush! I had by me the money sent to me last July by my uncle, and which you drew out of the National Bank for me. My husband knew nothing of this, and, as I knew that, after his winnings at play, he would not be in immediate want of money, I kept it back, meaning to apply it to this quarter's payment, and feeling certain that when that had to be met he would be in difficulties again. But poor people kept coming to me every hour for their money. I wrote to my husband, who answered that I must persuade them to be patient, as he could not entirely satisfy their claims at the moment. What was I to do? I used the money that I had put aside to pay these people.

"My husband came here about ten days ago. After his departure I learned that he had been trying to raise money. I also discovered that the person from whom he tried to borrow would only lend him the money on condition that his acceptance was endorsed by my mother.

My husband broke off the negotiations. I was not surprised to hear it. Last year he made a desperate attempt to induce my family to give him money, which was fruitless, and he thought, owing to a misunderstanding into which I need not enter, that my uncle, my mother, and I had combined to make game of him. Now you will understand his pride. I believe him capable of facing utter ruin rather than accept anything from us. There is good metal in his character, which always rings true when he receives a hard blow. When he heard that I had paid those trivial debts, he flew into a passion, and wanted to give me a bond by which he promised to repay me the whole sum. I reminded him then of the next payment of interest, and he told me that was no affair of mine. Various ill-omened phrases which have escaped from him at different times keep recurring to me. For instance, last summer in Rome, he talked to me of what he would do if he could not save his honour; but then he returned to the gaming table, intoxicated with fortune.

"Dear Clenezzi, the whole matter is very simple. All that the most devoted wife ought to do, I will do. But what course ought I to follow? I know not, and I am physically incapable of giving my attention to it. If you tell me that I must give up everything, down to my last ring, that I must live on charity, I would give it up and die; there! Now tell me what I should do. You will think; why does she not write to her people? Ought I to write? I will write. But, in any case, the money must be sent to you, and you must arrange matters with Boglietti as you think best, and knowing, as you do, how my husband feels towards the Carrès. What sum shall I ask for? Answer me without delay, as I expect my mother in a few days. She meant to come by sea, but she could easily change her plans, and come by Rome, and it would be well that she should bring the money with her. My uncle is scarcely convalescent, and I don't wish to trouble him with such a letter when he is alone.

"I am ashamed, my dear friend, of giving you so much trouble, when I can offer in return nothing but a little cold, worn-out gratitude. I scarcely dare to offer you even that! I will only say to you, do a good work. I should like to do one so much, but I can find none. Don't tell any one of this letter, and when you have time to give a thought to useless things, give one to your friend, ELENA DI S. G."

"*To Baroness*
Elena Carrè Di Santa Giulia, at Cefalù.

"ROME, *7th March* 1882.

"MOST CHARMING FRIEND,—For the last four days I have been shut up indoors with my old enemy. What could I do? The matter is more serious, perhaps, than you fancy. Forgive me, but I sent for you cousin, Signor Cortis, for whom I have great respect; I told him everything, and begged him to act in my place. I believe that just now he is overburdened with work—parliamentary committees, a newspaper to start, and the question of the redemption of the Venetian railways, with which he is very much occupied. But no one could have undertaken it with greater alacrity. Indeed, I had scarcely uttered your name when he offered his services without even giving me time to ask for them.

"For myself, I can only give you one bit of advice. Come to Rome.

"Forgive my bad writing, I can only use my left hand. I kiss your hand with the earnest hope of seeing you soon. —Your most devoted G. B. CLENEZZI."

"*To Baroness*
Elena Di Santa Giulia, at Cefalù.

"ROME, *14th March* 1882.

"Do not pity me, dear Elena; I could not refuse to do

a service for Clenezzi, who has an attack of gout. For the sake of this best of men I would do anything; I would even play the part of an intruder.

"I went to the lawyer, Boglietti, on Tuesday the 7th, but he was in Florence on business, and I learned that he would not return before yesterday evening. I saw him this morning, and had a talk with him, and am charged by Clenezzi to tell you what has been settled. Boglietti was very anxious about this quarter's payment. The sum, including capital, interest, and expenses, amounts to 16,800 lire. I tried to reassure the lawyer by telling him that if his debtors were not in a position to pay, the Carrè family would certainly provide the money. I took the opportunity of persuading him to abstain for some time from taking any action against your husband if he did not carry out his obligations. He promised that he would let me know at once if the money were not forthcoming, and that he would wait for it until the 15th of April. Now Clenezzi, who, by the way, is better, will send for your husband, and, speaking to him more or less in the name of the President of the Senate, who has already taken part in all this business, will ask him whether he is in a situation to pay this money or not. Should his answer be in the negative, then a delay will be promised him. Meanwhile, you and yours have free time till the 15th of April wherein to make the payment, or to enable your husband to do so.

"I have written to my mother to come to me in Rome as soon as possible. If it is to be done, it were better done quickly. She will arrive about the end of the month. I have taken from to-morrow, 15th, an apartment in the Piazza Venezia. A very noisy place—my mother will like it. I don't know why, but I fancy that if I am to live with her, I shall prefer noise to quiet. But what does it matter? Life with her, under any other circumstances, would seem to me intolerable; now I feel so indifferent, that I cannot in conscience make a merit of having yielded to your entreaties.

"I shall probably soon resign my seat as deputy. But what will this signify to you? Ah, Elena, Elena, perhaps I am wrong to write to you thus, but if my heart sometimes overflows, nothing but gall and bitterness can be expected from it. I have received a long letter from my constituents complaining of my conduct. Do not think that this has raised the gall! The letter has 226 signatures, but of those I know not how many are forged, and how many are those of non-electors, for an authenticated copy has also been sent to the President of the Chamber. These 226 fools have no idea of the service they are doing me. At any other time I should have laughed at their prose; now it is most lucky for me to be able to leave this sinking Chamber, and to present myself to the electorate at the general election with the support of an increased franchise. I do not know whether I shall resign at once, or whether I shall wait for the discussion of the army estimates, which rather tempts me. I shall have to decide quickly, for it appears that the Chamber is to be prorogued in the course of the next ten or twelve days. I will make a noisy exit, and will break as many windows as possible.

"I recommence at home this letter which I had begun at the Chamber, where I intended to speak to-day upon the redemption of the Venetian railways. However, I let it pass in silence, because every one was thinking of something else, and they had each his own project for redeeming the railways of their separate provinces.

"I went out in search of a breath of air, with my speech and many other weighty matters on my mind. I felt ill. I met a lady, who offered to drive me to the Villa Borghese; but I wanted to think over an article which I ought to have sent to a review three days ago, and of which I have not as yet written a line. I therefore declined, and drove to Villa Wolkonsky, where I found roses, ruins, ravens, and the solitude that one seems to require at certain psychological moments. I sat down in the shade of the Claudian Aqueduct, facing Santa Croce in Gerusalemme and the Romano desert, and I began to meditate upon my article: a sketch of Prince Bismarck. Standing out from the brick-work of the old columns, close to me, was a beautiful marble hand, with a well-turned forearm.

For a moment I did not think of Bismarck or of his idea of a cabinet composed of one responsible Minister. Was it poetry, Elena? Was it sentimentality? When can I have caught the latter disease? Be comforted, it won't last long. I told myself that henceforward little white hands and I had nothing to do with each other, and I finished my article with so much ambitious verbiage, that I shall have to omit half of it when I come to write it out. If I grow old without becoming a Minister, I shall go and be a hermit at Santa Croce in Gerusalemme, and, at the hour of noon, when the sun is doing his worst, I shall come up here under these lonely arches, among the fragrant and melancholy roses, to meditate upon that woman's hand and the days that are gone.

"I think that Aunt Tarquinia will be with you by now. Please say many nice things to her from me.

"If I have offended you in undertaking a commission confided by you to Senator Clenezzi, and in writing, notwithstanding your silence of a month, forgive me.

"Clenezzi wishes to be most kindly remembered to you and to your mother. He said to me only to-day: Tell her to come to Rome at once, without delay. I was just going to fasten my letter without repeating your friend's message. Forgive me for this too, if you believe in the devotion of your cousin,

"DANIELE."

"*To Daniele Cortis,*
Parliamentary Deputy, at Rome.

"CEFALÙ, *18th March* 1882.

"DEAR DANIELE,—Elena wishes me to thank you so much for all you have done, and to tell you that she wrote to Clenezzi merely because she knew how busy you were. What would you? You must be surprised at nothing. What will you say when I tell you that I write to you from Cefalù, but that I am staying at the inn within a few yards of my daughter's house? I don't know where I am! I found Elena fairly well in health, but very, very low in spirits. Poor Elena, if I am unlucky in having such a son-in-law, imagine what she must feel! Mercifully she is less sensitive, less nervous than I am; in her place, I should have died ten times over.

"It seems that we are to leave here in a few days. It will be thanks to you if we can have a little breathing-time before making this blessed payment; but still it is well, as Clenezzi says, to be on the spot. Please take a sitting-room and two bedrooms for us at the Minerva, not too high up. I will telegraph to you the day of our departure, that is, if we don't change our plans, for here they are changed every hour of the day. I don't recognise Elena.

"I left my brother-in-law pretty well. It was his wish that I should go to the inn. Ah, dear Daniele, amongst what people I have to live!

"We shall meet very soon, I hope. Try to get rooms looking over the Piazza.—Your affectionate aunt,

TARQUINIA.

"*P.S.*—An enigmatical letter has just come from my son-in-law, which has increased Elena's disquiet, and has simply terrified me. It is now settled that we shall arrive in Rome on the 24th, by the 1·45 express."

CHAPTER XII.

DIFFICULT WALKING.

"SIGNOR BOGLIETTI!" cried the messenger, entering the sitting-room of the Chamber, into which persons are shown who wish to speak to deputies. The room was crowded; here one was writing, leaning over the messengers' table, one was entering bashfully, while another was hastily quitting the room; a number of people bearing on their faces either weariness, nervousness, or vanity, waited in silence.

No one answered the messenger; everybody looked at his neighbour.

"Signor Cortis!" he called still louder. "Who wants Signor Cortis?" Then a man who was talking in a low voice to some others in an inner waiting-room, rose and passed into the dark corridor at the end of which Cortis was expecting him.

"What is it?" he asked drily. "Come in," and he beckoned the lawyer into a room where another visitor was confessing himself to his representative. Boglietti looked at these two and hesitated a moment. Cortis shrugged his shoulders.

"You can speak," he said, seating himself.

"I feel deeply grieved, Signor Deputy," he began, in a low voice, "at what I have to say to you, and, before coming to the point, I wish to make you believe—"

Cortis looked at the clock.

"Kindly come to the point," he said composedly.

"It is not my fault," answered the other. "I have been thinking over this delay; I have asked myself whether I had power to grant it. Perhaps I had not, but in any case that does not signify. Perhaps I might have had the power had a delay of only a fortnight been asked. But I have certain information—"

"Go on."

"Well, I know from a person who has it from the baron himself, that at this moment the relations between him and his wife's family are so bad that they could not be worse."

He paused a moment, as though expecting a remark from Cortis, which did not come.

"And besides," he continued, "I know that the baron is in great straits as regards other most urgent and most important debts. In short, had my own private affairs only been in question, I might perhaps have let the matter run on; but, as it is—"

"You withdraw your promise?" broke in Cortis, rising.

The lawyer also rose, protesting that he did not remember having given any formal promise, that he was deeply grieved. At that moment the other deputy, having got rid of his interlocutor, said to Cortis,—

"Are you not coming? There's a division."

"I'm coming," answered the latter, "and perhaps for the last time."

"Nonsense!" exclaimed his friend, disappearing down the corridor.

"I have just finished," recommenced the lawyer. "I therefore have been compelled to write to the Baron Di Santa Giulia this morning, warning him that no delay can be granted."

"Have you done this already?" asked Cortis, looking directly at him, with sarcastic coldness. "Come and see me to-morrow morning at nine o'clock."

"To-morrow, Saturday, the 25th," said the other, bending his head in thought, and stroking his beard, "I cannot come at nine; I cannot be with you before twelve."

"So be it; twelve o'clock. At my house. You know where it is?"

"Yes, signor."

Boglietti departed, and Cortis again looked at the clock. It was just three. Elena and Countess Tarquinia should have reached the Minerva an hour ago. Cortis had begged Clenezzi to meet them at the station instead of him. He entered the division-lobby, and ten minutes later, leaving Montecitorio, he was walking very slowly towards the Pantheon.

Someone who met him declared afterwards that he had never seen him so pale. He felt Elena near him, but, mixed with this feeling, was a load of other thoughts—other necessities, which he did not clearly understand, but which seemed to become heavier and heavier every moment. First of all there was his speech—that speech that he intended to have made the next day before announcing his resignation; a speech prepared to pass the walls of the Chamber, and to pierce the ears of future electors, so that he required for it all his nerve and all his courage. Then there was that fresh cloud that had come over the affairs of Di Santa Giulia, the necessity for settling something, the obscure postscript to Countess Tarquinia's letter. He had made an appointment for the next day with the lawyer without a very clear idea of what he intended to do, with merely an instinct that he must lift this weight off the baron, if necessary, by taking it upon himself. The Carrès would afterwards approve his action. How to reconcile this plan with the *convenances*, and with the feelings of the baron, he knew not; he would think that over during the night. His last cause of trouble was the imminent arrival of his mother. He was making this sacrifice for Elena, but what would he not have done for her! As he came nearer to the truth, he felt less and less that indifference of which he had written to her in perfect sincerity.

He thought now that all these preoccupations had combined to bring about this novel bodily weariness, this strange torpor, of which he had hitherto accused his excessive work and sleepless nights; now he laid it all to the charge of Elena, who filled Rome with her presence, and made the very air itself warm, soft, and enervating. In Piazza Capranica a man addressed him by name, and added, "This evening." He then remembered that he had convened for that evening, in his rooms, a meeting of political friends, subscribers, and contributors, secured or desired, to the new paper, to hear from him, Cortis, the outline of his speech, and they were to be asked to discuss it; because upon that speech the paper was to be founded. "This evening," he had said, and Cortis felt his heart grasped anew by the lofty ideal that he had set before his mind, and by the austere duty that he had imposed upon himself; he felt that all the weak fancies, the misgivings, had vanished, and that a fresh strength had been infused into him.

On reaching the Minerva, he found a crowd of old ladies and French priests. The porter, who was talking to a fine-looking capucin, noticed Cortis, and said to him at once,—

"The ladies have come. Senator Clenezzi has just quitted the hotel, leaving a message that if you came you were to go up to the countess immediately."

Cortis was known at the hotel. He himself had chosen Countess Tarquinia's rooms on the second floor. He went upstairs, and found her alone, in the worst of tempers, her face burning, and her still considerable good looks spoiled by the tiring journey. She received him badly declaring that politics had ruined him mentally and physically, that he was lean and wrinkled, and hideous to look upon. Why had he not come to the station to meet them, instead of sending that poor old donkey Clenezzi? Certainly politics was a much more serious disease than gout!

"And then," she continued, "it pleases your lordship to keep us waiting a century at the hotel before you come near us. It's no use contradicting me. I say a century!"

"And Elena?" asked Cortis.

The lady, piqued by his indifference, made no reply, and continued her lecture.

"I can't say much for the rooms you have chosen. It is evident, dear boy, that you have no women in your house."

"I shall soon have one, aunt," said Cortis quietly.

Countess Tarquinia felt that her remark had been thoughtless. She blushed scarlet, and held her tongue.

"Well," again said Cortis, "how is Elena?"

"Give me your hand and let us make friends again," answered the countess, restored to good temper. "Elena is very well, and I am very pleased with her."

She pronounced these last words in a loud voice, pointing to the door of the neighbouring room, then she covered her face for a moment with her hands, waved them in the air, and raised her eyes to the ceiling.

"I can't make her out," she whispered, making herself understood rather by her gestures than by her words; "I can't make her out."

"Oh!" said Cortis, feeling tired of her.

Elena stood in the doorway of her room, pale, smiling, her hair in disorder, her eyes larger, her whole appearance more delicate than ever. She looked like a girl. She shook Cortis by the hand, but there was no longer a smile on her face, not even a slight tremor of the mouth. They exchanged a few cold, stiff words in a low, uncertain voice. Then followed a silence. Elena looked at her mother.

"My good girl!" said Countess Tarquinia, "why

don't you speak? Very good," she continued, with a sigh, after vainly waiting for an answer, "if you won't talk, I will. Dear Daniele, we must put our heads together without delay. You understand? Poor Daniele, you have already done so much for us, and we are so grateful to you! Indeed we are, so grateful; it is true, really it is, from our hearts! Don't be hurt with Elena for not speaking to you, because, sometimes she is overcome by her feelings, poor thing, like her mother."

Elena raised her dark, shining eyes to Daniele. Neither he nor she uttered.

"You are aware, are you not," continued the countess, "of certain mad speeches that my son-in-law has made at Cefalù? Good. You know also about his letter? I wrote to you of it from Rome, but you do not know the end of the story. I will tell it you. I must begin by saying that no one ever wrote to us at Casa Carrè; that my brother-in-law and I were, so to speak, excommunicated until last summer, as if it had all been my fault! Well, well, perhaps it is better not to rake up those matters again. At last I find myself able to go to Elena; you know what distress I was in; I hope that not even a dog may ever have to suffer as I have done! Well, I started, and naturally I go to the inn, but never mind that. I go to the inn. No, indeed, I am not going to push myself into other people's houses! Besides, Lao would have beaten me. The fact remains that, four days after my arrival, just time enough for him to have become aware of it, this letter arrives from Rome."

"For you, aunt?"

"No; for Elena."

With the frowning face and sing-song voice of one who carefully repeats the impertinent words of a disagreeable person, the countess began to declaim as follows:—

"The baron knew perfectly well that his dear mother-in-law was at Cefalù, and that she had not dared to occupy a room in his house. This was the most deliberate acknowledgment the Carrès could make of their unworthy treatment of him (those were his very words). They would soon see, however, that their behaviour would produce still more serious consequences, but Elena might feel perfectly certain that he would not lower himself for fear of anything they could do. He would shortly have the pleasure of showing them, and her, and the whole world, how strong in him was the feeling of duty and honour ; he would give a slap in the face, he did not explain how, to his dear relations, and worse than a slap if they had in them a grain of conscience. Elena was not to pretend that she had been sent to Cefalù. He was generous, and left her perfectly free to go and live where she pleased. Henceforward, he should care for nothing in the world. In a short time he would leave her still more at liberty."

"Do you understand?" the countess went on. "I say that it is all nonsense, but it has frightened her dreadfully. Then I thought that I would answer him upon the point of our acknowledgment of the bad treatment he had received from us, and upon his humbling himself before us; and I think that I answered him kindly, weighing my words with the deliberation, though I say it who shouldn't, of a saint. I told him that, profiting by his permission, I should take Elena to spend some time in Veneto, but that we should remain for a few days in Rome, so as to see him. I added a few affectionate words about his anger against us, and our desire to help him by every means in our power. Elena added a note to my letter, wherein she said that she was coming to Rome to help him, even against his will, and told him the day and hour of our intended arrival, and the hotel at which we should stay. He has sent no answer, but let that pass; perhaps he hasn't had time yet. We arrive, hoping to find him at the station. Not at all! We ask Clenezzi about him, and Clenezzi, red as Bacchus, boggles over some story of having seen him this morning, that he was quite well, that he might be gone here or there. There was no time for explanations, but it is quite clear that our letters have had no effect. Now, tell me, this question of the day of payment is quite settled?"

"Yes, yes; quite settled," answered Cortis hurriedly, not wishing to worry them unnecessarily; for, although things were not quite settled at that moment, they would be at twelve o'clock the following day.

"And he knew of this delay?" asked the countess.

"He knew all about it."

"What did he say?"

"I have not spoken to him on the subject, but Clenezzi told us that he seemed pleased, and thanked him very much."

"Good; and now tell me, dear, what we are to do. It is evident that he doesn't mean to show himself. Ought we to write to him? Ought we to go in search of him?"

Countess Tarquinia began to gasp with anxiety, biting her lower lip and blinking her eyes, as if the idea of going in search of her son-in-law, after the insults she had received from him, had brought tears of rage from her heart.

Elena had not opened her mouth. Seated opposite to her mother, she seemed to have paid no attention whatever to her long speech, looking with tired, motionless eyes into space.

"What was the date of the letter?" asked Cortis, after thinking for a minute.

"Which letter?"

"Your son-in-law's; the last one."

The countess could not remember; she looked at her daughter.

"Elena," she said, "can you help me? That letter?"

"You have it, mamma," answered Elena sweetly.

A sudden blush overspread her face. She had not considered, before giving her answer, that now she would probably be left alone with him.

"I don't think so," said the countess, "but I will see."

Scarcely had she gone into her room than Elena stretched out her hand to Cortis, who seized it in both his own. Her eyes filled with tears, and she said, in a very low voice,—

"Forgive me!"

"Oh!" he answered, "but why?"

Elena saw in his face what he was on the point of saying; it was the reason for her coldness, for her silence of two months that he wanted to ask. She interrupted him hurriedly.

"No, no; it is not that that you are to forgive me. It is something else. I must speak to you; another time."

The door of Countess Tarquinia's room sounded as if it were opening. Elena withdrew her hand. It was not so. They looked at each other for a few seconds. Then the countess entered, having found the letter. She could not see Elena's face, but she could see Daniele. She stopped short, and said,—

"Are you ill?"

"No, aunt."

His voice was firm and clear.

"The 16th of March," added the countess, pointing to the letter.

"One minute," said Cortis. "I believe I wrote to Elena on the 14th, and the first mention of the delay was made to him at least three days later, because Clenezzi could not see him before the 17th, so he knew nothing of it when he wrote that letter. He will be appeased now. Does he know that you are at the Minerva?"

"Yes, we wrote and told him so."

"Well, then, if he does not come to-day, Elena might

go and look for him to-morrow, and meanwhile she might send him a note."

As he spoke, Cortis turned to his cousin, who said to him quietly, and without the least discomposure,—

"I am going to the Senate in an hour with Clenezzi."

"Bless me!" exclaimed the countess; "here you are making arrangements on the sly right and left, and never saying a word to us about it! And here are we spending our time in consulting what is best to be done."

"You are right, mamma. I thought you had heard of it. I am very careless."

Cortis went away a few minutes afterwards, notwithstanding his aunt's entreaties that he would stay at least till Clenezzi's arrival, so that they might make other plans together. She finished by telling him that for this once she would let him go, but that if he expected forgiveness for his other sins, he was to put himself at her disposition the following morning, and she would not take politics as an excuse should he fail.

"It's all very well," said the countess, "but it is a long time since I was in Rome, and I don't want to go away without seeing anything. To-morrow is Saturday; is not the Borghese Villa open? It will make an object for a drive, at any rate."

Cortis, his heart full of that hand so hastily withdrawn, of that look so quickly downcast, went down into the Piazza Minerva to wait for Clenezzi. He wished to warn him, to prevent him from taking Elena to the Senate. It was not right that she should see the baron just then; Cortis wished to see him first; he wished to reassure him as to the delay refused by the lawyer Boglietti. Clenezzi came limping and grumbling along the Via della Palombella. He hastened as soon as he saw Cortis, signalling to him, and at last coming up to him breathless and exhausted, crying: "Don't you know? Don't you hear?" and seizing his arm, he began to relate how he had had a visit from Di Santa Giulia, who was furious because he had received a letter from the lawyer retracting the promised delay. Clenezzi, amazed, could only say that he knew nothing about it. The other, the ruffian, had answered him brutally. Then Clenezzi had felt his good Bergamese blood boil, and had given him a piece of his mind, the beast. His hands and chin were still shaking with anger, and he growled like an enraged old mastiff. But, all the same, it was like the impudence of that Signor Boglietti! What right had he to make and break promises? An old simpleton, to say the least of it! And now, how could he take the baroness to the Senate? What could he say to her?

Cortis quieted him. It would suffice to tell Elena that her husband had left the Palace, and that it would be useless to search for him elsewhere. As for the business with Boglietti, he was not to worry about that. Cortis would settle it.

"My dear Signor Cortis," exclaimed the senator, clasping his hands. "You don't know how grateful I am to you! And now," he added, "I must go up to the ladies."

"By-the-bye," said Cortis, with a smile, "to-day, Friday, is not Trastevere open? Is not this the day to see—"

"Ah! ah!" answered the senator, breaking excitedly into his dialect, which he afterwards translated; "they are all ruined now."

The image of Elena, her gentle words: "forgive me," the action, voice, and look that accompanied it, took possession again of Cortis as soon as he was alone. Other images assailed him, but he would let them find no place in his thoughts; the conversation desired by her, the letter from her husband, his words: "in a short time he would leave her still more at liberty." Terrible words! He saw in his heart something that would have disgusted him had he not known that every human heart is like an open, clean, well-furnished house; thieves, who are not invited, may, without any blame attaching to the owner, sometimes break in and remain there for a space. He hastened on, without noticing that, while he was buried in thought, he had unconsciously reached the Piazza Venezia. Pricked by remorse, he turned back to the Senate, and having learned that Di Santa Giulia lived in the Via delle Muratte, he went straight thither.

To reassure him, to tell him that the payment of the 31st March would be provided for, to make him believe that this help came from the Government, and that attached to it was the condition of voluntary resignation of his senatorship; that was the only course to pursue. Di Santa Giulia was wont to boast that he had deserved well of the Left; perhaps he believed it. There was no other course.

The senator was out. Cortis wrote a message upon a card begging him to come and see him "on very important business," the next day, Saturday, at noon. He inquired of the portress who opened to him, whether the senator would certainly come in before next morning. She believed he would; but the senator had become so queer lately! He talked to her so oddly at times, that she would never be surprised if there were an accident! He must have great troubles, poor gentleman! The woman, a Tuscan chatterbox, would have gone on thus for ever so long if Cortis had given her the chance. But he had to return home. Passing a chemist's shop, he went in and asked for a sleeping-draught; he threw on to the counter a prescription borrowed from a friend, and said he wanted a dose rather stronger. For some time past he had suffered greatly from want of sleep. Physically robust, he despised every bodily requirement, and despising and ignorant of every kind of physic, he never took medicine except when suffering prevented him from work or action; and then he took it violently, fighting the phenomenon with the most powerful remedies. At home he ordered a cup of the strongest coffee, meaning to take the chloral that night before going to bed; then he shut himself up to work in his study, where ten or twelve chairs were prepared for the friends whom he expected at nine that evening.

CHAPTER XIII.

VERTIGO.

At a quarter past nine, a group of men was assembled in Cortis's room, talking and smoking, while he moved about among them with heightened colour and shining eyes, joking and chattering as though Elena, her husband, and Signora Cortis had never existed, and as if every difficulty had been banished for ever. There were some young deputies, in white neckties, quite ready to talk a little politics, and to laugh, later on, at some smart party, at what they had said; there were some old senators, who took matters gravely, and were not quite at their ease in the company of the former; there were two or three young men who took matters still more gravely, and who had just returned from a course of social science in Germany; there were also a few wealthy old gentlemen from the north of Italy, who had contributed largely with their purses to the foundation of the newspaper.

Cortis opened the proceedings by stating that all might be now considered ready for its publication. They had a subscribed capital of four hundred and fifty thousand lire. All was ready for printing—place, machinery, and persons. The editor and principal foreign contributors were engaged; the Italian staff would be very easily found. Cortis promised his own most careful assistance, at any rate until the opening of the new Chamber. The question to settle now was when it should make its appearance. Cortis was determined, as his friends knew, to take the opportunity offered by a protest from his constituents to make a speech the next day, the last sitting before the Easter holidays, and then to resign. He intended to state his political creed very clearly, appealing from the present to the future electorate. As he would eventually have direction of the newspaper, he considered it his duty to communicate to his friends the ideas that he intended to unfold in the Chamber, although they might not be new to some of them. If the idea pleased them, if the speech produced any echo in the country, it might, perhaps, be opportune to announce to the public the new paper as the result of this feeling, and to resign not so late that the speech should be forgotten, nor so soon that the connection between the two facts should appear premeditated.

At this point Cortis began to briefly explain what he intended saying, at greater length, in the Chamber. He spoke standing with his back against the high writing-desk near him, gesticulating and fixing his eyes first on one and then on another of his audience, some of whom were seated listening to him with reserve, one of whom was stretched on a sofa, and another who was standing in the window smoking.

"The order and the form do not signify," said Cortis. This will be the substance."

The honourable deputy who was smoking in the window came and planted himself in front of the speaker, riding on a chair.

"Some of my constituents," continued Cortis, "protest against me for expressing clerical opinions in the Chamber. I deny that these persons know the colour of their own opinions, and I very much doubt their understanding the sense of their own words; in any case, I mean to yield, and to resign my seat, while reserving to myself the right of making a few remarks upon the occasion."

"Your well-wishers," said somebody, "will not let you speak."

"Why not? In any case, it will be for the Chamber to decide. As for censure and blame, that is what I desire. I shall say that, grateful as I am towards my colleagues for the consideration they have shown me, I feel that the air of the Chamber is so vitiated that I can leave it without regret. And here, if they will let me go on, I shall say that those who believe that the disappearance, not of the old parties, but still more of every form of parliamentary government is at hand, may come thither to blow off the steam of their own corrupt ideas. I shall add that, on leaving the Chamber, I shall give clear and distinct notice of my resignation to the new electorate; and I certainly shall not go and preach a transformation of characters and opinions so as to constitute an inflated and lifeless majority. I have frequently heard in the Chamber mention made of a new party, which all desire, and to which nobody will belong. I shall be glad of the opportunity of letting my colleagues know that I am ready to sacrifice myself to the public weal, and that I am resigning my seat in order to go in search of this new party, followed by which I shall return, if possible."

"Hum! hum!" remarked some sceptics.

"Gentlemen!" exclaimed Cortis, "if you have no faith, why do you join in the undertaking?"

"Go on, go on!" cried the same sceptics.

"I shall be less haughty when the time comes," said Cortis; "I shall study my words. You see my speech will probably be much interrupted, and I shall have to make many asides to right and left, which I cannot foresee now, but the kernel of it is in the new party. I shall leave the Chamber with a prophecy that it will soon be filled by men raised above the superstitions and ignorance of a certain class of liberal individualism which regards itself as the leader of humanity, and will never consent to take a lower place; it has consented to do useful work, if destroying everything be useful, but now it will have to work for one much stronger, much more powerful, than itself, who, finding the way clear, will come to claim the leadership of the world, and will leave to those liberals a meadow in Arcadia, perchance, and a few sheep. These men, with the future always before them, will fill the Chamber, and, unlike the rhetoricians and mythologists, they will be convinced that in the arduous work of social revification which is imposed upon us by modern forms of production, the best instrument will be a strong monarchy, free and unfettered by any Chamber, but with a profound respect for religious sentiments. These men will be inspired by the most ardent patriotism, and will never make dishonest declarations in order to gain a rood of territory for Italy."

"There!" said Cortis, after a moment's silence; "I shall develop these ideas more or less. Now you ought all to give me your opinion frankly."

No one spoke. Cortis went and threw himself on to the sofa, where he waited, gazing at the ceiling.

"Bold," muttered an old senator. "A very bold speech!"

"Of course it is," said Cortis, with a gesture of indifference; "so bold, in fact, that perhaps I shall not be able to make it."

The deputy who had been sitting astride his chair rose and clapped Cortis on the back.

"I don't mind that," he said; "I don't mind the boldness of the sound, it is the boldness of the sense that I look at."

He added that, as far as he could judge from the brief exposition they had heard, the ideas seemed to him more radical than those which had been accepted as common ground by all present for the foundation of the paper. There had been much talk about social reforms, but this was too outspoken an advocacy of State socialism, and it might alarm the public. He would not discuss the principles, but certainly Italy was, as yet, insufficiently prepared, and these ideas had not been sufficiently published to cause people to flock to such a new standard. The honourable deputy did not approve of speaking disparagingly of a transformation longed for by so many people within and without the Chamber. There might be persons who were sceptical on this point, but in politics, it was never wise to give offence unnecessarily.

A young Sicilian, recently home from Berlin, a fervent believer in Christian Socialism, upheld Cortis warmly. He declared his speech to be even more than a Government or a party programme. Reserve and caution come with power. If they intended to start a movement which was to work upwards from below, they must be honest and courageous. Who did not talk of social reforms? He wanted to know how their great work could be carried out if not by a strong monarchy, by combination and by religious feeling.

The deputy replied; others intervened in the debate, recommending more prudent councils. Cortis shuddered, fidgeted on his sofa, wishing to keep silence, but he was not master that evening of his overstrung nerves, and suddenly broke out into a violent abuse of the nervous and timid, attacking his opponents with so much bitterness and vehemence as to amaze rather than anger them. When he had finished, no one spoke for a time, all looked round in astonishment. At last another senator began to speak at some length, and feeling his way with great caution, admiring the hardihood of some, praising the carefulness of others, congratulating himself upon having had any part in a discussion, honourable to all alike, though the ardour of conviction, and the desire for public welfare, had been once a truce expressed with considerable vivacity. After praising everybody, the senator, wishing to make peace all round, could only give a slight rap to those who had spoken most violently. According to him, the disagreement between them was rather apparent than real, a disagreement as to the opportuneness of what had been said by Signor Cortis, rather than as to their intrinsic value; although he himself, after hearing all that had been said, could not accept unreasonably the opinions and judgments of either one side or the other.

Having laid down this axiom, it did not seem difficult to the senator to hope that all would agree in the following conclusion. Signor Cortis had merely spoken for himself, and the newspaper was in nowise bound to accept that speech as its programme. He had spoken boldly, very boldly. During a few months of parliamentary life, Signor Cortis had distinguished himself, gaining much respect and much sympathy; his speech, should he succeed in making it, would certainly cause great excitement in the Chamber and out of doors, and would create an opportunity of studying the feelings and disposition of the public, and of founding the paper on firmer ground, either ahead of or behind the views therein stated.

Cortis nodded in silent but contemptuous agreement the others, some at once, others later, some aloud, others in a low, voice approved. There was nothing else to be said. The white neckties hurried away. Cortis came out last. He took the arm of the senator who had spoken, a man of great genius, learning, and character, and dragged him forcibly towards the Via Aracæli, although he wished to go towards the Roman College.

"If you thought me mad," said Cortis quickly, "you might have told me so sooner."

The other protested, but Cortis would not hearken to him, declaring his intention of sending society, paper and all to the deuce, and retiring altogether from public life. The senator tried to calm him, reminding him that as he had asked the opinion of his friends, he must not be hurt if that opinion were given clearly. Cortis denied having asked any one's advice; considering himself bound to those people, he did not wish to take any step without telling them, but he had considered himself sure of their entire approbation. Were not those the ideas which had been so frequently discussed since the question of starting the paper was first mooted? No, no; Cortis understood them, they were jealous of him, they feared that he would gain too much influence, too much authority. The senator did not think that, but the others did; they were envious, hidden enemies. Had not the senator heard them? Had he not seen them?

The few people whom they met turned to look at the tall, well-made man who was talking so energetically, in a voice which shook with so much emotion, to the other, tall and thin, very quiet in his old-fashioned overcoat. The latter tried to stop under a street-lamp to look at his watch, but Cortis would not allow it; he seized him more tightly by the arm, dragging him along like a naughty boy. At last they reached the Capitol, and then the poor senator stopped short, vowing that he would not be pulled a step farther.

"My dear fellow, do me a favour," he said. "Tell me where you are going?"

"I must walk; I must tire myself," said Cortis. "Did you not tell me once that you sometimes go into the Colosseum at night?"

"Thank you; yes, at eight o'clock. But it is half-past ten now. I am always in bed at this hour."

"Because I should like to have gone there with you. There are few people I respect as much as you."

"Thank you," answered the senator, with a modest smile and tired voice. "I salute you," he continued making himself very small indeed, as if to elude the grasp of his terrible companion. Cortis shook him by the hand, and let him go without a word.

He walked on rapidly, seeing before him the Chamber, the members with their eyes fixed upon him and upon the President; and facing him, under the left-hand gallery, the silent clock, marking as they passed the moments which were bearing away with themselves his irrevocable words, the hour which was one of the most solemn, the most serious of his life. Now the face of Elena, her look, would suddenly dash in among the other visions; but it disappeared again, quickly showing only that dark hall, those strong or hostile faces, that clock, with its inexorable hands. And he heard voices; he could hear the indifferent chattering of his colleagues, the interruptions, the contradictions, the abuse. They seemed to fall upon him like slaps on his face, and a flood of invective rose to his lips. He answered with abuse and sarcasm to right and left; he was alone against them all! Words, gesticulations crowded into his mind with increasing rapidity. And he walked on with teeth set and fists clenched, until in the Piazza dei Fenili he reeled with dizziness, and had to grasp at the parapet overlooking the Forum, waiting breathlessly till it passed away. When the huge spectral columns of Castor and Pollux ceased whirling round and round with the other great corpses of the Forum, all grey in the misty moonlight, he stood there watching almost unconsciously the three enormous pillars, the colossal fragment of the architrave curtained in the white clouds that veiled the Esquiline.

The peace of dead ages entered little by little into his soul. He then walked on slowly, thinking as he went, astonished at this novelty, this sudden attack of vertigo which not even his powerful will could prevent. He must be very calm, were it only for the sake of the morrow. He saw no more visions, and only heard his own footfall in the solitude around him.

All of a sudden he beheld the Colosseum rising black and huge out of the clouds. The little gas-lamps were insufficient to penetrate the darkness outside a space of two feet. He could just distinguish, far away through the doorways, the open arena. Cortis hid himself gladly in the darkness, seeming thus to pass from time into eternity, and reposing there. The moon shone out, whitening around him the vast, bare vertibræ of the amphitheatre. No living creature was visible. One single ray of light streamed through the arches facing him, coming from San Clemente: from time to time only the sound of wheels told of busy life in the distance.

Cortis leaned against one of the supports of the imperial box, in the shadow. The desolate silence, the vast, black and grey ruins reminded him of a spent crater in the moon, surrounded by black mountains. And with his sad dreams, the face and voice of Elena returned to him. Was she henceforth to live in another planet? Could she never be his? His heart began to beat violently. He clenched his hands on his bosom, fearing to faint. Good God! What meant this utter prostration of mind? where came this wave which, rising, seemed to cover his neck, his face, and which was so sweet, so bitter, and so powerful? What! he, Cortis, weeping! He turned to the old stone and hid his face.

A few minutes later a crowd of people filled the arena, stopping at the entrance with exclamations of—

"Oh! Beautiful! wonderful!" *

Cortis went away.

* In English in the original.—Note by the Translator.

CHAPTER XIV.

THEY WERE WORTHY OF THIS.

ELENA did not sleep that night. Towards dawn she fell into a brief slumber, and dreamed of her bright little room at Passo di Rovese, with its fresh breeze, its green leaves, and its roses; a dream for which she despised herself. She got up at six o'clock and went to hear mass at the Minerva church, longing to pray and to find a little peace. She could not. In church even more than outside she felt that her faith was dumb. And, as she sat wearily in her place, she envied all the devout people who had so many things to ask of God, who prayed so fervently as though they could actually see Him on the high altar bending down to listen to them. She, on the other hand, saw only her sad, useless life, and she desired nothing; there was nothing that she could beg from God without sin. Would He perhaps, in His mercy, extinguish her passion, the fire that burned up her very soul? Oh, no! her torture was too dear to her; she lived upon it. Rather would He allow her to die; but then what would become of her in the next world? What good had she ever done in this one? Perhaps some acts of charity, coldly performed. Even her one virtue of wifely fidelity, what religious merit had it? None. She had remained faithful, partly from a proud, human feeling of honour, partly in order not to hurt him, to be an obstacle in his path. What had been the fruit of this? Only this, that she had not sinned. What had she done with that treasure of love and enthusiasm which she felt in her heart? She had buried it. No, she must not beg death from God, but life: not love, not gladness, not peace, but only the power of doing right for His sake, of suffering with resignation. This thought was ecstasy to her, a sudden fire burned in her heart, and she sent up this prayer to God: she told Him that she would never beg Him to grant her happiness, not even in the future world, that she accepted and blessed His will, even though it should be to make her suffer eternally. She found repose in prayer, and a gentle breath of that peace for which she would not ask. Perhaps it was weakness, and the natural result of so violent an effort. Her prayer died away in her tired heart; even the power of thought seemed to leave her; there remained only a sense of quiet.

Then this idea occurred to her, that it was not worth while to hide her feelings any longer from Cortis. Notwithstanding all her attempts to make him forget her—to offend him—she had not succeeded, and she saw clearly that he had guessed her secret; both of these facts gave her great pleasure in spite of herself! And then? Pretence became a useless sacrifice. Poor Cortis! what comfort had she ever given him? Whose fault was it if he now had the sorrow of living with his mother. The latter had sent her a Pindaric letter of thanks, full of sickening expressions of affection and of unseemly allusions to ill-assorted couples, which had brought the proud blood to her face. Countess Tarquinia could not endure the notion, and was constantly talking of it, describing her sister-in-law as having been, when a girl, the most untrustworthy and most selfish creature in the world; life with her would be impossible! Elena was full of remorse at having even asked Cortis to allow such a person to live in Rome. She must beg pardon of him on her knees, and see if no remedy could be found. Mass was over, the church was emptying itself. Elena kneeled down a moment, not to pray, but to think, that if it were lawful to ask such a thing of God, if a soul that believed so little, and was so unworthy as hers, might hope to be heard, she would beg Him to provide for the deliverance of Cortis. As she left the church, it occurred, with a flash of irony, that she ought to have thought of her husband too. Indeed, the letter she had received at Cefalù had agitated her more deeply, more indescribably, than she would admit to herself; but now, knowing that the postponement of the payment had been obtained after that letter was written, and not knowing that her husband was hemmed in by other claims equally threatening, it did not trouble her so seriously. She had gone secretly the previous evening to the Via delle Muratte; the baron was out; she had left a letter for him.

What more could she do?

On the steps of the hotel she met Senator Clenezzi, and he, seeing her going up at that hour, gazed at her in open-mouthed surprise without even greeting her.

"My dear lady," he said at last, "is it you yourself? Do you know that it is scarcely half-past seven?"

Elena smiled.

"You ought to be pleased to meet me," she said.

The senator was quite puzzled by her manner, sighed, and suppressing the protestations that rose to his lips, merely answered: "To be sure." Then he talked to her of a very strange letter he had that minute received from Cortis. Elena started, and put herself into an attitude of silent entreaty. Clenezzi gave her the note, which was as follows:—

"My mother has arrived in Rome this morning unexpectedly. I do not know if I shall be able to go to the Minerva at half-past ten as I had intended. I have an engagement at mid-day, and then I have to speak at the Chamber. Please tell the countess this. If I cannot come, I will send the orders of admission for the sitting."

"Tell me," asked the senator, almost before Elena had finished reading the note, "what does he mean? I always understood from him, and from you, and from everybody, that Cortis was alone in the world, and that he had no relations except yourselves. I can't make it out at all."

Elena made no reply. Her eyes were still fixed on the letter, and she seemed deep in thought. Finally she handed it back to Clenezzi.

"Very well," she said.

Clenezzi saw that she knew more than he did, and that she did not wish to be questioned. He took his leave, promising to return about ten o'clock, and to put himself at Countess Tarquinia's disposal. He had reached the foot of the steps, when Elena suddenly turned and ran down after him.

"Go to Cortis," she said. "See my aunt, and when you come back here tell me about her."

The senator, taken aback, opened his mouth to excuse himself, but Elena had already left him and fled upstairs.

Countess Tarquinia did not awake for an hour. When she heard of her sister-in-law's arrival, she said plainly to Elena that people must lie on the beds they made for themselves, that she freely forgave her brother's wife, but that she certainly would not see her. She was sorry on Daniele's account, but she could not give way upon that point. If Elena would be guided by her, she would take the same line.

"Oh, no!" answered Elena, with such contemptuous indignation in her voice, and such a frown on her brow, that her mother hastily ejaculated: "Well, don't be so angry, for pity's sake." And then, having given vent to professions of exaggerated humility, of exaggerated respect for the talents and generous heart of her daughter, who listened shudderingly, she broke out into the whole story of the past misdeeds of her sister-in-law, not even concealing certain ancient quarrels that they had had together.

"I know all that," Elena rejoined; "but do you wish to make Daniele's sacrifice even more bitter to him than it is already, especially as you know the share that I had in it?"

"Your servant," returned Countess Tarquinia, "your most obedient servant! Did you ask my advice? and did Daniele ever say a word to me on the subject?"

Elena would not answer.

Clenezzi reappeared at half-past nine, and was received by Elena alone, as her mother had not yet finished her toilette. He had been to Cortis's house, but, concealing his real reason, he had alleged a wish to hear news of Di Santa Giulia's affairs.

"Well?" asked Elena.

"I also saw the signora, your aunt," said the senator, with a bow.

"Spare these civilities," said Elena, impatiently thrumming with her fingers. "There's no time for them. Tell me plainly what she is like."

"Plainly?" asked the senator. "Am I really to speak out? Well, then, she is a fright. I never saw such a woman."

"Tell me all about her."

"As to her appearance, she is tall, lean, and yellow; nothing but skin and bone. In my country we should say that she is only fit to be sent to Palazzolo to make buttons of. And her dress, her manner, her whole appearance! Cortis introduced me to her with a voice and look that choked my voice in my throat, but she immediately began to chatter to such an extent that I could not bear it more than five minutes. I ran away."

The senator paused a moment, and then began again in a grave voice,—

"But do you know what struck me?"

Elena grew paler.

"Cortis," he said. "He must be ill. One can see that. His face is quite changed. I am afraid of something serious."

She watched him, speechless, with her two eyes so wide open, so fixed, so full of sudden fear, that the senator hastened to attenuate, as best he might, the effect of his words, and of the sepulchral voice in which they had been uttered. At this moment Countess Tarquinia entered, beautifully dressed, and after a quick glance at each of them, she asked Clenezzi if there were any news of her son-in-law. Clenezzi somewhat thoughtlessly answered that Di Santa Giulia was expected at Cortis's house at twelve o'clock.

At Cortis's house? What new difficulty had arisen? The senator got a little bit embarrassed. He answered that they had to settle some final arrangements with the lawyer, some formalities relative to the promised delay. Elena did not speak; Countess Tarquinia was only too glad to accept any explanations which would leave her in peace, at any rate for that day. When all was said and done, Elena had left Cefalù with the consent of her husband; he had been informed of the day and hour at which she would arrive in Rome; they had sent to inquire for him at the Senate and at home; he had been written to in the nicest manner possible; what more could he want?

The countess inquired of Clenezzi whether he had arranged a good programme of amusements for the day. The only two things upon which she insisted were mass at St Peter's, and the drive to Villa Borghese. The senator proposed a visit to the Tiberine Museum, recently opened. Countess Tarquinia turned up her nose. Museums! She had seen so many of them. What was there to see in this Tiberine Museum? Clenezzi humbly acknowledged that he had never been into it. The countess resigned herself to it, and they were on the point of starting, when Clenezzi remembered that Cortis had said that he would do his utmost to come to the Minerva between half-past ten and eleven. Countess Tarquinia, terrified at the bare idea of having perhaps to meet her sister-in-law, hastily said that, as they were uncertain of his coming, it was not worth while waiting for him, and that they could leave a note for him with the porter. She wrote this herself, and told Cortis that he would find her and her daughter, towards eleven o'clock, at the Tiberine Museum.

As the countess was entering one of the chapels in St Peter's, Elena beckoned to Clenezzi, and hurriedly whispered to him,—

"What is the matter now with my husband? Why is he going to Cortis?"

"Nothing that I know of," answered the senator. "Only what I have told you."

The countess turned round to address a remark to her daughter, and their conversation came to an end.

Towards eleven o'clock her carriage arrived at the Tiberine Museum, from the Borgo S. Spirito, and Cortis's from the iron bridge.

"Do you know what I will do?" asked the countess, as soon as she saw her nephew. "I don't care about your museum, no more does the senator; is not that so? He shall come with me to do two or three things; and you, Elena, go to the museum with Daniele, and let him take you back to the hotel. Will you?"

"I shall be proud!" answered the senator, bowing, and raising his outspread hands.

Elena said not a word, she neither blushed nor paled; the heaving of her bosom alone betrayed her trouble. Before getting out of the carriage, the countess whispered to her to tell Cortis of her firm intention not to receive her sister-in-law. Elena resolutely shook her head.

"You must tell him yourself," she said.

Countess Tarquinia in her vexation bit the fan that she held in her hand, and then, scarcely noticing her nephew, she said to the coachman,—

"Via Condotti."

Cortis did not understand it all, and looked at Elena for an explanation.

"Mamma does not care about museums," she said, in a trembling voice, and forcing her lips into a smile, which accorded ill with the sad look in her eyes. "Will you accompany me?"

"Of course," replied Cortis.

He took the tickets, and, offering her his arm, entered with her the deserted, neglected garden, which strives to bloom in the solitudes of Sant Onofrio.

The far-away noises of Rome died in the silence. The great palms facing the museum in oriental gravity, the straight, thick rows of fir trees overshadowing the Gianicolo in black solemnity, seemed to cast a melancholy over the whole scene.

"I have never been here before either," said Cortis. "I daresay it is interesting."

His voice trembled a little too. Elena followed him, powerless. At the door of the museum he would have turned to the right to enter, but that powerless arm within his suddenly stiffened itself and pushed him straight on.

"Forgive me, forgive me," sobbed Elena, in a choking voice.

Cortis felt that the vertigo of the preceding evening was coming over him again, but this time he conquered it by sheer strength of will, and, squeezing closely Elena's arm, he walked rapidly with her down a grassy path to the left among some shrubs. Then he slackened his pace.

"No, no, Elena," he said tenderly, caressing her hand

and raising it to his lips. "What have I to forgive, dear? I have nothing."

She tried to stop her tears with her handkerchief, but a convulsive sob shook her whole frame.

"No, no, Elena—no, dear," repeated Cortis, whose gentle voice only seemed to increase her emotion.

She could only gasp with difficulty, as though speaking to herself: "Impossible, impossible!"

Little by little she became quieter, and raised her face to her cousin.

"Will you forgive me?" she asked.

"What?" answered Cortis, stopping short and seizing both her hands. "Your silence? your coldness? but if—"

Elena feared that he might finish the sentence, and interrupted him,—

"Yes, yes," she said, "all—even that. I did it for your sake, Daniele, that you might forget me for ever and ever!"

"I can do everything," answered Cortis, encircling her with his arm. "I can love and suffer as no one else in the world can, and I can die." She pressed his hand affectionately, as if to prevent him drawing it away. "Yes, indeed, and I would die rather than harm you."

"Oh," she said, "do you think I do not know that? Do you think I ever doubted it? I am not afraid of that; what I dread is being a cause of misfortune to you."

"I can die," repeated Cortis, "but forget, never. How should you be a misfortune to me, Elena? If you mean in my public duties, you know that there is no private feeling, however powerful, which should stand before—"

"I know that," broke in Elena; "but I fancied, and I wrote it to you, that you wanted an entire love, different"—to *mine* she meant to say, but the words died on her lips.

"You wrote that to me, and I answered you."

Cortis felt her trembling all over. Close by where they stood were a moss-grown column and some old semi-circular stone steps on the slope of the hill, half-hidden in the grass. Cortis made his companion sit down.

"Oh, Daniele," she said, "what most requires forgiveness is the letter about your mother. I was so thoughtless, so stupid! And now, through my fault—"

Cortis would not let her finish.

"No," he said, "not in the least through your fault. My mother is now with me in Rome because, of my own free will, I desired it. You have nothing to do with it. Perhaps my repugnance to living with her was mere selfishness. I said to myself: Any sacrifice save this one. And I was wrong. Nothing is a sacrifice when it is done willingly. Besides, I have never told her for a minute that I would keep her with me always. I told her to come for the present. I am trying an experiment, before leaving her quite alone, with perfect freedom. Indeed, you have done me good."

Elena seized his hand and attempted to kiss it.

"Oh!" said Cortis, drawing it away. Then, with a sudden rush, he seized both her hands, raising them slowly, as though they were heavy. "I am he," he murmured, "who can—"

He bent forward hastily, and kissed her forehead. She trembled violently, having neither strength nor will left, and being as one who neither sees nor hears. Cortis himself could not speak for some moments.

"Enough," he said; "we were both of us worthy of this."

They seated themselves in silence near together.

Elena first broke the silence.

"Do you go to church?" she asked him. "Do you pray?"

Cortis smiled, and inquired why she asked such a question.

"Because I should like to be able to pray as I once could, and I cannot. I have no faith, no faith, no faith!"

She pronounced these words in a low hurried voice, hiding her face in her hands, and rocking herself to and fro.

"It is a misfortune," he said; "I seldom go to church. I think more about my country than my soul, but in my heart I feel God deeply, and I trust that He may not be angry with me."

"Do you know," said Elena, "I should like to say so many things to you about my soul, so many strange things. But now I cannot find the words. And besides," she added, suddenly rising, "I have made you waste too much time. You ought to go." She clasped her hands with a sudden movement, and said, in a low voice: "Why is my husband coming to see you?"

"How do you know that?" exclaimed Cortis roughly. "Ah, Clenezzi!" he added immediately. "It is nothing of importance. Merely to settle once for all how these payments are to be met, and to put it all in writing. If your uncle were here he would do it. As it is, I do it and then tell him what has been done. It is all perfectly simple. Why did you think it was serious?"

He seemed almost angry with her. Elena did not insist.

"And there is another thing," she said; "you are not well. You ought to take care of yourself."

Cortis shrugged his shoulders.

"I?"

Elena did not try to contradict him, she saw it would be useless; but she ejaculated, *oh!* in a submissive voice which contained so much passion and so much entreaty, that Cortis felt it in his heart and made no reply. As a matter of fact, he knew that he had the fever; his head felt like lead, but he bore the pain with his usual pluck, helped by his highly-strung organism. And besides, the very knowledge that the heart that he loved had opened to him to-day for the first time, that he had received a full and complete answer to his questionings, that a new life had dawned for him, all this must do him good.

The silence of the woods around affected him. White and yellow flowers nodded to the southern breeze from between the old stone steps, a nightingale sang in the thickets in the garden, no human voice or step broke the silence.

Cortis would not have moved, but it was nearly mid-day, and he must go. They took the first path they came to, not knowing which led the other. It was only in passing the wide-spreading roots and the curious foliage of a foreign tree which seemed to have strayed into the middle of the garden, that Cortis noticed that they had taken a wrong turning, and told Elena.

"To-day I have to speak at the Chamber," he said presently, "and you are to come and hear me. I will send the orders to your hotel."

Elena leaned on his arm. They entered the museum for a minute, because they thought it was right and without any question, feeling, as they did so, an acute pleasure in the silent understanding that existed between their thoughts. They only looked at a little female bust, a poor little head leaning on a shoulder, white, with gentle features, rendered somewhat weak by the lapse of so many centuries, and by the river that had so ceaselessly flowed over them. It seemed as if the ancient artist had worked at it with a presentiment of the sad fate awaiting it, and had infused into it resigned and profound sorrow, which now, in the calmness of the quiet hall, seemed to say that she had suffered too much, and could never be consoled.

On the way from the museum to the hotel, neither Elena

nor Cortis spoke. Only when they arrived the latter said,—

"If your mother does not come to the Chamber, you will come all the same?"

She looked at him with large, passionate eyes, pressed his hand, and whispered,—

"Yes."

CHAPTER XV.

THE SIGNORA'S SECRET.

Boglietti, the lawyer, reached Cortis's house at a quarter past twelve, and was shown by the servant into the study, with the request that he would wait a few minutes, as his master would not be long. Five minutes later Signora Cortis, with her honeyed smile upon her lips, entered timidly, quite surprised at the delay of the deputy, her son, and so very sorry that the gentleman should be kept waiting.

The gentleman in question, somewhat taken aback by the appearance of this person, who looked and spoke like a quondam ballet-dancer, protested that it did not signify.

"Pray sit down," said the signora. "If you will allow me—"

She took a chair also, so as not to leave him alone. Boglietti, not at all inclined for this unexpected conversation, begged her not to trouble herself, but his somewhat confused words always meeting that same honeyed smile, he gave it up.

"The deputy, my son," continued the signora, "is so occupied. You must forgive him."

"Oh," replied the lawyer, "of course, I know that. But," he added, "I must congratulate you, signora, now that I know that you are his mother."

The signora clasped her hands, and raised her eyes to heaven.

"Yes, indeed," she said, "a happy mother. No one knows how happy."

The lawyer feared lest she should make her happiness clear to him, and, as soon as he could without rudeness, he looked at his watch.

"I expected," he said, "to meet another person here, about whom your son wrote to me this morning. I do not know if he has already been here."

"May I know who it is?" murmured Signora Cortis, leaning forward, and expressing in movement and face the most eager curiosity.

"Some one whom, perhaps, you may know—Senator Di Santa Giulia."

She jumped up from her seat.

"The senator?" she cried, "Baron Carmine? Here?"

"But—I believe so," answered the other, surprised.

The signora dashed out of the room, and immediately returned.

"He has not come," she said; "and now tell me, I beseech you, why is he coming here? Oh, sir," she added, opening her arms tragically, and shaking her head, as the lawyer hesitated a moment, "it is a woman, a mother, the mother of Cortis the deputy, who asks you this!"

"Bless my heart, madam," he replied, "don't be so uneasy. There is no question of a duel; their business is pacific."

"Pacific!" exclaimed the signora, with stagey irony. "Surely you know that between certain people there can be no peace. Indeed," here the signora wagged a prophetic finger, "indeed! there can be no peace!"

She was silent, with her finger still uplifted, and her head turned towards the door listening.

"The bell rang," said Boglietti. "It may be the senator."

She seized his arm.

"Signor," she said, "I beseech you! Remember that you have not seen me or spoken to me!"

She disappeared, and the lawyer was still gaping in open-mouthed astonishment at the door which had shut behind her, when, from the other side of the room, he heard the loud voice of Di Santa Giulia saying from the other side of the room,—

"Good morning."

The baron had got thinner and paler, and in his face the expression of mistrust and discontent had deepened; but his loud voice, his upright figure, and his arrogant manner had not changed.

He seated himself in a corner of the sofa, nursing his knees, and lolling his head back among the cushions.

"It is a real pleasure," he said, "to find myself with you, my charming attorney! You write a good letter, you know; your style is perfect. Your letters are most delightfully worded! I can't say quite so much for their contents, which sometimes seem cavalier, but—"

The lawyer, red as a poppy, tried to protest. The other was not in the least put out, and signed to him with his hand to keep quiet.

"Gently, gently. Don't excite yourself. How you northern people take things. You are Piedmontese, aren't you? I said *they seem*, and there is a great difference between *they seem* and *they are*. For instance, the face of Senator Di Santa Giulia *seems* like the face of an earthquake, but in reality he is the mildest creature in the world. Of course law is your business. Who would ever think of confounding an attorney with a gentleman? There is no question of law there. And now, tell me what you want with me, you and my reverend cousin Father Daniele of the Society of the Jesuits. Did you not write to me that you wanted the money on the 31st of March. Is to-day the 31st of March?"

The lawyer made no reply. He stroked his whiskers and looked the other way.

"Well?" asked the other.

"Are you speaking to me?" asked Boglietti. "Who invited you to come here?"

"Cortis."

"Well then, please speak to Signor Cortis."

"Here I am," said the latter, entering at this moment. "I beg your pardon."

"What for, what for?" asked the senator. "I have been having a most agreeable conversation with this pleasant gentleman. I may as well go on with what I was saying. I was just asking him what the devil you two want with me here?"

"*We two* have nothing to do with it," answered Cortis. "It was I who begged you to come here."

"Very good," answered the other; "and did you also invite this gentleman?"

"I did."

"Well then, I suppose you wish to speak to me about something which is some concern of yours, or about which, at least, you have some right to speak to me."

Cortis's eyes sparkled for a moment with anger, but the light soon died out.

"Because," continued the other, raising himself and his voice, "if it were about—"

"I begged you to come here in order that I might speak to you," broke in Cortis; "when I have spoken I will listen to you."

"Let us hear what you've got to say!" said the baron, throwing himself back on the sofa. "May I smoke?"

He pulled out a cigar and lighted it without waiting for an answer.

Cortis, seated at his writing-table, began to speak, pressing his head and his temples with both hands. The lawyer kept his eyes fixed on him, and Di Santa Giulia smoked and stared at the ceiling.

"Both time and will fail me," said Cortis, "to waste unnecessary words. I have a proposal to make."

"To whom?" asked the baron.

"To both of you. Someone, who does not wish his name mentioned, is willing, under certain conditions, to take upon himself the debt of Baron Di Santa Giulia to—"

"Don't bother me any more!" cried the senator. "This unknown person is my mother-in-law; may the devil fly away with her! Don't bother me any more!"

He flung his cigar on the floor in a passion.

"I will look after my own debts!" he said.

Cortis kept his patience wonderfully that day.

"Your mother-in-law has nothing to do with it," he said.

"Well, then," said the baron, "though it is hardly likely, it can only be that old carrion at—"

"Hold your tongue," exclaimed Cortis, bringing down his fist violently on the writing-table.

"I would have you to know," said the baron, in his strident voice, and leaning over toward Cortis, "I would have you to know, and I don't care a rush if this gentleman knows it too, that I have debts, many debts, but that I am a ten, a hundred, a thousand times more noble than your most noble Signori Carrè, and your most highly virtuous aunt, and that most highly-born gentleman, her brother-in-law, who gave me without any difficulty, somebody who was worth a great deal more than they were, and more than I am, and who now fight with tooth and nail to defend a paltry sum of money; they refused it to me when it would have been of real use, they persuaded that person to lie, I believe, for the first time in her life; they made game of me, and now that they are afraid of their good name, and for their reputation as generous and honest people, they come and offer it to me!"

"Who is offering you anything?" said Cortis.

"And now," continued the other, without heeding him, "now I say, No!"

Cortis made a gesture of weariness and fatigue, and replied, in a low voice,—

"It is quite unnecessary. Nobody from Casa Carrè offers you anything."

The baron shrugged his shoulders.

"Bless my soul!" he exclaimed. "Who then—"

"Do not try to discover. I shall not name the person, who is neither a friend nor a relation of yours."

Cortis spoke very low, in a tired voice, closing his eyes frequently, and passing his hand over his forehead.

"And pray why," asked the baron, "is this person so anxious to pay my debts?"

"The reason is no business of yours. But there is one condition. The President of the Senate has already called upon you once to resign your position as senator of the Kingdom. That is the condition."

The baron was silent for a moment.

"So," he said, with an ironical smile, "you would wish me to believe that you are charged by the government?"

"I have not mentioned the government."

"The government, dear Signor Cortis," replied the baron, "is under a sacred obligation to do this for me, and much more handsomely too; and I may as well add, that even if you do not consider me worthy to continue to hold my seat in the Senate, I shall only resign it of my own free will, and your condition is an outrage. But in any case, before coming to a decision, I wish you to declare to me plainly whether it is the government that makes me this offer or not."

"I may only tell the lawyer," answered Cortis, "the name of this new debtor. It will be then for him to say whether he will accept him or not. I have no declarations to make to anyone else."

"So be it," exclaimed the senator, rising. "Then there's an end of your declarations, conditions, anonymous persons, and everything else. I am here, my dear cousin, and dear Signor Boglietti. You have written me a letter to which I will send an answer of one sort or another before the 31st of March. Now, good day to you both."

"One moment," said Cortis, raising his hand towards him. "I have power to take away the condition."

"What's that to me?" retorted the senator.

Cortis rose.

"Stop!" he cried.

The baron made a gesture of contempt, opened the door, placed his hat on his head, and said, without turning round,—

"Good-day!"

"Great beast!" exclaimed the lawyer, as he heard him going downstairs.

Cortis had re-seated himself, and was leaning his head in his hands.

"I am the person," he said.

The lawyer looked at him without understanding him.

"I will pay," continued Cortis. "Don't you understand? I am a friend of Count Carrè. Were he here, and could be informed of everything, he would pay. Now there are special reasons why the matter should be hurried on. Therefore, if you have no objection, let your client put me in the place of Di Santa Giulia, and I will undertake to pay the entire sum in a fortnight."

"Only think!" exclaimed Boglietti.

"And will you kindly inform the baron, at once, that he is absolved from any liability towards the bank? Nothing more."

"But do you know that what you are doing is splendid?"

"Not in the least," answered Cortis. "As I have

already told you, I am simply *negotiorum gestor.* Will you have something to drink?"

No, the lawyer would not drink at that hour. Cortis rang and ordered a cup of strong coffee and some brandy.

"We ought to put this into writing," said he.

The lawyer answered that there was no hurry. He would prepare the deed at his leisure, and Cortis should sign it next day. But Cortis insisted upon, at least, some preliminary step being taken at once, and Boglietti left the room, saying that he must, in that case, fetch some papers from his office, and would be back in a few minutes.

The door facing the writing-table opened very, very slowly, and Cortis's mother peeped into the room to see if the lawyer were really gone, then she burst in.

"Daniele, don't," she groaned, in a choked voice, clasping her hands. "Don't do this!"

"What is the matter?" he asked.

Signora Cortis threw herself on her knees at the writing-table, buried her face, and sobbingly repeated,—

"No, no, no!"

He asked her kindly two or three times what was the meaning of this scene, but as he could get nothing from her but groans, he lost patience, and told her abruptly either to speak or to go.

"Oh, dear, dear!" she cried, "don't sign."

"What do you mean? What am I not to sign?"

"Nothing for that man who went away first, nothing!"

"I see that I must have double doors made. But why am I not to sign?"

She only sobbed in reply. Then Cortis remembered the mysterious words she had said to him at Lugano.

"In heaven's name," he said, "get up and speak. Get up, I tell you!"

His mother rose, and, holding her handkerchief to her

eyes, went slowly, bent double, towards the sofa. When she reached it, she removed her hands.

"No," she said, as if to herself, "I cannot allow it." And she seated herself, hiding her face afresh.

Cortis shuddered.

"The lawyer will be back in a minute," he said, "and then you cannot stay. If you have anything to say, say it at once."

She rose slowly to her feet, and stood upright and pale as a ghost. For the first time, perhaps, Cortis saw real passion burning in her eyes.

"You know," she said, in a low voice, without a gesticulation, "that he was a friend of your father's?"

"Who?"

"Di Santa Giulia."

"I know that he was introduced to him when he was a lieutenant of cavalry, and that he rarely came to our house."

"Yes, but we often met him out of doors. And do you know the place, the year—Alessandria, between '53 and '55?"

Cortis hid his face, placing his hand on his forehead as if it hurt him to think. He removed it quickly, pointing at his mother with his forefinger, and arching his eyebrows.

"Yes," she said; "the time of my misfortune."

She was silent. Their eyes met, and spoke to each other. A sudden fit of shivering seized Cortis, a sudden pang of agony made him wince. He stretched his hands to his mother, his eyes wide open.

"He?" he asked, in a choked voice.

She drew several deep, long breaths, watched him intently, and did not answer.

Suddenly Cortis's face became hard and cold.

"That is the second you have accused," he said, stretching out an arm towards her.

"The other was dead," answered his mother. "I hoped to save myself. Besides, I have proofs."

"What proofs?"

"I have a note which he wrote me when, after I had been driven from home, I went in search of him to Valence, whither he had been sent with a detachment."

She was speaking impetuously now, with a totally different accent to that which she usually employed, feeling herself confronted by a scepticism, which, though often merited, was, on this occasion, undeserved. This irritated her, and in her irritation her voice bore in it, unconsciously, the ring of truth.

"I have the note here," she said, drawing a paper from the bosom of her gown. "I knew beforehand that you would not believe me. Perhaps you will believe this. I have always kept it, feeling certain that some day my moment of vengeance would come. It has come now. I know that I may be injuring myself, but I don't mind that."

Cortis pressed both hands upon his temples, and, opening his mouth, drew several deep breaths.

His mother handed him the note in silence. He watched her hand and the piece of paper which it held, and they both trembled violently. He dared not take it.

A ring was heard at the door-bell.

"Please go away," said Cortis; "here is the lawyer."

"The lawyer? Send him away at once."

"Please leave me," answered the other imperiously.

The actress reappeared in her. She brandished the note before her son, drawing her head back between her shoulders, and keeping her gaze fixed upon him. Then she placed it with much gesticulation on the writing-table, and left the room slowly, not, however, without turning round at the door to raise and wring her clasped hands.

Cortis took up the note. It proved to be one of the visiting-cards of Baron Carmine Di Santa Giulia, officer in the Genoese cavalry, and bore on it these words in pencil and in his handwriting :—

"You have deserved it. Had I been in the doctor's place, I should have done as he has. Woe to us if good and beautiful ladies adopt this system. Besides, your husband is a soldier, and above me in rank. I have already turned over a new leaf, do you likewise. Good luck to you. After all, I don't feel at all certain of the paternity that you wish to foist upon me."

"Here I am," said the lawyer entering, "have I not been quick? I have brought the stamped deed and all."

Cortis raised his head and looked at him with glassy eyes.

"If you will allow me," continued the lawyer, approaching the writing-table, "I will just write two or three lines."

He thought that, perhaps, Cortis would give him his own place, but as he did not offer to move, Boglietti resigned himself to fetch another chair, and settled himself down to write as best he could.

"By this—present—private—deed—"

He laid down his pen and interrupted his jerky soliloquy to turn to Cortis.

"I thought I would do it thus," he said, "so as to save expense. Don't you agree?"

Cortis scarcely raised his head, and made no reply; and the other, taking up his pen again, continued his work, muttering one by one the words as he wrote them down.

"To acknowledge—in—the best manner—that—"

Cortis suddenly seized a pen with convulsive grasp, twisted and tore it to pieces, and threw it away from him.

"What is the matter?" asked the lawyer.

Cortis jumped up, seized him by the shoulders, and pressed him forward.

"Write, write!" he exclaimed; and then began to walk up and down the room.

The other watched him in stupefaction. Cortis, stopped, and, stamping his foot, cried,—

"Will you write?"

Then he walked straight to the door through which his mother had passed, and, finding it ajar, closed it with a tremendous bang, knocking out the key, which fell on the other side. He waited a moment as if trying to think what had caused that tinkling sound, and then he went and sat himself down upon the sofa. The lawyer, who could find no reason for this storm, looked at him furtively. He appeared to have turned to stone. Boglietti continued to write in silence.

After ten long minutes, he laid down his pen and looked at Cortis afresh; he saw he had not changed his attitude.

"There!" he said, "it is finished now. I beg your pardon," he added, seeing that the other did not stir, "has anything happened to you?"

Cortis shook his head excitedly.

"Now I will read over the deed to you," continued the lawyer, and he began to read, stopping every now and then to correct a word or to dot an *i*.

"You are perhaps saving a life," he said presently, seeking to move Cortis from his silence by a little flattery.

"Are you sure of that?" he asked anxiously.

"I can't be sure. Nobody can be quite sure of a thing of that kind. I, naturally, have made some inquiries. I have heard of certain things, certain speeches; a story of a revolver which he showed to his landlady; mere gossip, perhaps. It may have been done for swagger, or it may not; that depends on the man's character. You know him better than I do."

Cortis was still silent. His eyes, fixed, wide open, seemed to be gazing at something in front of him on the floor.

Yes, visions were passing before them, constantly changing, like shadows pointed out to him by the rapid motion of a large hand hidden behind his back. There was the face of his father, which suddenly took upon itself the appearance it had worn during the different scenes and actions of his life, and finally putting on the marble quiet of death; this figure reopened its eyes, raising its head from the pillows, and changed itself into quite another set of features: Cortis now had before him the likeness of the man who had left him a short time previously, who, in his turn, looked at him smoking and sneering.

"Will you sign this?" asked the lawyer. "First you, and then I."

Cortis, with burning face, raised his clenched fist, and growled from between his teeth,—

"I will sign nothing."

The lawyer started, leaned back in his chair, stretching his arms and arching his eyebrows.

"Nothing!" repeated Cortis, in a voice of thunder. Boglietti looked at him for a moment, then, shrugging his shoulders, rose and collected his papers.

Suddenly a terrible idea occurred to Cortis; the whole room seemed to ring with these words: "What if Di Santa Giulia kills himself?" And it would be he who would have killed him by his refusal, and who would also have set Elena free. Remorse seized his heart; and, mingled with it, he felt a bitter sorrow, a terror of not keeping his usual calmness, his iron will.

"And now," he said, "when the payment falls due, what will you do?"

"You know quite well. I shall at once denounce him to the public prosecutor for malversation of funds."

A knock was heard at the door. Cortis raised his head, but did not answer. It was repeated more loudly. The wailing voice of Signora Cortis was heard,—

"Daniele! Daniele! One word, I beseech you!"

"Wait a minute," answered Cortis resolutely, with a frown. He shut his eyes for a instant, and then, turning to the lawyer, asked, "What time is it?"

These words were said in his usual clear, commanding voice. The latter looked at his watch.

"Half-past one."

Cortis drew out his own watch.

"I am just half-an-hour slow," he said, setting it right. Then he went straight to the writing-table, seized the pen, signed his name to the deed in great haste, and handed it silently to the lawyer. When the latter, amazed, had signed his name, Cortis motioned to him to go away, and said aloud, "Come in!"

The signora, as she came in met the lawyer as he was going out. She glanced at him rapidly, read satisfaction on his countenance, and with frightened eyes interrogated her son, who was standing in the middle of the room.

"Please say that I don't want that coffee and brandy now," said Cortis. "I must go to the Chamber. Let my bed be ready for me when I come in."

"Oh, Daniele," exclaimed his mother, "are you ill?"

"No, I am tired; I am sleepy."

He took up his hat.

"Daniele," groaned the signora.

He took two steps towards the door, then, turning back, rang for his servant, and threw himself upon the sofa, and said,—

"Get me a cab."

The servant saw how upset and unfit to go out he was, and ventured to beg him to stay quiet.

"I must go," answered Cortis, and he dragged himself up, leaning forward on his knees. His mother watched him, not daring to speak to him.

Two minutes later he started, with his eyes staring,

and almost reeling. On reaching the staircase, he said to the servant,—

"Should anything happen to me, go and tell Countess Carrè of it at once, at the Minerva. Do whatever they tell you to do," he added, emphasising his words by laying his hand on the man's shoulder.

CHAPTER XVI.

IN THE CHAMBER OF DEPUTIES.

"I WAS sure of it!" whispered Countess Tarquinia to Elena, fanning herself in great anger, because the hall was almost empty. "We have come an hour too soon. I told you so. Two o'clock would have been quite early enough, or even half-past."

Many fans were beating in unison with many grumbling voices, which were making the same complaint in the gallery to the right of the president. Others were placidly and slowly marking the possession of phlegmatic patience, or a train of thought which was travelling over a road many miles away from Montecitorio. One practical man was pointing out the hall and the galleries, things and persons, to some ladies, in a loud voice, looking round at the faces of the neighbours in the hope of reading thereon the respect and admiration due to his experience. But the ladies seemed to prefer studying each other obliquely. Only when a deputy entered the hall, and the knowing man mentioned his name, were the fans stilled, and heads bent forward to the great open space.

Countess Tarquinia, exceedingly smartly-dressed in maroon and very pale blue, with two bracelets of burnished gold, four inches wide, attracted a great deal of attention. She looked like Elena's elder sister. The latter, dressed in black, with no ornaments save a turquoise cross at her throat, was suffering from the impatience of her mother, from the inexhaustible chatter of the man near her, from finding herself among so many strangers, and being stared at by so many more. She would have been satisfied if she could have seen Cortis; that would have calmed her impatience; but he had not yet entered the hall. Some few deputies were writing in their places; others were wandering about the gangways with their hands in their pockets; others were standing in groups, staring up at the galleries. One of the latter, an acquaintance of Countess Tarquinia's, suddenly saw her. He went upstairs to her immediately, and offered his services, if he could be of any use to her while she remained in Rome. She answered by a beaming smile, quite crimson with pleasure at this public homage. The deputy had not recognised Elena at first, and tried to excuse himself, as best he could, by saying that he thought she was in Sicily.

"That belief of yours is very old and very strong," said Elena, with her quick smile. "You always think me in Sicily, even when you see me in Rome."

He blushed scarlet, and protested, but Elena interrupted him by asking what the business of the Chamber was that day.

"Well," answered the deputy, "first, there's the budget statement. Did you not know that? It is on that account that the galleries are so crowded. And then, though you will know more about this than I do, there is the *coup d'éclat* prepared by Cortis."

"Indeed!" exclaimed the countess. "What is that? He has said no word to us about it."

"Then it can't be true. You know that his constituents have sent up a protest against him. It is said that he intends to resign his seat, and to do it in a speech which will be daring, to say the least of it."

The people near leaned forward to catch what he said. Some one turned round to repeat, in a low voice, what had been said. Another, who had not heard very well, whispered, "Who?" And the answer was given in the same low voice: "Cortis, that clericalist." Elena overheard, and shot a quick glance of displeasure at the speaker. Countess Tarquinia was quite miserable, would not believe it, and asked the deputy how, and when, and by what means the story had got about. She knew about the protest, but she knew also that many of those who had signed it had already repented of what they had done. The deputy answered vaguely; he did not know much, and regretted that he could give them no further information, and, so saying, he took his leave.

"He is quite capable of it!" muttered the countess to her daughter. "Sometimes he gets extraordinary ideas into his head! And fancy not saying anything to us! Of course, that was only to be expected. But I vow that I shall go away as soon as he begins to speak."

"Why?"

"Because who knows what may happen, and then I shall faint! Goodness gracious, are you made of stone? I shall go away. And you, I suppose, will remain?"

"Certainly."

"Do so, and then have people coming to me and saying—"

The conversation was carried on in whispers, and the countess's last remark was made in almost less than a whisper, but Elena heard it, her face crimsoned with contempt, and she guessed that some accusation had been made for which she had given no open justification.

"What do you mean?" she asked.

"Nothing."

As a matter of fact, no one had spoken to Countess Tarquinia about any suspected tenderness between Cortis and her daughter; but a certain pious gossip had written to her about it a long time before, of course with a good motive. Elena spoke no more. Her heart beat violently with grief, contempt, and disgust, as if some horrible curiosity had come to peep into it. And now she felt as if she, too, would like to go away; staying there was disagreeable to her; she felt that, when Cortis came in, when he began to speak, she would betray her thoughts. Meanwhile, the fan of Countess Tarquinia moved up and down unceasingly, showing more weariness than ever.

"How tiresome!" she said.

A lady near her said timidly,—

"I was told that they met at one?"

Countess Tarquinia made no answer. The delay was not her principal cause of annoyance.

"They will soon begin now," said the knowing man. "Do you see that deputy beginning to write just above the second gangway? That is Minghetti. And there is Depretis."

The countess forgot her own troubles for a minute in order to gaze, with every one else, at the minister who was just entering in his usual listless manner.

A lady whispered,—

"How old he is!"

"Look," remarked Countess Tarquinia to her daughter, "is he not the image of the chemist at Passo di Rovese? The very image!"

Elena did not heed her. She, too, had been startled on seeing the minister come in, and had received a shock from it, as it made her feel Cortis's absence still more keenly. Her heart beat fast. "What if he were ill!" she thought. And in imagination she saw him lying in bed, his eyes glittering with fever.

"The president has not come yet," said some one. "He is generally in his place half-an-hour before this."

Then a gentleman, who had come in a few minutes before, said that he had seen him coming out of his room with Cortis.

"There!" whispered Countess Tarquinia. "Did you hear that? No doubt they have been talking over this speech."

"Farini! Farini!" said the knowing man to his neighbours. "Do you see Farini?"

The president of the Chamber entered at this moment hurriedly, and, having exchanged a few words with one of the officials, took his seat. Elena waited breathlessly for whom should come in behind him.

The minister Magliani made his appearance, then came the ushers, bearing the boxes and portfolios, which they placed on the ministerial bench. Thirty other deputies entered one by one; the president's bell broke in upon the hum of conversation, with its shrill tinkle, a clerk began to read something aloud in a sing-song voice, to which nobody paid the slightest attention. But still Cortis did not appear. Elena, however, knew that he had had an interview with the president, and she was more at ease.

"Where does Cortis sit?" asked her mother. Elena did not know. The knowing man hastened to answer with polite officiousness.

"There, signora, by that third gangway, near to the pale deputy with a black beard. Here is Signor Cortis. He has just come. There he is."

Elena was looking to the right, and Cortis entered on the left, leaning on the arm of another deputy. He crossed the open space in front of the tribune, and went to his place without raising his eyes to the gal ery. Elena could not see his face clearly, but something in his walk and in his attitude, caused her great anxiety.

"That really is Daniele down there," said Countess Tarquinia. "But he looks like an old man, doesn't he?"

The other made no reply.

Somebody said "hush," because the president was reading something which demanded the attention of the Chamber. Every ear in the gallery was bent to listen.

"Resignation," said some one, when the president had finished reading.

"Whose?"

The person could not catch the name, but it was certainly not that of Cortis. Silence! A deputy has asked leave to speak. Who is it? This one here? no, it was that other one over there. It was C. who proposed that the resignations should not be accepted, and that the deputy P. should have leave of absence for a month. People murmured in the galleries and said: "The daily comedy." A second deputy rose, then a third, and after him a fourth. They all spoke alike. The question was put to the vote, and the Chamber approved. Then Cortis rose, and, in a hesitating voice, said,—

"I ask permission to speak."

"Upon what subject?" asked the president.

"I wish to make a declaration. As I do not desire to detain the Chamber, which is now justly impatient to hear the honourable Signor Magliani, I beg you, sir, to give me leave to speak after the budget statement."

"Very good," answered the president.

While these few words were passing, Elena had not moved a muscle.

"That's all right," said her mother. "We will hear Magliani, and then go away. Did you notice Daniele's voice? The boy can't be well."

Elena was still silent, watching Cortis with a fixed, searching look, which, in her, denoted intense passion. He was there, with his elbows on the bench and his head between his hands. He never raised it, and Elena suffered, and at the same time was angry with herself for suffering, despising the selfish sentiment that reigned in her own heart. Of course he was entirely occupied with thinking over what he was going to say, how could he think of her?

Meanwhile, the minister had begun to speak. Nearly all the deputies had crowded into the benches round him, so as to hear better. From the president's gallery his white head was visible, moving from right to left, leaning forward every now and then to look at the papers spread out on the table, glancing at some figures, and then raising itself again. The fluent tongue continued its exposition of everything connected with the public finances with that ability which some admired and others deplored. As the minister said himself, he did not attempt oratorical effects; but nevertheless frequent murmurs of approval filled the hall, caused not only by the genius of the man, not only by the profound knowledge of every detail relating to his office which he displayed, and which were mysteries to most of his audience, but also by the reports of his boldness, and, above all, by the lustre of his extraordinary success.

"This is amusing," whispered Countess Tarquinia, after a time. "He quite takes away my breath. How long will he go on?"

"I don't know," answered Elena. "I mean to stay after he has done."

"Amen!" answered her mother.

The figures, the subtle reasonings flowed on, but few of them reached the president's gallery. Every moment some one got up and crept out, on the tips of his toes, along the benches. Few people remained to attend to the speech of the minister, and to hear the cheers of the Chamber. On the other hand, the public galleries were filled to overflowing. From the senators' gallery, Clenezzi frequently looked across to the countess and her daughter, vainly seeking to be recognised by them. Suddenly the minister ceased and resumed his seat. A noise rose from the floor of the hall, like the buzzing of a cloud of flies suddenly disturbed.

"That's over," said Countess Tarquinia. "What is Cortis about?"

At that moment Cortis had crossed his arms upon the back of the bench in front of him, and laid his head upon his arms. It was not his turn yet. Another minister rose to present a report, then Magliani, who had only asked leave to rest for five minutes, took up his discourse again. Elena was very uneasy. She saw that Cortis was feeling ill. She feared that he would not be able to speak as he intended, and that he would suffer morally in consequence. She would have rejoiced to see him get up and go out; she was indignant with all those deputies who were sitting round him, who never troubled to inquire if he were ill, or to advise him to go away. Had Cortis no friends in the Chamber? She longed to go down to him and lead him out, and wondered if she could not charge T. with the task. She borrowed an opera-glass from a neighbour to see where he was sitting, trying to make a sign to him to come up into the gallery. But first she looked at Cortis. Just then some one touched him on the shoulder. He started and raised his head. Then Elena could see his face clearly. It was on fire, perhaps from having been hidden so long in his arms. She saw him exchange a few words with the man who ..ad touched him, and then shake his head in token of refusal; then he looked up at the gallery, but without recognising any one, and slowly subsided into his former attitude. And that man did not speak to him any more, did not carry him by force out of the Chamber! T. was intently listening to the minister's speech, and never looked up at the gallery. Elena thought of going down to the parliamentary office in the Via della Missione, and sending for Cortis. But she would not. If he was thinking over his speech, her interruption would be inopportune. If only she could get at T. instead! The minister just finished his speech, amid loud applause. Deputies from every side crowded round him. In the galleries many people already prepared to go.

"Dear child," said the countess, "won't you come away?"

Elena did not answer. Perhaps she did not hear. She

was standing upright, leaning over the balustrade of the gallery, waiting breathlessly till the president should call upon Cortis.

"The hall will soon be empty now," said the knowing man. But instead of going away, nearly all the deputies resumed their seats.

"The honourable Signor Cortis," said the president, "has leave to speak!"

Elena's eyes involuntarily turned towards the clock facing her. It marked five minutes to four.

Cortis rose. From every quarter of the Chamber, except from the centre, all looked at him with diverse expressions; some with lively curiosity, others with contemptuous indifference, others again with predetermined condemnation. In the centre, where certain conceited mediocrities had writhed under his sarcasms, they continued to talk and laugh, despite the president's bell; Elena meanwhile, very pale, bit her lips. He seemed to be waiting for silence, leaning his body forward to the bench upon which his hand rested. The president rang his bell once more, and said,—

"Speak, Signor Cortis."

At the same moment Cortis began,—

"I must beg the Chamber—" here he stopped, seeking for a word. He passed his hand over his forehead, and began again in an enfeebled voice,—

"The state of my health compels me to beg, before proceeding further, the indulgence of the Chamber."

He paused again, perchance in order to struggle with his weakness and to revive the force and courage of his mind and body. His voice appeared stronger when he next spoke,—

"It is probable that the Chamber will adjourn to-day, and I cannot postpone an action which I regard as a duty to my constituents, my country, and myself.

"Before quitting this assembly, perhaps for ever—"

As he uttered the words *perhaps for ever*, his voice failed, and his tongue seemed paralysed. He said a few more unintelligible words, and would have fallen had not his neighbours hastily supported him. A cry was heard from the president's gallery, but nobody paid any attention to it. Ushers and deputies rushed to Cortis, and he was immediately carried out of the hall.

Elena, at first, had not understood, and had leaned forward to catch the broken words that he uttered. Upon seeing his neighbours support him, and seeing him abandon himself in their hands, she rose and uttered a stifled cry, looking in the same direction as every one else, for all in the galleries were now aware that something had happened, were standing on the benches, leaning over the balustrades in eager curiosity. When Cortis was lifted by two of his colleagues and carried out, she suddenly, without herself or any one else knowing how, broke away from her mother, who, alarmed, had tried to hold her, and rushed out of the gallery.

The doorkeeper, seeing a pale and excited lady coming towards him, tried to stop her, and asked what she wanted, but she repulsed him with a haughty gesture, and, passing on, found herself in the corridor joining the gallery on that side of the Chamber. The corridor was empty, silent. She stopped a moment, not knowing which way to go. Then a gentleman who had followed her said,—

"Signorina, * don't be alarmed, it will be nothing; I have seen your mother, who is also somewhat upset."

The expression "Signorina," which, used at that moment, might mean so much, would have pierced Elena through and through had not all her thoughts and senses been fixed elsewhere. She fancied she heard steps and voices on her left, and hastened in that direction without

* Miss. Note by the translator.

answering; she found herself at the head of the staircase leading to the rooms of the president's office.

A crowd of people were coming up. P. and another, noticing Elena, advanced towards her and took her aside so as to prevent her seeing Cortis, who was being carried up behind them.

"It is nothing, baroness," said P. "A fainting fit, quite unimportant, it will soon pass."

"Nothing indeed," repeated the other; "you may be quite easy."

"Where is he? I wish to see him," asked Elena convulsively. "Has he a doctor? I want to help him. He is my cousin!"

"Yes, yes," said the men; "you shall see him and help him. B. and G. are with him now. All that he wants is quiet and rest."

Two or three other deputies joined them and made a hedge round Elena, while the sad procession passed rapidly by, and entered the president's offices.

Elena saw it; she did not speak, but she attempted to follow it. She was prevented. Calming herself, she begged P. to go and see after her mother in the gallery, and begged the others, sweetly, almost smilingly, to let her into the sick man's room, where she could see the doctors. She declared that the uncertainty was harder to bear than the reality. Then they respectfully allowed her to pass. Some one coming up the staircase, and who could not see her, said in a loud voice: "Have they taken him in there? It is a bad omen; that was poor ——'s room," and he named a young Lombard deputy, full of genius and fire, and who also had been struck down at his post, and who, having been carried into that room, died there shortly afterwards. Elena stopped for a moment, her hand on her heart, then she made her way into an ante-room, dark, and full of people talking below their breath. Some one gave some orders from a still darker room on the left; between the two rooms there was a constant stream of messengers passing to and fro. A little light entered through a glass door from a well-furnished, cheerful room. Elena turned to the left towards the person who was giving orders. He said to her somewhat roughly,—

"Are you his wife—his sister?"

"No."

"Well, then, I am sorry, but you can't come in."

"But I wish to know—" said Elena, trembling.

"What? What we none of us know yet? You shall come in later. Wait there."

He pointed to the light room, and returned to his patient with a messenger who had just arrived bearing something in his hand, and the door was closed.

Then the deputy who had at first addressed her in company with P. went up to Elena and told her there was a fear of congestion of the brain, certainly not a very slight attack, but, on the other hand, not a very serious one. They had placed him in an arm-chair, and were now getting a bed ready. He persuaded her to believe that, for the moment, she could do nothing; her help would be very useful later on. He took her into the light room, and made her sit down upon a sofa behind the door. From there she could not see what went on in the ante-room.

"Do you feel unwell?" he asked. "Can I get you anything?"

Elena shook her head, murmured an inaudible "No, thank you," and kept her eyes fixed upon the lamp which, though it was not yet five o'clock, was burning on the table.

"The sittings often finish late, and here they light the lamps in good time," remarked the deputy, for something to say.

She made no answer. After some time she begged him not to put himself out to remain with her, as she could perfectly stay by herself. At this moment P. entered. Countess Tarquinia was waiting for her daughter in the passage. Elena, rising from her sofa, went to her mother, who was leaning upon Clenezzi's arm, and who seemed half out of her mind.

"Oh dear, Elena!" she said, "why did you leave me in this way? For mercy's sake let us go home! I can't breathe, I can't stand; I can do nothing, I cannot remain here!"

"Courage, mamma," answered Elena; "I can't come just now. I will come later, perhaps, when I have seen what turn things have taken. And then I shall come back here, naturally. I am strong, and can be of use."

"Oh dear, oh dear, won't you come now?"

"No; I will beg the senator to call a cab and take you to the hotel."

"Of course I will," said the senator, his honest face looking serious and full of woe. "Make use of me. I will take the countess home, and then I will come back and accompany you if you like."

"There is no need for that, thank you," answered Elena hastily. "I cannot say for certain now when I shall come."

"I expect," said the senator, leaning towards her, "that you will have that lady here presently who arrived this morning."

Elena started.

"I don't know," she answered. "In any case, I shall come back here."

"Elena, Elena," groaned her mother, "do remember that you have no strength to throw away."

Elena raised her eyebrows, shrugging her shoulders contemptuously.

"Now I am going," she said, and, darting away, disappeared in the ante-room. A moment later she slipped behind a messenger into the sick-man's room.

She left it two or three hours later, very pale, but calm, and talked with several members of the staff of the president's office, who offered her, with the utmost courtesy, every assistance that they could give, promising to leave nothing undone to help Cortis, of whom they spoke in terms of high esteem and sympathy. They expressed an opinion that the danger had been overcome by the letting of blood, which had been instantly done. Elena only asked to be allowed to send a telegram, which she addressed to Count Lao in these words :—

"Daniele somewhat seriously ill. I want you immediately."

Then she sent a note to Clenezzi to inform him that she could not move unless her mother had absolute need of her; and she returned to Cortis, by whose side she now found another person, a long, lean woman, who could do nothing but sob and groan.

CHAPTER XVII.

AN INTERVENTION.

"THE express from Florence?" inquired Senator Clenezzi of a railway official, as he arrived quite out of breath about four in the afternoon at the Roman station.

"Twenty minutes late," answered the man.

The senator breathed, raised his hat, wiped his forehead with his handkerchief, and looked at the omnibuses drawn up in the yard outside the station. He was no longer afraid of arriving too late, but, little by little, the traces of a much more serious preoccupation showed themselves on his old face, the senile trembling of his lips and eyebrows displayed the trouble of his mind.

"Are you going by train?" asked a young man of Clenezzi in the Bergamo dialect.

"My dear boy," answered the old man, "forgive me for not having seen you before."

"Are you travelling?" repeated the other.

"Madonna! Don't laugh at me! But how glad I should be if I could wake up to-morrow morning and look out upon our market-place. You know it well, young man; there are many beautiful things in the world, but I tell you this, there is but one Bergamo."

"You are on duty here, are you not? Looking after some pretty ladies, eh? When there are pretty ladies about, Senator Clenezzi—"

"Come, come, don't talk nonsense. Count Carrè is coming by this train, and I shall have enough to do to look after him. Are you going to Naples?"

"Yes, signore."

"Pleasant journey to you then."

At ten minutes past four the train from Florence arrived. The doorway of the station was crowded, and amongst the crowd stood the senator, with his mouth open and his eyes staringly fixed upon the stream of passengers that passed him. Faces of every age and shape, Italian and foreign, passed him; faces which looked greedily right and left at the crowd; faces which expressed disgust at the throng and its curiosity; but still that pale face, with its well-shaped nose and black beard, never came. The senator's eyes became momentarily more anxious. Now, nearly every one was gone, the crowd had dispersed. Was it possible? He moved forward, looked, and his face beamed with pleasure as he went to meet Count Lao, who came behind everybody else, walking very slowly, smoking, with his hands in his pockets, and the collar of his great-coat turned up. He was followed by a porter laden with portmanteaux, shawls, and rugs.

"My dear count," said the senator, "I am here to greet you in the name of your ladies."

Lao gave him a slight nod of acknowledgment, and immediately asked,—

"And Cortis?"

"He is getting on. Let me see, this is the 28th, is it not? Three days have passed. There is no comparison between this and the first day."

"So much the better!" exclaimed Count Lao. "But they might have telegraphed to me again to give me fresh news. I came expecting to find him almost dead."

"But, you see, they did not know when you would

start, or where to telegraph to. And besides, you might have seen bulletins in all the papers."

"I never read the papers," returned Lao shortly, shaking his head. "So he is getting better?"

"Oh, without doubt; he will soon be well again."

They got into the omnibus belonging to the Minerva. Lao hastened to shut every window, and enveloped his legs in a rug, grumbling,—

"I was broiled in the train, and here I am frozen. He is getting well, and I shall die instead."

Clenezzi, who only knew him slightly, looked at him as if he were some curious animal.

"Have you caught cold?" he asked.

"Caught cold? If that were all! I tell you I am going to die. It would bore me horribly to die in Rome, because every time I have come I have caught the fever, and if I were to rise again here, I should certainly catch it anew. And now tell me, what has been the matter with Cortis?"

The senator told him all about it. By this time the threatened symptoms of congestion of the brain had disappeared, and, with them, some of the danger.

"Is he still at the Chamber?" asked the count.

"Yes, he is still there."

"And my sister-in-law and niece? Always there too, I suppose?"

"Baroness Elena is always there, except for a few hours in the night, and a few moments in the day."

"But they are fairly easy now?"

"Yes, but you know that there are other things too."

Count Lao, deafened by the noise of the omnibus and of the traffic in the streets, cursed every vehicle in Rome, and leaned forward, opening his eyes, towards his companion.

"What has happened now?" he asked.

The senator looked out of the window till some of the noise was over, and then repeated,—

"There are other things too. You know that Cortis's mother is here?"

"Daniele wrote and told me she was coming," answered the count, "but I didn't know she had already arrived. I wrote back to him, and said: 'You are an ass.' One expects a big heart like his in an animal, but not in a man."

"Well, that is one source of trouble," said Clenezzi. "And besides that—you know already—there is my colleague, your relation."

Count Lao frowned, and, clenching his fists, emitted a noise between a groan and a roar.

"And that's enough, in all conscience!" said the other. "Here we are. Now you will hear all about it."

The omnibus was just turning into the Via Piè di Marmo. An instant later, Lao was very slowly going up the stairs of the hotel, and Elena was hastening down to meet him.

"I saw you coming," she cried, stretching out her arms to meet him. "How glad I am you are here!"

Lao clasped her silently to his breast, kissed her forehead, and, when he raised his face, said, in a voice full of emotion,—

"Good-bye."

Elena stretched out her hand to Clenezzi rather to send him away than to thank him for his trouble. He read in her face that she was impatient to be alone with her uncle. Lao took her arm.

"Let us go upstairs," she said.

"Gently, gently," answered Lao, "remember that I have eight hours of that infernal railway in my spine, without counting the ten or twelve of yesterday. I thought that if I did not sleep at Florence, I should arrive dead, and then what would you have done with me? There are no miracles now-a-days, you know."

"Dear uncle," whispered Elena, pressing his arm tightly, "our rooms are on the second floor, but I ordered one for you on the first, and we will go straight there. Mamma went to lie down an hour ago. She told me to wake her as soon as you arrived, but we may put it off for a little."

"I hope to Heaven," said Lao, "that my room does not look to the north?"

"No, no, uncle."

It was some time before all the trunks, rugs, and shawls of the traveller were finally disposed in his room. At last, however, uncle and niece found themselves sitting alone on the sofa, hand in hand.

"And so," he began, "Daniele is doing well?"

"Yes, pretty well."

Elena answered quietly, without raising her eyes to her uncle's face.

"That fellow who comes from Bergamo—what's his name?—Clenezzi, told me so. He told me all about Daniele. And he said something about the worries that you have."

"It is necessary that you should know everything without delay, uncle, before you see mamma, because, well, you know what she is, and how impossible it is to talk things over with her. She gets into such a state—so excited; in short, it is better that you and I should have a chat together first."

"Talk away," said Count Lao. "If you don't mind, I am just going to take a little sulphate of quinine. It is a good thing on first coming to Rome. But you talk."

He rose, opened a bag, and began to arrange his medicine-chest with the greatest care, taking out a quantity of bottles and boxes, looking at some of them with great attention, and repeating, "Speak, speak!" because Elena had thought well to stop her narrative for the moment.

She told him that her Aunt Cortis had arrived at the Chamber shortly after Daniele was taken ill, and had made a scene because she had not been informed at once. She had expressed her intention of remaining near her son. By some fatality Daniele, in his delirium, talked of nothing but politics and his mother, saying things that were very painful for her and for other people to hear. Then she would begin to sob and bewail herself, turning first towards the sick man, then towards any others who might be present, declaring that this was all the effect of his illness, that her son really loved her dearly, that this was untrue, that the other was untrue—so much so, that at last the doctors ordered that the patient should see as little of her as possible. She would not hear of this, and was always striving to make herself as visible as she could by his bedside. Elena made no other comment upon the zeal of her aunt than was implied in the use of this adjective. She had considered it right to help her in all her maternal anxiety, although the assistance given by such a woman could not be of much use, and her chatter was intolerable. But, on the evening of the 26th, when the acute delirium had ceased, Daniele, seeing his mother return after a brief absence, had become very angry, and had bitterly reproached her for leaving his house uncared for, and coming where she was not wanted in the smallest degree. Elena had tried to quiet him, but in vain; his excitement had increased to such a pitch that, at last, the doctors had requested Signora Cortis to leave the room, and not to set foot in it again for some time. Her aunt had left the room in a fury, and, meeting Elena just outside, had assailed her with the most bitter invectives, accusing her of conspiring with the doctors, and of wishing to take away her son's heart from her. The doctor and one of the officials happening to come out shortly after, she abused them to such an extent that she was at last turned out altogether, and she had retired swearing that she would apply for justice to the president, the ministers, nay, to the king himself.

Lao, who had listened to the last part of his niece's story with a quinine pill between the thumb and finger of his left hand, and a glass of water in his right, now swallowed the pill.

"And what next?" he asked.

"She has been here three times yesterday, and this morning. Mamma always refuses to see her. At the Chamber, orders were given to the doorkeepers not to let her pass, but I begged that they might be cancelled. She came yesterday, and again to-day; but she has not come into Daniele's room, and I have not seen her. Now, I fully expect she will assault me in the street, and mamma is in terror."

"Indeed!" said Lao. "She is quite capable of it! But let me arrange matters. Where does she live?"

"Close by; in the Piazza Venezia. Do you know her?"

"Don't I?"

Lao raised his right arm, waved it in the air, and let it swing again loosely from the wrist.

"Is there anything else?" he asked.

"The worst," answered Elena, in a low voice, with downcast eyes.

"Let us hear the worst then."

"My husband is here."

"I thought as much; I should have been better pleased to hear he was at the devil."

Elena stamped her foot on the ground in vexation.

"If you talk like that I will not go on," she said. "I will not say another word."

"What nonsense!" growled her uncle. "Go on! go on!"

"Listen, uncle," said Elena, very red. "Three days ago I telegraphed to you on Daniele's account, but I would equally have telegraphed to you had it been on my husband's account, and if you begin like that, it will be useless for me to say anything more."

"Go on!" cried the count.

Elena shrugged her shoulders, bent her chin on her breast, and looked at her hands.

"If you speak like that I will not, so there!" she said.

"Yes, you will," said her uncle, "if I have to say 'go on' for the next half-hour."

Elena raised her face, looked at her uncle for a space, and then said, in a low voice,—

"Ruin."

"Go on," said Lao undisturbed.

Elena forced herself to relate all that she knew of her husband's affairs down to the meeting between him and Cortis about the bank business.

"What had Daniele to do with it?" asked Lao in surprise.

"I believe he took it up in order to try and help my husband," answered Elena, in the tone of one who deplores what he has to tell.

"He?"

"He. I would never have allowed it. I did write to Clenezzi once from Cefalù, asking him to take certain steps on my husband's behalf, relative to the affair which you know about. Clenezzi was ill, and charged Daniele with it, and that is how he came to be brought in."

"Very good," said Lao, half ironically, half resignedly. "And what next?"

"Yesterday Clenezzi came to me saying that he felt it his duty to tell me of a serious occurrence. There is no further question of the debt to the bank; but there seems to be a perfect storm coming of debts of every sort and kind, which cannot be kept hidden any longer. A great scandal is imminent. Clenezzi added something else."

"What?"

"That his appearance is alarming."

Elena's voice trembled as she pronounced these words; a deadly paleness overspread her face. Lao did not understand.

"Alarming? What do you mean?" he asked.

"Some extreme—"

She could not finish her sentence, because Lao interrupted her by waving his arms in the air.

"I wish to heaven he would!" he exclaimed; "if only he would put a bullet through his head, it would be the best thing he ever did in his life!"

Elena's eyes flashed.

"Instead of that we must help him," she said; "immediately! And you and I must do it!"

She seized, as she spoke, one of her uncle's arms with the energy of a madwoman.

"Go away," said her uncle, rising and throwing off her arm. "Go upstairs. Go away and call your mother, and dress her and don't bother me. Good heavens! here have I been travelling for eight or ten hours, and you give me no opportunity of washing and changing my clothes. Go away, I tell you; go away!"

"I will go, uncle," said Elena resolutely; "but we will help him."

He put his arm round her, and said, with affected gentleness, as he led her towards the door,—

"Go away, now, dear; go to to your mother; wake her; don't worry me now, and when I am dressed I will come upstairs."

As he spoke, they reached the door.

She still kept repeating: "We will help him, we will help him!"

She left the room, but returned in a moment, and knocked at the door.

"You can't come in," cried Lao.

"I am just going to the Chamber," she said. "Mamma is on the second floor—No. 39."

Lao answered aloud, "All right," and grumbled between his teeth,—

"Go, and be blessed thirty-nine times, you stupid creature! She may go on sleeping!"

And he continued his toilette, exclaiming at every moment as he washed his face or buttoned his vest,—

"Pretty business! Body of Bacchus! Pretty business altogether!"

The toilette took a very long time, because Count Ladislao was as careful and particular as a woman. At last, however, it came to an end, and then he went up, full of thought, to the second floor in search of No. 39.

A chambermaid pointed it out to him, and he was just going in when he heard a strange voice. He turned to her, and asked whose room was 39? She replied,—

"Countess Carrè's."

"She has somebody with her?"

The woman did not know; she had seen no one go in.

"Hang it," grumbled the count; and, hearing the voice of his sister-in-law, he entered without further ado.

Countess Tarquinia, as red as fire, was standing in the room, exclaiming,—

"I am surprised—"

Opposite her stood Signora Cortis, her two black eyes flashing, and her face very pale. She had raised her arm against her sister-in-law as though to ward off her words, to beat them back if possible, and to get one in herself at the first opportunity.

Lao stopped in the doorway.

"I am surprised," continued the countess, "and I am glad that my brother-in-law should hear what I say. I am surprised at your boldness—"

Signora Cortis, turning her back upon her, went towards Lao.

"Count Ladislao, if I am not mistaken?" she said timidly.

Lao scarcely bowed, and answered,—

"At your service."

"Oh, count!" she continued, "you must remember me, and I remember that you had a large heart; I appeal to you."

"To me?"

Lao stepped backwards, and opened the door, saying,—

"Then come to my tribunal."

The signora hesitated a moment, and seemed disturbed.

"No," she said; "I cannot leave this room without a promise."

"Oh, indeed," said Lao.

"Promise!" exclaimed Countess Tarquinia disdainfully. "What promise?"

"Let us hear," said the count. "Did not the signora appeal to me? If she will not leave the room I will hear the case at once."

He made a sign to Countess Tarquinia, who hastily vanished into her bedroom, shutting the door behind her. Signora Cortis advanced to retain her, but was too late.

"I am not being treated with common civility," said she.

"Well," exclaimed Count Lao, pretending not to have heard her, "what is this promise that you require? Let us sit down, if you don't mind, as I have travelled eight hours to-day. I am rejoiced at your resurrection."

"It would be better if I were dead," answered the signora, in a tragical voice.

The count maintained a significant silence. Leaning back in Countess Tarquinia's arm-chair, with his hands in his pockets, one knee crossed over the other, he was swinging his foot and watching the signora, who had sunk down upon the sofa and covered her face with her handkerchief.

"Merciful powers!" he suddenly exclaimed, as if speaking to himself.

The signora raised her head, and interrogated him with her eyes.

"Oh nothing," he said. "I was just thinking of the visit I paid you at Alessandria in 1853."

"Oh, count," whimpered she, smoothing out the handkerchief on her knees, and watching, with bent head, her unconscious work. "I have been very wicked, but I have also suffered much. You, if you can remember me as I was, will see that in my face."

"Of course I can see it," answered Lao. "And now, if you will take my advice, you will tell me what you want of my sister-in-law."

"Tarquinia has treated me badly. When all's said and done, if a son forgives, who has any right to throw stones? And besides, I am not at all sure that, once upon a time, Tarquinia did—"

"Hush," said Lao, frowning, and shaking his right hand, which was extended towards her. "Come to the point," he continued.

"A mother!" exclaimed the signora, raising her arms. "Fancy treating a mother thus! But where are the feelings, where is the virtue of these people?"

"Who cares to know where they are?" said the count. "Have the kindness to come to the point."

"The Magdalen," continued the other, as if inspired, "the Magdalen, Mary of Egypt, and many others, have become saints."

"Pretty saints," murmured Lao.

"But such women as these of to-day are without charity! To treat thus a poor unfortunate creature who has absolutely nothing left to her but her son and her God! How can they?"

"Look here," said Lao, sitting upright in his chair, and drawing out his watch, "I will give you one minute to come to the point."

"I am coming to it," said the signora, with a sigh. "You were nicer to me once."

"Naturally."

Her voice now changed suddenly; from whining it became dry and hard.

"I want you to know," she said, "that I have been driven, in violation of all right and propriety, from my son's sick-room, and that in that room there comes and goes, as mistress, a person--"

At this point the signora probably saw something terrible in Lao's eyes, for she stopped and began afresh,—

"Another person, in short. But that is not all. My son is recovering miraculously fast; I have prayed so much, count! They ought to be thinking of moving him to his own house, where he would be much more comfortable, poor dear! Heaven knows how much more comfortable he would be! Not at all. Do you know what they want, and what they propose? They propose to move him straight into the country, and not to his own house even there, but to Passo di Rovese, to the Villa Carrè! It is too much! I oppose it, and will continue to oppose it by every means in my power!"

"By what means, my dear creature? I know nothing about such matters, but it seems to me the most natural thing in the world for the doctors to order Daniele to go into the country and have absolute rest. It seems to me the most natural thing, especially now that the Chamber is closed, to leave the sick man quiet until the time comes for moving him into a sleeping-carriage on the railway. It seems to me the most natural thing in the world that his relations and friends should prefer to have him with them rather than leave him to mope in solitude at Villascura during his convalescence."

"His relations?" exclaimed Signora Cortis. "His friends? And his mother? Does she count for nothing? Would not Daniele be comfortable at Villascura with his mother?"

"Listen to me," answered the count coldly. "You have settled all this very quickly in your own mind, but as the house in question is the one wherein his father died, Daniele might feel some slight difficulty. In fact, it is clear to me that he does feel it; he has mentioned it to me in his letters. But he is not a doll; he can say himself whither he wishes to go, and with whom."

"That's all very fine!" broke in the signora, with intense bitterness, "he can speak for himself indeed! When there is always at his elbow some one who forever talks to him of Passo di Rovese, and who seeks to keep me away from him by every method. And I know why! There are two reasons. The first is that you and my sister-in-law could not bear me when poor Cortis married me. She thought he was marrying beneath him. There is another reason, which is not connected with Tarquinia, and which is somewhat more delicate, and which I will only mention in an extreme case, that is, if I see Daniele being carried off to Passo di Rovese. But then I will say it so that even Daniele shall understand it. There will be a scandal, what does that matter? but at least we shall see if Daniele will go! Are you all afraid of a scandal? Will you promise—"

"What? What do you mean?" broke in Lao. "What is this scandal?"

"In an extreme case, I repeat, in an extreme case I will tell you."

"But what extreme case?" said the count, his eyes and forehead denoting the storm that was brewing. "Let us suppose that the case is extreme now. If they have said they will do this, they will do it as sure as fate. You know they won't wait to ask your permission."

Signora Cortis bit her lip, smiled, and slowly said, with affected sweetness,—

"And dear Elena, who so earnestly desires *to do this*, will she not ask leave of the Senator Di Santa Giulia?"

Count Ladislao impetuously tossed his head, then,

half-closing his eyes, scrutinised the signora for a moment, and finally, rising from his chair, pointed to the door with the forefinger of his outstretched left hand, saying, with a calmness that was threatening,—

"Have the goodness to leave the room."

"I will go—I will go!" answered she, getting up. "I will go, because now I am quite content to do so. Of course the senator will grant his permission, as he is having his debts paid by my son."

Count Lao was on the point of seizing and putting her out of the room, when the door opened, admitting Elena, who, on seing her aunt, remained for an instant in amazement.

"Let her pass!" thundered the count.

Elena did not stir; she interrogated with her eyes, first one, and then the other.

"Elena is not accustomed to letting me pass," remarked the signora with irony.

"It does not depend upon me," answered she. "I have just come from Daniele, and I have to tell you that he is asking for you."

The signora extended her long, fleshless arms and skinny fingers towards Elena. With her big Rembrandt hat on the top of her head, her hair in disorder, her pale face and long, yellowish neck, her black cloak awry on her shoulders, she looked like a Fury unaccustomed to modern clothes.

"He has always wanted me!" she screamed, as she left the room with great strides.

Elena looked at her uncle. He was livid and trembling.

"Tell me at once!" he cried. "How much has Cortis paid?"

Elena gazed at him in surprise.

"Uncle!" she said.

"How much has Cortis paid, I ask you? What has he given your husband?"

Elena understood neither the question, nor the angry voice, nor the furious countenance.

"I know nothing about it," she answered; "I have told you all I know."

"What put it into his head to mix himself up with all these matters?"

Elena blushed.

"Uncle, uncle!" she said. "Ah!" she added, with a start, "I do remember now that he told me that he was simply acting for you, and doing what you would have done, as there was no time to ask you, and you would certainly approve all he had done in your place."

"But then he should have written to tell me!"

"You are not aware, uncle," answered Elena, "that Daniele saw my husband at noon on the 25th, just before going to the Chamber?"

"Is she gone?" asked Countess Tarquinia, putting her head through the doorway of her room. "Heaven be praised!"

Lao took no notice whatever of her.

"Was no one else present?" he said.

"The representative of the bank at Cefalù, Boglietti, the lawyer, was to have been there," answered Elena.

Lao took his hat, and said, with determination,—

"I am going to him."

"Where?" asked Countess Tarquinia in surprise. "What has happened?"

"Will you not go to Daniele first?" inquired Elena, in her turn.

Count Lao hastily replied,—

"No. If I went to Daniele I should abuse him, and that would not do just now."

"But tell me," repeated his sister-in-law, "what has happened?"

Elena quickly answered: "Nothing, mamma," and added that she too was going out in search of her husband. Henceforward Daniele did not need her. Her uncle asked her if it were a fact that they thought of moving him to Villa Carrè. Yes, and the doctors had even gone so far as to say that he might travel the next day, but they did not yet know who could accompany him. She herself did not intend to leave Rome without having first done all in her power for her husband; and she looked to the others to help her.

"I am to see him this evening," she added.

"I know nothing; I want to know nothing," cried her uncle. "I am going to look for this Signor Boglietti."

"Boglietti?" said the countess; "where does this Boglietti spring from?"

"I will explain it to you, mamma," said Elena, as Count Lao was leaving the room.

The countess called him back.

"Come here," she cried, extending her hand. "Do you know that we have not greeted each other yet?"

"Ugh!" said Lao, raising his arm as if to say: "Why do you bother me with such rubbish now." And that was his greeting.

Elena immediately inquired of her mother how her Aunt Cortis had got in.

"Allow me to tell you that you have got a precious donkey for an uncle," answered the countess. "What manners! Of course, I suppose I ought to be accustomed to them by this time, but there are some things to which one can never accustom one's self. That woman? How should I know how she got in? She stood before me without my knowing anything about it. Imagine what sort of person she must be to walk in without asking anybody. I tell you that if I stay here three days more, I shall die of consumption. My dear child, for mercy's sake let us take Daniele with us and go away. What are you doing there? Are you not going to take off your hat?"

Elena put down the parasol that she held in her hand, and let herself fall on the sofa.

"I will rest a minute," she said, "and then I must go out. I told you so."

"Go out again?" exclaimed her mother, surprised. "I did not hear you. In such a state?"

Elena's face, and indeed her whole person, showed signs of the most profound distress.

"I am quite well," she said, leaning her head upon the back of the sofa. "Will you go with Daniele, mamma?" she went on, in the same weak, tired voice. "You and Uncle Lao?"

"How, I and your uncle? And you too?"

"No, mamma. You were not listening just now."

The countess could not get over her astonishment.

"But, goodness me!" she cried, "what are you going to do?"

Elena's hand was still resting on the sofa. She half closed her eyes, and replied almost inaudibly,—

"Stay here."

Then, raising her head and voice, she continued,—

"You know why I came to Rome."

Her mother started in her arm-chair, and seized her arms tightly.

"For your husband? You mean to say that you are going to stop in Rome for your husband's sake? Listen, Elena. You know how much I once did to set matters straight, how much I suffered. You must remember, at Passo di Rovese! You were up in the clouds at the time, and could not condescend to occupy yourself with such matters. And you know how he has behaved to you and to us. One minute! You are his wife, and you came to Rome to help him; I praise and respect you for it. I also came, disposed to receive him kindly, and to do anything in my power for him. But now! now that he behaves in this manner, that he never lets us see him, alive or dead, as if he did not care a straw for you, for us, or for anybody, I tell you plainly, that I think you would be foolish if you did not leave him to reap as he has sown, since such is his desire. And besides—forgive my saying so—there are debts and debts; Clenezzi has told me something about these. I ask you, how can any one who respects himself have anything more to do with such an individual?"

Elena smiled slightly, and said,—

"I never heard, when I married him, that under certain circumstances I could have nothing more to do with him. You see I married him in real earnest, mamma."

Countess Tarquinia gazed at her daughter without speaking, then covered her face with her hands, and burst into tears, repeating through her sobs,—

"Forgive me! Forgive me!"

Elena pacified her with caresses, and with her affectionate voice. Her mother was not to blame herself; she had been deceived too, that was all. As she thus spoke, Elena's mind turned to that other guilty mother, to the goodness of Daniele, and she redoubled her tenderness, feeling that she was hard and bad in comparison with him.

"I must do my whole duty," she said.

The countess inquired where her uncle had gone, who that Boglietti was. She had understood nothing of what had passed. Elena explained it to her very briefly.

"And you," added her mother, "where are you going?"

"To see my husband," answered Elena. "He does not expect me, but I have arranged it all with his landlady. She told me that he is generally at home soon after seven. I shall not start till I have spoken to him."

"What a beast he is? Who knows how he may treat you! And when are we to leave here, Elena?"

"I don't know: it must depend upon how Daniele is; to-morrow, or the day after."

"Because the other day, after leaving you at the Tiberine museum, I saw in Noci's shop some lovely little arm-chairs, and I should like to get two of them—one for the town-house and one for Passo di Rovese. I badly want a tea-service, too, for the country, but I have no money."

Elena, who was in the act of leaning over her mother to kiss her, felt all her affection freeze within her, and she stood there a moment as if turned to stone.

"It must be dinner-time," remarked the countess; "it is past half-past six."

"I must be there at seven," answered Elena drily. "Good-bye."

"And dinner?"

Elena made no answer; perhaps she did not hear the question. She had already left the room, and, as she acknowledged the chambermaid's deep curtsey, she thought to herself that probably within that woman's breast beat a heart less vulgar than that of Countess Carrè.

CHAPTER XVIII.

NOCTURNAL STRUGGLES.

ELEVEN o'clock was striking on that night of the 28th March, the moon was shining on the houses and deserted pavements in front of the august black mass of the Palazzo Madama (the Senate), when Baron Di Santa Giulia came out thence alone. He stopped at the door, and turned round to look at the large, brilliantly-lighted hall. The porter came towards him obsequiously, thinking that he was looking for something.

"What do you want?" asked the baron roughly. "Have I not even the right to stand here now?"

The man stared in surprise.

"I thought as much!" sneered Di Santa Giulia, and, turning his back upon him, walked off in the direction of the church of St Louis of France.

He had, that evening, resigned his position as member of the Senate, laconically, without a word of preamble or conclusion, and had entrusted the sealed letter containing his resignation to a colleague, the president's secretary. Nobody had lately called upon him to do this; it was done of his own free will; and the resolution was taken some time since, with others still more serious, part of the preparations he had secretly made when he found there was no longer any hope of saving himself from utter ruin. Henceforward that was hanging over him; he saw no escape from the desperate remedies which he had hitherto desperately opposed. Now he would rest, and let everything fall to pieces; he could do nothing else.

Boglietti had written to him on the 25th, informing him of the settlement made with Cortis, and adding that he was now free from any debt to the bank; but the baron had proudly sent back his letter, swearing that he would never accept the offers of Signor Cortis. As a matter of fact, they did not sensibly relieve his difficulties. He was deeply sunk in many other debts, and of a no less serious nature than the one to the bank. Merely to pay his gambling debts, and to secure his reception in the more or less private gaming-houses that he frequented, he had, after trying all the best-known money-lenders in Rome, laid hands upon certain bonds which he held in trust for a minor, had pledged them, and turned them into money. This transaction had now come to light, and a prosecution was imminent. Notwithstanding all these sacrifices, cards had swallowed everything, and he now found himself unable to pay his gambling debts. No one would play with him any more; the door to fortune was closed, that of the criminal court was open.

But in his savage nature, made up of power and corruption, the proud determination to ask nothing off the Carrès remained stronger than ever. Three hours before he resigned his seat, Boglietti had met him in the street and dragged him, against his will, to his office, alleging the necessity of speaking to him at once. There he had communicated to him a proposition which had just been made, he would not say by whom. The lawyer undertook to settle with his creditors, to save his honour and liberty, and to pay to him a sufficient yearly allowance, on condition of his emigrating to America for ever. Di Santa Giulia, rooted in the idea that this was a plan of his mother-in-law and his wife, would not even listen to the attorney when he protested that he did not even know Countess Tarquinia or her daughter by sight, and that the proposal came neither from them nor from Cortis; he rushed furiously out of the office, leaving Boglietti calling after him that he would not take "no" for an answer, that he had better sleep on the proposal, and that he would wait upon him the next morning for a definite answer.

And now he walked frowningly homewards, his head high as usual, his hand in his pocket, playing with the key of the box containing his revolver, experiencing a sort of gloomy satisfaction at having at last come to the bottom of the abyss, feeling that he was close upon a terrible exit, but one which should set him free and be worthy of the pride that mingled with his debased nature. At least he was out of the Senate. That act seemed to him to have been decisive, and he felt that he had laid his coat by the river's brink, as so many do, before disappearing for ever in its waters. That gloomy conceit was fixed in his mind. He saw in imagination so many things and persons connected with him in his mind by feelings of rage or anguish. Yesterday, nay, a few hours back, he was choked and oppressed by visions of overdue payments, summonses, accusations, usurers, gambling-debts, bailiffs, judges; now they all seemed far away, and he seemed to be alone in a large empty space, like the space that a crowd leaves around a corpse. As he crossed the Piazza di Pietra, he thought again with fury of Boglietti and America. The Carrès, without a doubt! To free him! In America! Boglietti was to come to him next morning for an answer, was he? What if, when he came into his room, he found him on his bed with a ball through his heart? Curse those stuck-up people! What did they think he was? He might have every vice under the sun, but he was not a coward! He would stain them with blood and disgrace; his only satisfaction, by heaven! He had thought his wife better than the rest of them, even after her treachery at Passo di Rovese, but now she showed that she was cast in just the same mould. What sort of wife had she been to him? Upright? yes, except on one or two occasions; hard and cold as a crystal; faithful to herself, not to him! That is if she were still faithful! He had received an anonymous letter containing accusations against her and Cortis. At first the baron would not believe them; now he was inclined to. He liked believing them, and it pleased him to fancy that high and mighty virtue prone and sullied. In America? Did they want to purchase his absence? No, no; his wife should marry her man if she pleased, but she should bring him blood and curses as her portion.

He stopped in the Corso and looked up and down as though for the first time. It was empty; the two long rows of lamps seemed to the baron as if they were accompanying a funeral. He thought to himself that he would have no such pomps, and the idea tickled him.

Better to go alone, without a lot of humbugs behind him, who would only laugh and chatter, and not care what became of him at last. He would have no funeral, and he would go to no church. So be it. Neither God nor saint would have helped him. At this moment his pride seemed to fail him, and a feeling of alarm came over him; but it quickly disappeared, and the man walked on without another thought.

He entered a little café in the Via delle Muratte, a few steps from his own door, and knocked violently upon the table to arouse the waiter, who had fallen asleep on a bench, with his arms folded under his head. There was nobody in the poor little place except Di Santa Giulia and an old priest, with face and hands the colour of wax, and who came there every night just before twelve o'clock for a cup of chocolate.

"Do you really believe, father," asked the baron, without any preface, "that there is another life?"

The old priest looked him straight in the face and quietly answered,—

"No, signor."

After which he unfolded a dark-blue handkerchief, looked at it all over, wiped his mouth with it, folded it up again carefully, and, having replaced it upon his knees, said in a sweet, gentle voice,—

"I do not believe it, I know it."

Nothing was audible save the splash of the fountain of Trevi. The baron drank a glass of rum, and went out without another word.

There was a light in his windows. Why? He fancied he saw, on the dark balcony, a figure which retreated as soon as he stopped at his door. On the staircase stood the landlady, with a candle in her hand.

"Why is there a light in my room?" he asked.

"A visitor, Signor senator. A lady has been waiting to see you since seven o'clock."

The baron thought at once of his wife.

"Who is it?" he asked angrily. "You should have said that I was not coming in."

"It is the baroness, Signor senator."

"Ah!" he exclaimed, as though to say if that be the case you have done quite right. But his accent and look expressed how disagreeable the visit was to him. He went to his room with hasty steps, cursing between his teeth.

Yes, she was there. Her tall, refined figure was erect in the middle of the room, close to the table whereon stood a large, unshaded lamp.

"You here?" he said, stopping at the door. "What do you want?"

Her shoulders heaved with nervous palpitation. She hesitated a moment before answering, and then said calmly,—

"Remember that I am alive."

"I knew that already," answered the baron, taking off his hat and throwing it on his bed.

Elena raised her eyebrows.

"I should not have thought so," she answered.

The baron took off his overcoat, threw it also on to the bed, then closed the shutters of both windows; afterwards he removed his hat and coat from the bed, put them on a chair, and began to walk up and down the room, and round his wife, who neither spoke nor moved. He suddenly stopped at some little distance from her, and, in a furious voice, said,—

"And now, what do you want?"

She turned towards him, took hold of the back of a chair, and answered, as she pulled it in front of her,—

"Why have you never let me see you? Why have you not answered one of my letters?"

Her voice was low, very quiet, almost affectionate.

"To please you," he answered. "Thank me. Was not that what you wished?"

Elena swallowed her contempt with difficulty. She raised herself from the back of the chair upon which she had been leaning, and said with severity,—

"That is no answer."

Her husband crossed his arms over his breast.

"Are you getting angry?" he asked. "Was it not enough for you that I wrote to you giving you leave to go and come when you pleased, with whom you pleased? and have you not taken advantage of it? do you find fault with me for not having come to kiss your mother's hand? Don't break that chair, as it does not belong to me."

"I beg your pardon," answered Elena gently, putting down the chair.

She had come with the firm intention of being as humble and affectionate as possible, of putting up with all the indignities she foresaw she would receive at the hands of the man whom she wanted to save from the abyss; and now she was ashamed of herself for having failed at the very beginning.

"I would once more beg you to believe," she continued, "that you are wrong to be angry with mamma. If any one were in fault that time at Passo di Rovese, it was I. I have told you so many times, Carmine, and I have begged your forgiveness. I did not mean to do any harm, but I will beg your forgiveness again, if you wish. If you will not believe me, I cannot help it. Remember that, out of respect for your wishes, I allowed my mother to lodge at the inn at Cefalù; and it hurt me the more to do it because I know that the poor thing is not to blame in the slightest degree. Yes, I did come to Rome with her, but I wrote and told you why I had done so: to be of use to you! Mamma had taken into her head that she would carry me off into Veneto, and I wrote and told you so; but I always told her that if I moved from Cefalù it would be to come to Rome, to help you to the best of my power."

"All very fine," broke in the baron. "And then followed this miraculous combination: the Chamber met, and the reverend Signor Cortis, not knowing how the deuce he should finish a speech, managed, by the help of the saints, to have a fainting fit; and then, by the most extraordinary chance, you, who had come to Rome to help me, went and looked after him night and day, etc., etc. Is not that so?"

"What do you mean?" asked Elena frowning.

"You know very well what I mean," answered the other. He took some letters out of his pocket, and, going to the lamp, chose out one, which he flung on the table. "For you," he said.

Elena's heart beat in spite of herself as she took the letter, as though things buried in her own heart might be written therein. She hastened to look at the signature;

there was none. Then she glanced at the short note in which she was anonymously accused of trying to get round Cortis, so as to make him her lover. She recognised the handwriting of her aunt.

"I know who it is from," she said coldly; "I recognise the writing. And do you believe this?"

"I know nothing about it," answered the baron surlily. "Who is it from? I seem to recognise the writing too."

"You don't believe it!" exclaimed Elena. There was so much fire in her eyes and so much pride on the brow raised towards him, that her husband was dumb for an instant.

"And what if I did believe it?" he said at last. "In any case, if, as I hope, we shall never see each other again, you may tell your cousin to respect my name, as it is a mere fluke that I am not his father. It simply depended upon my having known Signora Cortis four or five years earlier."

Elena started.

"It's perfectly true," continued the baron. "Tell him that when I was quartered at Alessandria I knew his mother very intimately."

"You?" exclaimed Elena.

"Yes, I. Do you know the story? It was I, and not the artillery officer. Go and tell that to your sanctified cousin. Let him know it! What do I care? Nothing matters to me now. And besides, it's only justice. Tell him from me, if his mother has not told him already; as I hear that that witch has reappeared from hell. Certainly she had not told him the other day."

Elena hid her face in her hands. She was stunned, and felt a dumb horror, an agonised longing to go far away at once; a violent resistance to that longing rose somewhere in the secret depths of her soul.

"Ho, ho! what an impression!" said the baron, with an

ironical drawl in his tone. "We are weeping! Poor cousin!"

"I am not weeping," answered Elena proudly, uncovering and raising her face. With her left hand she pushed the hair off her forehead, and looked straight at her husband. "I am suffering, but I am not weeping."

The baron's face contracted, a deep roar issued from his mouth.

"And am I not to believe that he is your lover?"

Elena did not move or flinch. Her eyes were fixed, her figure like stone, as she answered, in a low voice,—

"No, it is not true."

They remained thus for a minute, looking straight at each other, motionless. Di Santa Giulia suddenly broke out into a storm of gesticulations and words.

"I am at liberty to believe that it is true; I am at liberty to tell you that I do believe it, and I choose to tell you so. And now go; go where you like, with whom you like! Go, I say! I have better friends than you in this room; friends who can be of more use to me than you can, who can free me in a minute from you, from—"

Here followed a string of imprecations and curses against men and things.

Elena, meanwhile, had recovered her self-control.

"I will go," she said; "but not before I have done my duty."

A violent trembling came over her, and rendered her incapable of proceeding. She was obliged to sit down, and wait till she grew calmer.

"I promised," she went on at last, "to be faithful to you; and, whatever you say, whatever you think, faithful I will be to the end. You wrote sinister words to me at Cefalù, and now you repeat them to me." She stopped; she could not speak much. "I know not if it be true that your affairs are in so bad a state," she said, "and that you have a dreadful deed in contemplation. I am here to do everything in my power to help you. I will work, give lessons, suffer hunger!"

"Never mind the heroics; they're not wanted," sneered the baron. "Am I not going to America?"

"To America?" exclaimed Elena, in astonishment.

"Don't play the hypocrite! As if you didn't know that!"

She started; no greater insult than that could be offered to her. She bit her lip and restrained herself, however, saying only,—

"As if I didn't know what?"

"That your people have offered to pay my debts on condition that I take myself off to America. They offer me money and liberty; they send me to die a long way off, because they think that their blood is sufficiently tarnished, and that they have disgrace enough upon them now, I suppose! But they are mistaken; neither payment nor America!"

Elena started to her feet.

"It is not true!" she said.

"What is not true?" cried the baron. "There is no other dog in the world who could have the smallest reason for making me such a proposal. And you," he continued, in a tone of ironical kindness, "have come, have you not, to sound me, to try by your kind interest to discover whether I will accept or reject the proposal that has been made to me."

"But I tell you it is not true," protested Elena. "I tell you that my mother and I are quite unable to pay your debts, and that my uncle absolutely refuses to do it!"

In her surprise, she spoke in such a tone of sincerity that the baron was shaken for a minute, and was silent.

"Indeed!" he exclaimed presently, returning to his

original conviction. "It is so! How is it possible that it should be otherwise?"

Elena was in despair.

"Heavens!" she exclaimed, "what can I say or do to convince you?"

The baron thought for a moment.

"Should you be glad," he asked, "if I accepted this proposal and went to America?"

Glad? She thought that did she but love that man she would have willingly died with him.

"Glad? No," she answered. "I should be glad if all this could turn out to be a bad dream; but—"

She did not know how to express that a great weight would be taken off her mind, a great fear of not having done, of not knowing how to do, everything in her power to prevent the accident that would leave her free.

"Well, *but?*" exclaimed her husband. "Listen to me, faithful wife," he added slowly, looking her straight in the face. "If I go, will you come with me?"

Elena received this blow in her heart without flinching. It was a terrible, an unexpected blow—a terrible and unexpected manner of putting her words to the proof. She did not flinch, but, on the other hand, she made no reply. She felt in herself something of a soldier called upon to die, and who goes out to meet death gravely, silently, with beating heart.

"Ah, you are silent!" said the baron.

"Have you already said that you would not accept?" she asked.

"Yes; but they are coming to me to-morrow morning for a definite answer."

"And if I come, will you accept?"

"Bless my soul!" he exclaimed, half amazed and half perplexed, "if you come, I shall begin not to understand it at all."

"Will you accept, then?"

"Perhaps."

"No, no!" exclaimed Elena, with determination. "You must promise that, if I come with you, you will accept."

The baron threw himself on the sofa.

"I will think about it," he said.

But Elena would not allow a shadow of a doubt, and insisted. Her husband could not believe that the Carrès would allow her to expatriate herself.

"Well," he said, "if you will really come, I will accept."

Fully convinced that the offer originated with the Carrès, he felt equally certain that it would come to nothing in consequence of that condition.

Then Elena asked him whether, under no circumstances, he would accept an offer from her family without the condition of going to America. He answered with a "Never!" full of pride and indignation, wondering whether, after all, Boglietti had not been instructed by the Carrès.

"I will come," she said.

The baron looked at her, brought down his open hand on the back of the sofa, and said,—

"Very good!"

Then he went to his chest of drawers, pulled out his revolver, and laid it on the table near the lamp.

"This is the friend who would have helped me," he said. "I swear to you that I would have killed myself a hundred times over before accepting any help from your people."

Elena took up the revolver.

"It is loaded," said her husband.

She continued to hold it nevertheless, and appeared to study it carefully. Her hands shook, and her lips were drawn and set. She did not really see that little shining barrel. She saw only the man she loved so dearly, by whom she knew herself loved; she saw him at the moment of their last farewell, and knew the anguish it would cause him.

"It is the one you gave me when we were engaged," said her husband.

Elena replaced the revolver on the table, looked at it again, until she had succeeded in choking back he tears.

"And now?" she asked gently.

"Now," answered the baron, "I will accept. They may settle my affairs. It will take some little time, as I don't know all my debts myself. After that, we will go."

Elena had not strength to inquire how and when.

"Do you know I think I am a great fool to believe that you will come?" he suddenly exclaimed.

She rose with disdain, and prepared to return to the hotel.

"No, no; I believe you," he said soothingly. "What a hurry you are in! Stay a little longer. Be pleasant to me."

Elena wished to go at once. Her husband roughly offered to accompany her; the landlady, who had had an ear at the keyhole all the time, offered to lend her own bedroom for the night; it was quite ready, close by. Elena refused with such vehemence that the woman apologised for the suggestion.

"Let her do as she pleases," said the baron. "Between this and the Minerva the streets are quite safe, and my wife is afraid of nothing,"

The landlady lighted Elena as far as the street, saying that she had hoped she would stop. The senator grieved her! He had so many worries! He said such things!

Elena answered with a nod of thanks and went out, walking slowly through the dark streets, not knowing very well whither she was going, letting her instinct guide her, feeling nothing but a dead pain at her heart, and intense mental fatigue. And, as she passed the rare gas-lamps, she watched their flames flickering and quivering, and disappearing above her head as she walked beneath them. Little by little a strange idea took possession of her; she fancied that she had lost her way in an immense unknown city. Suddenly her instinct failed her. She knew not which road to take; and she had to stop to collect her thoughts and look round carefully before being convinced that she had reached the corner of the Via dei Pastini. She hastened forward, and a minute later entered the Minerva.

A waiter had orders to tell her that her uncle was waiting for her in his room, and that she was to go straight to him, no matter at what time she came in. Now she must hide, dissemble this new suffering! She did not think she could do it, and was on the point of telling the waiter, who was leading the way, that she would let the count sleep, as it was now so late; but she did not say this, and the man knocked at the door, showed her in, put down the candle, and withdrew.

Count Lao was in bed, reading. He threw down his book, and, raising his head from the pillow, turned to gaze at his niece.

"Oh!" he said, "I thought you were never coming."

Elena did not approach the bed, and merely answered that she was very tired and sleepy. The count silently watched her.

"Good night," she said, with some hesitation.

Her uncle did not answer immediately, and then, with an imperious movement of his head, said,—

"Come here."

She took two steps towards him, very slowly, then stopped, and whispered,—

"What do you want?"

"Sit down there," he said.

Elena begged him to let her go, again alleging her fatigue and want of sleep.

"Sleep! Nonsense," returned her inexorable uncle; "you can sleep to-morrow. Take that chair, sit down, and tell me all about it."

She did not obey even now. She had been glad to come to bid him good-night, but they must think a little of the people of the hotel, and not keep them up.

"You goose!" exclaimed her uncle. "Come, don't worry me any more."

Elena found it was useless to attempt further resistance. She seated herself near the bed, avoiding, as far as possible, having the light of the candle upon her face.

"So," he said; "have you been with your husband?"

"Yes."

"How is he?"

Elena made no answer.

"Is he alive or dead?"

She was silent for a moment, covered her face with her hands, then, suddenly throwing herself on her knees beside her uncle's bed, she seized one of his hands.

"Uncle, uncle!" she exclaimed, with a sudden outburst of passion, "we must save him, and never let him know it was we who did it!"

This time her uncle did not lose his temper.

"Save him, do you say?" he returned, smiling. "Save him? That's more easily said than done. A fine piece of goods to save! If you like to save him, do so; you are quite welcome; I certainly will not throw away my money upon him. Get up, get up!"

He spoke with the greatest gentleness, and, when he had finished speaking, he lightly kissed Elena's hair.

"If only I could do it!" she said despondingly. "If only I could save him! I should be doing a good work! I know it, indeed, I do!"

It was a bitter moment! Count Lao had not thought that his words would sound so harsh.

"You know perfectly well that I have not the means," added Elena, rising.

"Come, come," he said, "such scoundrels as he is never go to the bottom. They always find somebody to pull them out. He won't kill himself, never fear. I would bet that he will fall on his feet."

A sudden ray darted into Elena's eyes.

"Do you know anything about it?" she asked.

"I? No. I know nothing. What should I know?"

"Because, as a matter of fact, somebody has been offering to pay his debts."

"There you are!" exclaimed the count. "I told you so. And what does he say?"

"There is a condition attached to the offer, you know."

The count lost his patience, and declared that he knew nothing in the world about it.

"Yes," continued Elena, "there is a condition, which is that he should go to America for ever."

Lao said nothing, and showed no further curiosity in the matter.

"He accepts," she went on, after a short pause. "He will go."

Lao shrugged his shoulders, and muttered,—

"So much the better."

They were both silent for a short space.

"Well then," he said at last, "why make yourself miserable? I can't make it all out. Do you think it would be more respectable for him to go to prison? What better could he do? Upon my word, I don't understand you."

Elena rose from her chair without a word, approached the chest of drawers whereon stood the candle, took it up and studied it for a moment, then, replacing it, turned slowly round, placed both her hands on the bed, and leaned forward as though to kiss her uncle, but instead, stooping down to his ear, whispered,—

"And what if I were to go too?"

He burst into a loud, ironical laugh.

"I am not joking, uncle. Indeed I am not," she said.

Then her uncle, who had been lying on his side, turned over on to his back.

"Tell me the truth!" he exclaimed, seizing one of her arms; "would you really serve me this bad turn?"

"I am afraid it is my duty, uncle."

"Duty! rubbish! Who ever heard that it was the duty of the wife of a scoundrel to accompany her husband to America? Have the goodness to go to bed. Go, I say, go!"

Elena was surprised to find that her uncle received her news with such relative tranquillity.

"I am really going, you know," she said.

"That will do!" exclaimed the count. "Have done. The condition is that he should go alone. That is understood, of course."

"No, it is not, uncle."

"Yes, yes! alone; absolutely alone!"

"I beg your pardon, uncle."

"I tell you it is!" exclaimed Lao, beside himself. "Who should know better than I? Who is the ass that is paying, if it be not I?"

Elena could scarcely draw a breath; all the blood in her body seemed to rush to her heart. She looked at her uncle with staring eyes, clasping her hands over her breast, unable to speak. She had fancied that the offer had been made by Clenezzi, acting for the president of the Senate, instructed by the government.

"I cannot have explained myself clearly enough," said the count. "I cannot have explained myself properly to that fool of a lawyer, but I will see to it. Nothing is settled yet. Wait till all the terms of the treaty are drawn up properly."

Elena threw her arms round her uncle in a sudden frenzy of affection and fear. She kissed him over and over again.

"No, no, no!" she said excitedly, "I am not going; don't say any more about it! Thank you; oh, thank you! I did it on purpose to see if you would move in the matter, if you would try to save him, if you would let him off going to America. I have been stupid and unjust, uncle! He will go alone, you know, quite alone. Never mind anything else now. Thank you, uncle!"

And she kissed him again, caressing him passionately, smiling at him with a deadly pain at her heart. Should she betray herself, or fail for one moment in the part she had undertaken, she might kill her husband and remain free.

That thought was horrible to her.

"I suppose I did not make it clear to the lawyer that I meant him to go alone," grumbled Lao. "He might have guessed that I meant that. My head was in such a whirl, what with my journey and that Cortis woman, and—"

"No, indeed!" broke in Elena. "He did tell him; he will go alone. I did it on purpose."

"Listen to me," exclaimed Lao. "If there be anyone else who would pay his debts, would it be worth our while to do it for the sake of sending him to America? Clenezzi has told you of the scandals that are impending; a question of the criminal court, you know. Now we can find a remedy for that; but do you think he can stay in Italy? Do you think he can continue to hold his seat in the Senate?"

"No, no," she said, jumping at the suggestion. "You are right; I had not thought of that. Yes, I see, it is better for him to start, to go right away. Do you suppose he wants me? He was furious with me for going to see him, and let me walk home by myself at this time of night! He can't bear the sight of me, nor indeed of any of us. Therefore I do beg this of you most earnestly; never let him know or suspect that the offer comes from you. Never, never!"

"I told the lawyer not to mention it," answered the count; "but, of course, he will guess."

"So far he has guessed nothing; he must not guess anything, he must be allowed to think it comes from the government."

"The government!" ejaculated Lao, with an incredulous smile. "Do you know," he continued, after a short silence, "it occurred to me that with your stupid heroism you might play me the trick of going with him; but it may be that I did not mention that to the lawyer."

He reverted to the explicit understanding which should be imposed upon the Baron Di Santa Giulia, and Elena once more implored him to be silent.

"Well, well!" answered Lao, "we will see. Meanwhile, you must leave Rome at once."

"Yes, uncle; anything you like; as soon as you like."

"Daniele," he continued, "is now, I believe, well enough to travel. You and your mother will accompany him to Passo di Rovese."

Elena's heart leaped in her bosom. What pleasure, what pain, what burning fire! She would have liked to refuse, to escape this bitter trial; she could not.

"Yes," she murmured, leaning over her uncle and hastily kissing his forehead, "anything you like. Good night."

"Good night," answered Lao. "You are full of attentions for your husband, and you never give a thought to me, who am half dead on your account. There is not an inch of my body which is not hurting me at this moment. But what does it signify if I die! He is the only person who matters! It's all very fine; you may say what you like, but it is so. I must be content to be a dummy. Good night; shut the door carefully."

Countess Tarquinia was asleep.

Elena went straight to her own room, and, having placed the candle on the table, sat down in the arm-chair near the bed. She still felt that pain at her heart, that heaviness in her head; but they were worse now than before. She watched the flame of the candle as it flickered and quivered like the lamps in the street, and in her heart she felt a load of tears that could not struggle to the surface. She did not undress, she did not move. A mist every now and then passed between her and the candle, enlarging its flame immoderately; then her heart would beat with violence, and she fancied the tears were coming, but they never rose, and the candle resumed its brightness.

Towards morning she laid her head upon her untouched bed, and, falling asleep for an instant, saw herself in a dream at Passo di Rovese. She thought she was going to bid a last farewell to the old fir-trees. And lo! the oldest and dearest of them all, the large, sad fir-tree, which seemed tired out by its age, had yielded to destiny, and lay prone, thrown down by the tempest. At this sight she wept in her sleep; she awoke, and the tears were still flowing, relieving her as they fell.

CHAPTER XIX.

"OUGHT I TO GO?"

CORTIS, who had been threatened with congestion of the brain, had recovered rapidly, partly thanks to his excellent constitution, and partly thanks to the skill and attention he had received. He was tired of remaining at the Chamber, although he was in nobody's way during the parliamentary recess. He longed for his mountains, and his doctors ordered him absolute rest, fresh air, as speedy a departure as possible, and, what was the most important, freedom from the irritating proximity of Signora Cortis. They kept him where he was, however, so as to save the useless risk of two moves—one to his own house, and thence into the country.

This threatened congestion had left behind it a profound depression, a deep sadness which often brought the tears to his eyes. He had no faith either in the future nor in himself. He fancied himself tossed on to the bank out of the political current, left high and dry like a wreck. He made anxious inquiries as to who came to ask after him, always ready to imagine inattentions, slights, or indifference. All this caused Elena much pain, although the doctors assured her that they were ordinary and transitory symptoms. She scolded him in her gentle voice, forbidding him to repeat such ugly things. He was so grateful to her, and obeyed her for a little time, and then he would begin again. He could not bear to be without her, and begged her to forgive him for all the trouble he caused her, excusing himself on the ground that he had lost everything, and that only her friendship remained to him. He wished her to promise to come to Passo di Rovese, and to stay there for a long visit. She avoided giving this promise as well as she could, trying, at the same time, not to irritate him as she had done on the first occasion that there had been any mention of it, when she, not knowing whether she could come or not, had referred to her husband. Cortis had looked black, and had not opened his lips for an hour.

It had been she who persuaded him to send for his mother on the 28th, and to speak to her instead of sending her a message, as he had intended. The latter went straight to him from the Minerva. Cortis signified to her, very clearly and coldly, his intention of starting for the north of Italy, and his wish that she should remain in Rome. He spoke in a manner that allowed of neither remark nor answer. All the same, the signora could not be quite quiet; she told her son, in a grave, sad voice, that it was very difficult, almost impossible, to believe that any affection should make up to him for that of his mother. She added, as she took leave of him, that she felt the duty of forgiving all who had injured her, even those cruel ones who had deprived her of her son's heart. She knew well whence the blow came, and she prayed that Heaven would open her son's eyes, and show him the dangers attending certain equivocal friendships. Her own friendships were not equivocal now, in Rome.

After the signora's departure, Cortis's attendant found him trembling, and in a most excited state; he feared a fresh attack of fever, and wanted to send for the doctor, but Cortis angrily forbade him, desiring him instead to send for the baroness; and then, just as the man was starting, he called him back hastily, and revoked the order.

Later on, towards evening, the doctor, Senator Clenezzi, and finally Count Lao, came. Cortis was much moved at sight of the latter. He immediately asked for Elena, and learned that she had gone after her husband, and that she would probably not come that evening. He then relapsed into profound silence. Meanwhile, the doctor complained to Lao of the little rest the sick man was allowed, for so he still called him, although the slight attack of congestion had been rapidly overcome. His nervous condition was still very excitable. Those nerves of his required absolute material and moral rest, impossible to obtain in Rome, under Cortis's conditions, for he suffered if he saw people, and equally if he did not. He must have rest without delay, and fresh air; for such benefits he might safely face the fatigues of a long journey. Besides, as he understood that the deputy owned a fine country-house, and as his relations were near him, and would keep him company, the best thing for him was to make the move at once.

"To-morrow?" asked Lao, looking at Cortis.

"Why not?" replied the doctor. "To-morrow be it."

Cortis did not utter.

Then Lao described Passo di Rovese to the doctor, and the life that Cortis would lead there, at any rate for some time; because, until he was absolutely well and cured, Daniele was not to be allowed to go to Villascura, but would be kept a prisoner at Villa Carrè. As he spoke, Lao frequently looked at Cortis; he watched for signs of thawing. There were none. Then he went on to speak of the walks that the patient could take in his own gardens at Villascura, mentioning the woods, the hills, the lake, and the fountains. Cortis, lying on his side, with his face to the wall, did not stir; he seemed to be asleep. Lao went on to say that his niece was in love with that garden; she would certainly go there every day. She was so fond of the fine trees. Her favourite was a magnificent plane-tree, with a trunk divided in two, which grew far from the house, near a picturesque path.

"A lime," said Cortis, without turning round.

"Bless my soul," exclaimed Lao, "did you speak? A lime, to be sure, so it is."

Then Cortis remarked, with a cunning that was quite new to him, that Elena naturally would remain in Rome, that she would not come north. Lao protested against the word "naturally." Why "naturally?" She would perhaps come at once, but, at latest, in two or three days. Cortis would see her next morning. Then they could settle all the arrangements with the doctor, who, perhaps, would have the kindness to come next morning at his usual hour. Cortis recovered his temper, so much so, that the doctor begged Lao to accompany him without talking any more, for fear of over-exciting the patient, and causing him a bad night.

Next morning Lao appeared about nine o'clock, alone, and explaining that Elena had come in late, and was tired. She would come, perhaps, about midday. For his part, he would be kept in Rome by business, he did not know how long; but Elena and her mother were ready to start with Daniele immediately. The latter sat up in bed. Did not the express to Florence go at 10.40? There were nearly two hours yet. Lao began to laugh, and said,—

"Just look at him! He is like a boy!"

"Indeed!" said Cortis, somewhat mortified. "It would be impossible for the ladies, but I could catch the train if I were alone."

At this moment the doctor arrived, and, after a short debate, it was settled that, as the least evil, and to pacify Cortis, they should start that evening; and it was further settled that they should travel by the night train in a sleeping-car, and that the doctor should accompany them at least as far as Bologna.

Lao was just going to warn the ladies, when Cortis called him back to beg him, with a sudden, inexplicable earnestness, to ask Elena to come to him as soon as she could.

She was scarcely up when she received this message from her uncle, and she went at once to the Chamber.

Cortis received her with tears in his eyes, asked her if she knew that he was starting that very evening, and whether it was true that she and her mother were prepared to travel with him. Elena answered yes, simply, without further explanations. He went on to say that he had been so rejoiced to hear this from Uncle Lao, that his happiness had driven everything out of his mind till a few minutes previously, when he was staggered by the doubt as to whether he were committing a bad action or not. Now, he wanted to ask her whether he ought not to give up all his happiness? He gave her an account of his mother's visit, and repeated her last words to him. He added that, if the world were really so malignant, he ought perhaps in duty to warn her of it, and to renounce the pleasure of travelling with her, and of accepting the hospitality of the Carrès' house.

"Why?" she asked. "On account of the world? What matters the world?"

Cortis made no answer, but, taking her hand, raised it to his lips and pressed them upon it with fervour. They exchanged a long look in silence. Her lips trembled convulsively, her gaze was one of terrified intensity. She fancied that she was committing an act resembling treachery, seeing that Cortis had no suspicion of the terrible resolution she had taken, or of the mortal sorrow in store for him. Knowing that she was hiding this from him, who loved her so dearly and so nobly, Elena felt herself carried towards him by an indescribable affection, remorse, and desire—by a longing to confess all to him, and to weep on his breast. A mute force kept her back, perchance an unknown spirit from above.

"No," she whispered gently, as she slowly withdrew her hand; "the world does not matter to me; but we must be calm, we must behave like old friends of sixty years' standing, otherwise I cannot come."

"You may be able to," he said, in a broken voice, looking like a child caught in a fault. "Forgive me; I am not yet very strong, but I soon shall be. To-day I seem less nervous than I was yesterday."

She made no answer, smiling at him. She longed to tell him that he was so much better than herself, that she had felt, a moment previously, so weak, so much in his power, had he taken advantage of it, that she did not deserve all his dear, timid words.

They were both silent again for a while. Cortis opened his mouth as if to speak, but no sound came.

"What is it?" she asked.

He hesitated before answering.

"Nothing."

But Elena understood that he wished to speak, and waited. At length he murmured, without looking at her,—

"And will he allow you to start this evening with me?"

"Ought I to speak or write to him?" she answered. "In any case, I am coming."

Cortis begged her to write. He feared a conversation. One could never tell what might be its result. Why should she not write at once? There were pens, ink, and paper. The messenger could take her note.

"Ought I to write from here?" she asked, still uncertain, speaking to herself.

She decided, and seated herself at the table. She had in her head all that she wanted to say, but she was in doubt as to how she should begin. How it made her heart beat to write there in his presence!

"I thought your uncle looking well," said Cortis.

She made no answer, and wrote thus,—

"I start this evening for Passo di Rovese with my mother and Daniele. I am right in going now, and in such company; but, wherever I may be, at whatever moment you may require me, I will keep my promise. Meanwhile, do not say a word about it to anybody. I wish to have started before the matter is really known, and thereby save myself much useless sorrow.

"When the time comes, you have nothing to do but write to me, telling me the date and place of departure, the name of the boat, and everything with the greatest precision. I should like my journey to be as direct as possible; and I should also like to start from Venice, which is four hours only from Passo di Rovese. But I fear no boats start from thence to America."

Elena ceased writing for a moment.

"How long it is," said Cortis gently, "since we have found ourselves together at Passo di Rovese in May! We must read some Shakespeare in the gardens. Forgive me, I see I am interrupting you," as she made no reply, sitting with her hand over her eyes, buried in thought.

At this moment a cry, an agonised cry, burst from her heart. "Ought I to go? Ought I really to go?" And her beating heart answered, "No, no." What might happen at Passo di Rovese? What if strength failed her, and she fell? It had been too easy to promise; it would have been easy to start then and there, without having time to see anyone, without having time to think!

She began to write again,—

"I beg you to give me as many days' notice as possible, because I shall want a little time."

She had hardly written these lines when she bitterly repented having done so. Ought she not rather to have desired the very opposite, a sudden call? a call that might come in the morning, and take her away at night, without leaving opportunity for temptation; and instead, her weak hand, her vile hand, had written those words! And now? She did not like to tear up her letter and write another in presence of Cortis. Her heart beat violently, as if by its vehement "no" it had already half conquered her.

"I cannot write," she said rising; "I cannot find the words. I had better see him."

Cortis, terrified, begged her to do nothing of the kind, and to finish her letter. She might alter that one, if she liked, or write another.

Elena resumed her seat, and said,—

"I will try."

Immediately various arguments rose before her why she should not change those last lines. That would not be a departure; it would be a flight. She must have some time to get ready. She would have to go from the country into the town; she must give a pretext for her preparations. It was not easy to find one then and there. A very sudden determination, joined with a condition of moral uneasiness, would be too marked to escape observation altogether, at any rate from Uncle Lao. She must make some preparations for so long a journey; and as they were to be made secretly, so they would require more time.

But then her heart made another suggestion. What if she destroyed her letter? What if she went away now without either writing or speaking?

"Well," she said, "perhaps I had better let this go as it is."

Cortis rang, and told the messenger to take the letter to the Senate.

"I can send it later on," whispered Elena; but Cortis could not see any reason for this delay. She wrote the closing lines, and directed it, seeming to hear around her, as she did so, the thundering of the sea. There was still time.

"And if he were not well?" she said, in a trembling voice. "I might do without writing?"

"No, no," answered Cortis. "I am sure he is perfectly well. Give it me," and, taking the letter from her hand, he gave it to the messenger.

"Take this at once," he said; then, turning to Elena, he asked: "To the Senate, or to his own house?"

She did not seem to have heard him.

"To the Senate, or to his own house?" repeated Cortis.

"Number 54 Via delle Muratte," she said, in a low voice.

The man departed with the letter. O God! If Cortis should repent of his haste, and if he should call him back, if he should suspect, if he should guess! But nothing of this could happen now. The messenger had already gained the staircase.

"What is the matter?" asked Cortis.

She had no time to answer, as Clenezzi entered at that moment. She ran to meet him, turning her back on her cousin, and received him with so much cordiality that the old man was quite flattered. Cortis had sent for him to beg him to go and collect certain papers at his house that he wanted to take with him. But the senator, who had hastened in response to the summons, could not drag himself away from Donna Elena, and stood there smiling, bowing, and making pretty speeches.

"I say, senator," cried Cortis, after some time.

"Here I am," answered he, "at your orders. Pray make use of me. I am quite at your disposal."

"And I am going away," said Elena. "We shall meet at the station this evening."

Before Cortis or Clenezzi could detain her, she had turned and disappeared.

CHAPTER XX.

A HIDDEN DRAMA.

No blade of grass stirred round the oval lake in the gardens of Villa Cortis, no leaf trembled on the horn-beams that grew around it. The water, brown as far as the middle of the lake from the neighbouring torrent, and silvery beyond, had no ripple on it; and even the white clouds hung motionless in mid-air, tempering the sun till it gazed sleepily into the depths, while every sense was lulled by the trickle of the stream that fed it. The silence was full of unseen life, quivering with expectation. As soon as any breath of wind came from the south, every blade of grass, every leaflet whispered the news to one another; the lake alone knew that it was not the great south wind that blows in May, bringing joy and life to every wood, to every meadow, and to itself also; the water did not add a ripple to its surface, and when the breath died away, everything once more resumed its stillness and its silence.

"How quiet it is," said Cortis, in a low voice.

Elena, seated near him on the trunk of a tree lying in the grass near the beginning of the path that leads from the lake to the house, did not answer immediately. She seemed absorbed in contemplating the water.

"Too quiet," she said presently, without moving her eyes or her face.

"Why too quiet?" asked Cortis.

"Because it makes one forget too easily; here one is too much shut off from the world; one's only thought is to stay here, even though one be not comfortable. It makes one soft, inert. Does it not?"

Cortis picked up a pebble, and threw it into the lake, which gave out a little cry, as of pain; then he remained watching the wavelets till their ever-widening circles touched the bank.

"I don't feel that," he answered. "I am thankful to be out of the world, and would gladly keep out of it."

"Oh, Daniele, don't say that; it hurts me to hear you."

It was easy to see, from her grieved voice, that she meant what she said, and that he did really cause her pain by such words; it was easy to see also from the great eyes which she turned towards him, looking at him at first with sad tranquillity, and suddenly with passion.

Cortis took one of her hands, which she abandoned to him.

"Why?" he inquired tenderly, "why does it hurt you? You know I have no intention of burying myself in sloth. For the present, at any rate, I am out of the political sphere. I was born thirty or forty years too soon. I mean as far as militant politics are concerned. But there remain science and books. I do not in the smallest degree abandon my ideas. Only I see that our country is not yet ripe for them, and it would be well if some one would help to prepare it by making these ideas known, and by discussing thoroughly their theory before attempting to put them into practice. I shall stay here; I shall read, write, and perhaps even travel; that may be necessary to me. And we will discuss together all that I write, will we not? For I hope you are going to spend a long time at Passo di Rovese?"

Cortis pronounced the last words in a very low, almost timid, voice.

She smiled at him in silence, her half-closed eyes moist. Then she whispered,—

"You must go back to the Chamber, to please me. You must look after your newspaper."

"Oh, that is all over and done with," answered he.

Elena started; her hand, which had been lying dead, pressed his.

"How 'over and done with?' Have you answered?"

The previous day Cortis had received a letter from Rome, asking him what his intentions were regarding the new paper. As he had not been able to make his speech, did he think that it should appear at once? Or would he wait for another opportunity? Did he persist in his intention of retaining the editorship until the re-assembling of the Chamber? Or would his health make that impossible?"

"No," he said, "I have not written yet; I shall do it to-day."

"No, you must not!" exclaimed Elena.

Cortis began to laugh.

"I say, yes I must; and you shall sign it."

Her eyes glittered.

In the grass near him was a small, yellowish volume of Shakespeare, in the Tauchnitz edition. He took it up, and began turning over the leaves, saying,—

"Where is the passage you dreamed of in Rome?"

Elena snatched away the book.

"Promise me," she said, "that you will show me your answer?"

"Yes, I promise you I will."

His grave face and his voice expressed a surprise that was almost painful.

"Are you afraid of me?" he went on. "Do you wish to send me away?"

She leaned towards him for an instant, carried away by a dumb impetus; her lips fashioned a kiss. Then, drawing herself back, she looked at him again, and, opening the book, hunted through it, turning over the leaves again and again for some time. At last she handed it to her cousin, pointing to a passage, which he read: "My little body is aweary of this great world."

The sad words thus silently pointed out to him made him feel cold, as if with a secret foreboding. He read them again, and then raised his eyes to Elena, as if to question her; but her eyes were turned towards the sleeping water.

"'The Merchant of Venice,'" he said; "I had forgotten the line."

At that moment the sound of a bell was wafted to them across the silent lake; other bells took up the sound, and repeated it from all sides.

"Mid-day?" said Elena, getting up, surprised to find it so late.

The post usually reached Casa Carrè at one o'clock. The hours of the morning were always the most painful to Elena. After the postman had been, she could breathe a little, allowing herself to enjoy her home, her mountains, the presence and voice of her friend, with the certainty that, up till one o'clock the next day, she could live in peace, indifferent to letters.

"Are you in a hurry?" asked Daniele. "Let us listen to these bells for a little."

She was silent, and turned to gaze through the hornbeams across the valley to her own home. A twinkling ray of sunlight was travelling over the neighbouring field, which sloped away from where she stood, touching, as it passed, the black tops of the fir-trees, which were putting out their fresh shoots.

Down there, on Villa Carrè, on the bed of the Rovese torrent, and even beyond that, on the bare sides of Monte Barco, were large patches of sunlight. She could not see that, behind her, Passo Grande, the frowning, had become deep blue, almost black, above its steep precipices and declivities under a heavy crown of clouds. Elena could not see this threat, but even the pallid smile of the sun seemed to her sad. She was grieved at Cortis's nervousness, his love of nature, of solitude, of bells! It was so new in him.

He had not thoroughly recovered yet. Would he get well? or had some cord in him snapped?

Daniele listened to the bells, which always told the same incomprehensible story, and made the very solitude feel devotional.

"I seem to be a child again," he said; "to have gone back to the days when my grandmother made me say the *Angelus.*"

"I could pray better here than in church," said Elena.

"How would you pray?" he asked, with a smile. "What would you ask for?"

"I deserve nothing, Daniele," she said sadly.

There was so much affection in that unwonted "Daniele," so much grief, such genuine confession!

The mid-day bells were still ringing, but Cortis heeded them no longer. He had something to say—something that caused him much uneasiness. He rose, took Elena by the arm, and drew her away towards the light-green shadows thrown by the horn-beams along the path.

"Listen!" he said. "Do you remember that I once wrote to you about Pergolese and his unknown, and I asked you whether they were now together? Would you not pray for such a reunion in another life?"

"No," answered Elena, in scarcely audible tones; "I could not. Have I hurt you?" she added. "Forgive me!"

He was silent.

"You have so much faith," she said; "I have not. I cannot ask God to make me happy. I might ask Him to make you happy, I desire that so much; but I have not courage to ask those things of God; I have no right. And I do not think it would be well to ask them. It is all I can do to say, Thy will be done,' and to beg Him to enable both of us to bless it, whatever it be."

Cortis pressed her arm, and, seizing her left hand in both his own, pressed it violently in silence. For a long space neither spoke again.

When they reached a place whence a little shady walk turns to the right from the larger path, Cortis stopped, and asked Elena if she would like to go and bid "good-day" to her lime-tree. The lime-tree was not the only thing in that direction; the column with the clasped hands and the Latin inscription was also there.

"Let us go to-morrow," she said gently, "if you don't mind. We will come later; shall we?"

She preferred to reserve that pleasure until after post-time, when she would be more in a position to enjoy it. And besides, she felt too uneasy at the words of Daniele on the subject of future reunion, too much in danger of letting him see how much she loved him; for he did not yet know how much! It would not be right. She did not wish that he should know it, for, when the terrible day came, he would only suffer the more.

She fancied she noticed a shadow of displeasure on his face, and immediately added, with a blush,—

"You see, I should like to be at home when the post arrives. It is so many days since Uncle Lao has written."

So many days? Why, it was only a fortnight since their arrival, and he had written several times. At most, it was not more than five days since they had heard from him. In any case, he ought to have written sooner, and Elena said she was uneasy. Cortis asked what was keeping Lao so long in Rome. He knew of one matter, but that was finished. That affair, whereof Cortis gave Elena no further explanation, perhaps forgetting that he had given her a glimpse of it in Rome, was the cession of the debt to the bank agreed upon with Lawyer Boglietti, and concerning which Lao had already written to him from Rome, thanking him for what he had done, and informing him that the payment had already been directly provided for by himself.

Elena answered that she believed him to be taken up with very serious business; more than that she could not say. Cortis thought of the affairs of Di Santa Giulia, but said no more till they reached the gate of the garden, where a very fine, warm rain began to fall, visible in the trembling light of the sun's rays, but not audible.

"Let us go in," he said, "and wait; at any rate let us get an umbrella from the bailiff."

She would not, however, and, drawing herself from his grasp, took the path under the house leading up the hill.

He was somewhat struck by such impatience.

"Look here," he said, after they had gone a few steps, "I don't know why I should continue to live in your house. I can perfectly well come here now. I am not an invalid any longer; I am as strong as ever again."

"Do as you please," said Elena, in a humble voice. "Do what seems best in your eyes; perhaps it would be best so!"

He had expected a different answer, and was not content with this one. It seemed to him too coldly discreet, and not quite just towards him. Quick by nature to take offence, he was, since his illness, more than ever inclined to do so. Elena's words, wrongly interpreted, drove out of his head for the moment the other matters which had previously disturbed him.

So it happened that neither of them desired to talk; and the warm rain, which was now falling faster, murmuring round them first on the shrubs, and then on the great walnut trees, and finally on the hedges of the high road, favoured their silence. Elena walked a little in front, as he had not offered her his arm again. There were no patches of sunlight now. The fields were lost, the road ahead of them steamed in a dark mist, through which the ghosts of the distant mountains were just visible.

Elena walked on hurriedly, without even opening her parasol. He had told her once to open it, and then had not spoken again. Her little round black velvet cap was useless, except to filter the water drop by drop down her neck and into her ears. When they had passed the solitary house, which is called "The Factory," Cortis suddenly joined her, took her parasol and opened it, at the same time taking her arm, without a word. She let him do as he liked, smiling at him with ineffable tenderness, thankful that the slight cloud had passed away from between them, but not wishing to speak. Then she stretched her hand over the low wall to her right, where the edge of the field was covered with anemones among the long grass; she picked one and gave it to him.

They had just reached the gate of the Villa Carrè when the postman came out. Cortis called him, and inquired whether he had brought any letters.

"For you, sir, yes; you always have a bundle. Nothing for the countess; only the newspapers."

"And for me?" asked Elena, with beating heart.

"No, signora; nothing for you."

Another day gained! Elena drew a long breath of relief, but involuntarily pressed Cortis's arm with her own. He looked at her, and was surprised at the expression of joy that beamed in her eyes. Had she really wanted news of her uncle? She guessed his surprise, and blushed, saying hastily that she was sure her uncle was enjoying himself thoroughly in Rome, and had forgotten all about them; it was better that he should.

They passed through the gate, and took a path that, a hundred feet further on, leads direct to Elena's studio, and thence to the villa.

"Shall we go in?" asked Cortis, as they passed the studio.

Elena smiled, thinking that he had forgotten how wet they both were, but, nevertheless, she made no opposition.

"We will not sit down," she said, with a laugh, as they entered; "my poor sofa!"

Cortis had not thought of that. He regretted his carelessness, and wished to go out again. But then she would not consent, not wishing to seem to blame him. They could stand, and there was no need to hurry indoors. And she smelled the violets and the white banksia roses in a bronze vase on the table. Cortis, meanwhile, was looking at the books.

"Oh!" he exclaimed, "your 'thanks and greetings'!"

He had found the volume of the *Mémoires d'outre tombe* that Elena, when starting for Rome, had given to her mother to be restored to Daniele. Cortis had afterwards left it in the countess's drawing-room, and Elena, having found it there, had retaken possession of it.

"Did they not go?" asked Elena, with an affectionate smile. "Were they too cold?"

How sweet, how pure were her smile and her glance! He took both her hands in his, and looked at her in silence. A step was heard upon the gravel. Elena hastily withdrew her hands. Shortly afterwards a servant entered, and said that the countess had seen them come in, and wished to speak to them directly.

"What has happened?" asked Elena.

"I believe that a telegram has arrived," answered the footman, "and that Signor Lao is coming."

"That is why he has not written," said Cortis.

Elena made no answer; she tried not to let him see her face, because she ought to have been glad of this unexpected news, and it was hard enough to appear calm without appearing glad.

Neither was Countess Tarquinia overjoyed at the

intelligence; she would not have complained had the absence of her brother-in-law lasted a little longer. Now she could do as she pleased in the house; nobody grumbled, nobody made grimaces when she spoke, nobody said "Nonsense!" to her; in a word, she could breathe while he was away.

"This will interest both of you," she said, handing the telegram to her daughter. "He telegraphs from Bergamo, do you see? And what possesses him to bring that poor old Clenezzi up here? The old man would be much happier in his own house. I can't make it out. What can he have gone to Bergamo for?"

In this way she poured out, poor woman, her own annoyance, ending at last by declaring that if one lived with a madman, one must expect all sort of things to happen.

"What can have happened?" asked Elena, as she went up to her own room.

Can everything be settled? Can the day and place of departure be fixed? Heavens, can the dreaded letter be on its way? Just before leaving Rome, her husband had sent her a note, in which he undertook to give her five or six days' notice before starting. She seemed to see her uncle already, to hear him say, "He will start on such and such a day," and a shudder ran through her, which broke the thread of her thoughts. At what time would her uncle arrive? She longed for him with feverish anxiety. Her state of suspense was worse than any certainty. And she was without a soul to whom she could pour out all her woes, without a helper, without a comforter! Had her faith been like that of Cortis, she could at least have prayed that her uncle might bring home good news, some happy, unexpected explanation. But what was done was done, and could not be altered now! She could only say: "Thy will be done."

She was standing in front of her window, her hands

pressed against her cheeks, her eyes staring, her thoughts upon those words of the prayer which did not, as yet, come from her heart. She heard Cortis's voice. He occupied the room on the ground floor, below hers, and he was speaking to somebody. Ah, no, her heart would not, could not utter those words! It wanted life, love, happiness. She drew her two hands slowly down her cheeks, drawing down her eyes at the same time. "Daniele!" she murmured, in a heart-broken voice. She closed her eyes; for one moment she was all his in imagination; his heart and his name were hers.

Countess Tarquinia came to consult her daughter as to which room should be got ready for Clenezzi; as to what dinner she should order, whether of meat or "maîgre," as it was Saturday; and the countess did not know the senator well, and was quite in the dark as to his habits and ideas. She could not bear being worried about such trifles!

"At any rate," she said, "we shall learn something about your husband. He has not written to you once, has he? That's nice behaviour! You know you can stay here as long as you like, and as long as he leaves you free."

She knew nothing of Lao's secret actions; she only knew, from Elena, that that evening in Rome she had left him fairly composed, in hopes of some solution which could not be, as he said, worse than his present condition, and that he was quite willing to leave her free to come and go as she pleased.

Elena did not answer, but followed her downstairs to look at the room next to that occupied by Cortis, and which they thought of getting ready for Clenezzi. In the hall they found Cortis reading his letters; he smiled silently at Elena as she passed him.

"Tell me, Daniele," said the countess, reappearing in the hall a few minutes later, "tell me what I am to give this senator to eat. Fish or flesh?"

"Elena knows," answered Cortis.

Elena made a gesture of surprise.

"I know?" she said.

Cortis pretended to be annoyed to find how carelessly she read his letters. He had certainly written to her that Clenezzi was in the habit of going once a week to eat a "maîgre" dish at Trastevere, where a Lombard cook prepared it for him. What was it called? *casonsèi.*

To be sure, Elena remembered it now.

"For shame!" said her mother. "You deserve a good scolding—forgetting things just when they are wanted."

She went off to see if her Milanese cook knew how to prepare this dish. Elena waited till the door was shut, and then asked her cousin if he really thought that she did not read his letters.

"Do you know," she continued; and she wished to add, "how often," but she did not complete the sentence. Cortis understood, and, taking her hand, made her sit down beside him on the sofa.

"I know," he said kindly; "I can guess."

She left her hand in his, and looked in silence, first at him and then at the door. She thought that she would be gone in a few days, and that she might permit herself this little indulgence. Then she said, in a low voice,—

"You have had a lot of letters?"

"Yes; friends in Rome."

She looked at her imprisoned hand, and said, in a still lower tone than before,—

"What do they want?"

"Oh, nothing! To hear how I am—when I am going to them."

"Not yet?" she said.

"Certainly not!"

Elena freed her hand, lightly caressing his, and looking at them, as she murmured,—

"But later on—when you are well—quite well and

strong, as you were before." She pressed his hands now, raised her face, and smiled at him tenderly and sadly, saying: "Then you will go?"

"Thank Heavens," exclaimed Countess Tarquinia, re-entering, "he knows the dish!"

"Really?" said Cortis, rising, and without answering Elena. "Then your dinner is settled. In the evening, give him a bottle of wine, a little Donizetti or Pergolese, and the old fellow will be perfectly happy."

"Elena will look after the music," said the countess; "I can't play. At what time will they be here, did you say?"

They could not arrive before half-past six. There were still four hours to wait. It had stopped raining. The countess had one or two visits to pay in the neighbourhood. She ordered the carriage, and started soon afterwards.

"What letters we wrote to each other!" said Cortis, returning to his place near his cousin. "It seems impossible!"

"Why impossible?"

"Do you ask me?"

Elena dropped her eyes, saying, shyly and gravely,—

"I don't wish you to love me."

"Why not?"

"You know. Because I do not believe it would be for your happiness."

Cortis leaned towards her, and said, smiling,—

"But you don't believe that any longer, do you? you have no more doubts of that kind?"

"I still believe it," answered Elena, covering her face, "only I have not my strength now. Do you know," she added suddenly, dropping her hands, "that I longed to die in Sicily?"

He seized her hands, watched her quivering lips, and saw that she was breathing quickly, as though she feared he was going to carry her away. She had a moment of horrible giddiness, closed her eyes, paling as though she were going to faint, very quietly withdrew her hands, and drew herself away into the opposite corner of the sofa. At that moment a servant passed through the hall with some things that were wanted for Clenezzi's room.

"Let us go out for a little," said Cortis; "it is not raining."

"I am too tired," answered Elena, "you go alone." Cortis neither spoke nor moved. The servant passed back through the hall.

"It would have been better," murmured Elena.

"What?"

"To have died."

"You must never say that again!" exclaimed Cortis so vehemently that she feared he would be overheard, and motioned him to be more careful, and to lower his voice.

"You must not say that!" he went on in a quieter voice, but with a still excited accent. "You don't know what you are saying. You don't know how I love you. I never permit myself one guilty thought, Elena, never! But do you think that I was born for that base happiness which the majority of people seek for? I must love, and I must suffer for what I love. Then I am happy; I feel as though a breath of life were suffusing my whole being, as though the blessing of God were upon me. I feel that I am a man, with all the dignity and the strength of a man. It is the same when I think of my ideas, my country, which I love so dearly. You know, my conscience tells me, that that should stand before everything else. For those objects I am glad to suffer. The more I have to fight, the more I am hurt, the more I suffer, the better I am. If the prospect of returning to Rome and the Chamber is distasteful to me, it is simply because I fear to do no good there, and not on account of the opposition

I shall meet with. And if I love you, Elena, how—how do you think that my happiness can consist in anything but in continuing to love you, sacrificing for you, now and always, everything that I ought to sacrifice, but trusting meanwhile, that you love me, and that your love is as strong and noble as my own? How can you expect me to marry? Why should I? To have my life encumbered and my heart empty? You are my love, my life, my happiness, even now, while we are living like spirits, praying God always to help us, and to unite us some day—I do not say in this world. For I do pray thus, you know, and my faith is strong!"

It was now Elena's turn to breathe deeply, drinking in his passionate words and looks. It was too much! She suddenly rose, pressed his hand very hard, made no answer to him, rushed out into the garden, and threw herself on to one of the iron seats that stood outside.

A cold, stormy wind had risen in the north, and was shrieking through the fir trees, and blustering among the shrubs and the westeria, round the dead cypresses, among the grass in the meadow, confounding its voice with that of the Rovese torrent rushing down on the right, thrown headlong from the bare, bleak rocks of Monte Barco. Down in the valley the sky was clear. A streak of blue sky touched the snow and the sunlight on the distant peaks of Val Posena. There were no clouds on the summit of Passo Grande; its outline stood out darkly against the light background of clouds which were scurrying away southward; and opposite to it, between Val di Rovese and Val Posena, the obelisk-shaped rocks of Corno Ducale were bathed in a pure golden light.

Elena felt better for the sight of the sky and mountains; the furious wind seemed to her like a spirit of purity and peace cooling her forehead and bosom, quieting her imagination, her blood, and her heart. And all the various noises made by the wind, its sudden rushes through the trees, its different tones of complaint or contempt, did her good, though she could not now talk to them as she once could, when in some secluded corner she could listen to them, alone and happy, and so many pleasant thoughts came into her mind, so many dreams. Neither could she any longer talk to the mountains, but she could nevertheless, while gazing upon their dear venerable forms, hear the voice of her heart as clearly as in her own room.

Ah, foolish, imprudent heart, what was it saying?

"I will go," it said, "but yet supposing I did not go?" And then it beat loudly, as if it would break, struggling violently against a weak will, and pointing out the joy, the infinite joy of being near him, and of knowing that it would be always so to the end of life. "No, no," she said to herself, "I will go, I must go. It is my duty to go!" And having thus quieted her conscience, she returned to her imaginings, allowing them to please her fancy for a moment.

"Contessina!" cried a maid from the balcony, "don't stay out in the wind!"

She started as though some one had guessed her secret, and, rising, she took refuge in her little study, whither, at least, no prying eyes could follow.

The volume of the *Mémoires* was lying open on the table as Cortis had left it. Elena took it up. Again that same page, that same word, "jamais ternie." She could not take her eyes off them; they seemed to have been written for her, and to have reached her at an opportune moment. She defended herself, saying that her will had never sinned, only her fancy. There was not as yet one spot, not one tiny spot upon her life! As she read on, almost unconsciously, she came upon the following words:—

"Depuis t'avoir vu, mon cœur s'est relevé vers Dieu et je l'ai placé tout entier au pied de la croix, sa seule et véritable place."

A great silence fell upon her, stilling her powers of thought and feeling. She fancied, too, that she would like to be able to perform this act of adoration before the Cross. Taking up the book again, she read,—

"Il n'est rien tel, mon ami, que l'idée de la mort, pour nous débarasser de l'avenir."

Here again she stopped.

It was quite true that she had longed for death in Sicily. Now she did not, although the future loomed terrible before her. How could she have ever longed for death? It seemed impossible. Perchance, in some dark corner of her heart, hope had taken stronger root than she was aware of; perhaps she dreaded facing, in an unprepared state, the mystery of the other side of the tomb, concerning which she and Cortis felt so differently. What a shock it would be to him should she die without faith!

She tried to imagine what this faith was like, but she could not. She was tortured by expecting the arrival of her uncle, and each time the clock struck her anxiety increased. She tried to continue her reading, but had to put down the book again. She was tired, and could not keep still. Remaining there wearied her, but meeting Daniele, or sitting with her mother, who had come home, would have wearied her even more. And it wanted nearly three hours to half-past six!

She was standing on the threshold of her sitting-room, when the noise of wheels and hoofs resounded in the portico. She instinctively stepped back; she feared now that it might be her uncle. Was it possible, so soon? What would she not give if it should prove not to be he, and if he would not come for another hour! She had not yet considered whether she should ask for news of her husband, or wait for him to begin. She had not yet decided upon her own behaviour, for it would be difficult to dissemble before him, who knew so much, and who might have some secret suspicion. It was he, beyond a doubt! There was Cortis's voice greeting them noisily, there was Clenezzi's voice too. Her mother told a servant to fetch the contessina. She took her courage in both hands, and advanced towards the group.

Senator Clenezzi came forward alone to meet her, hat in hand, and crying,—

"There she is! there she is! Your uncle brought me, you know! I should never have dared, dear baroness!" he said, bowing and smiling, as soon as he was within reach of her hand.

Elena answered with some words of greeting, and immediately asked after her uncle.

"He is well—very well!" answered the senator. "He hurried in for fear of the wind; that is very serious, in his opinion. Never saw anything like him. I was nearly stifled in the carriage."

Elena interrupted him by asking after her uncle's temper.

"Good, first-rate, could not be better! I wish you could have seen him this morning when we started! He insisted on coming by the early train, so as to gain an hour or two here. He was like a boy!"

"Tell me," said Elena, "do you know if he finished his business in Rome? Need he go back there?"

"I think not. He told me that now he must begin to economise, and that he should not stir from here for a long time, but that he was certain of having good company here, always. Let us go in, baroness, otherwise he will be in a fury."

Indeed, Lao was at the hall window, tapping on the glass and calling them. Elena, who had at first been frozen by the senator's words, recollected herself, and ran towards him with a smile.

At eight o'clock, two hours after dinner, Clenezzi was still dilating enthusiastically upon his Bergamese dish, which had been a perfect success.

"Beautiful house, beautiful country, countess," he cried, entering from a stroll with Daniele; "but what *casonsèi.*"

He thought that the countess was alone, but, on the contrary, she was receiving that evening. The billiard-room was lighted up, and Count Lao was playing by himself, as he did in moments of great good humour, whereby he retained the conviction that neither his eye nor his hand had lost its cunning.

Lighted card-tables were set out in the drawing-room, and there were also candles on the piano, in addition to the large lamp on the oval table near the sofa, on which Countess Tarquinia was sitting with Signorina Zirisela. The parish priest, the doctor, and Signor Zirisela, who had just begun a game of cards, rose at the entrance of Cortis and Clenezzi with a diabolical grating of their chairs and their feet, although Don Bartolo, the fourth player, kept his seat, grumbling, "Come on, come on; what's all this fuss about?"

Signorina Zirisela also got up, very respectfully, as did also Doctor Picuti and two or three other men who were watching the game. Poor, short-sighted Clenezzi did not know whither to fly; he made a series of bows, vaguely, while Countess Tarquinia recited to him a whole litany of introductions.

"And Baroness Elena?" he asked, looking round.

At that moment Elena entered the room. She had heard Cortis pass, with Clenezzi, under her windows, and had come down at once. Lao laid down his cue, and silently beckoned to his niece to come to him in the billiard-room.

Elena obeyed with beating heart.

"Have you nothing to ask me?" he said.

"I was waiting for you to speak, uncle."

"What's the use of that? Are you not interested more than I am?"

Elena answered by a glance so grave, and so sad, that her uncle repented of his rudeness, and said, hastily,—

"Well, well. Let us hope it's all settled now; but it has been a serious matter."

"All settled!" exclaimed Elena. "How?"

"Ah, how indeed! there will be no prosecution, and he owes no money now, except to me."

"And he?" she asked, in a low voice.

"What do you mean?"

Elena had not courage to ask how her husband was. Lao certainly had something to say to her, as he did not demand further explanation.

He took her arm, and, drawing her towards himself, whispered,—

"Do you wish to know how much it has cost me?"

"I beg your pardon, Elena," said Signorina Zirisela approaching timidly. She called Elena always by her Christian name, but did it with the manner of a person who fears to take a liberty, "the countess and that gentleman are asking for you."

"Go along," said the count; "we will have our talk later."

Elena hesitated.

"Do you know what they want?" she asked.

The signorina had not understood exactly. Perhaps it was to make some music. They were all talking, at any rate, in the room where the piano was. Elena remarked that they did not seem to want any music. She was still in doubt when her mother appeared at the door of the hall and called,—

"Well, Elena?"

She obeyed without a word, and Lao turned to continue his game of billiards.

"I am glad that you made that speech after all," said Doctor Picuti, rising and blushing very red, and going towards where Cortis was standing. The latter said,—

"Never mind it now, it's over and done with."

"That will do; now we will have some music," said Countess Tarquinia. "Elena, come and play something!"

"Bravo, bravo!" said Clenezzi, in a low voice, but before Elena had time to express her decided refusal, Doctor Picuti, resolved to speak at any cost, suddenly pushed his way into the circle, and said solemnly,—

"Will you allow me, countess; will you allow me, deputy?"

Some one, most inopportunely, had introduced the subject of the protest made by the electors against Cortis, and Zirisela, from the card-table, had muttered, in joke, some words about little bellows producing a great fire, but remaining hidden the while, thereby hinting that Doctor Picuti had acted the part of the bellows with regard to the protest.

"There's neither fire nor bellows in question," continued Picuti.

"Who mentioned you?" asked Zirisela.

"I know what I am saying," retorted the other angrily. "I know what sharp tongues we have about here, and how they set to work to ruin an honest man, without ever mentioning his name."

"Ah, Picuti, Picuti!" broke in Don Bartolo, "the hen that lays the egg is always the first to cackle."

"Come, come, Bartolo," grumbled the parish priest, drumming upon the table with his cards, "*intende animum tuum ad ludum.*"

"Yes, yes, *ad ludrum, ad ludrum,*" muttered the chaplain, fixing his eyes upon his own cards, and fingering them one by one.

Meanwhile Doctor Picuti, after having retorted, "You hold your tongue, who can generally hold it so well," cried,—

"Signor Cortis, shall I tell you who were the scoundrels?"

"Hulloa, hulloa, what next!" exclaimed Zirisela, putting down his cards, and turning round so as to face the speaker.

Then Cortis could no longer restrain himself from silencing them all.

"That will do," he said, "let it pass. I don't know who did it, and I don't care to. I bear no malice against any one. And besides, you electors under the old law are all dead and buried. Why should I be angry with you? I am myself more dead and buried than any of you."

"What, what!" they all exclaimed.

"Yes, yes; dead and buried; and that's the long and short of it," answered Cortis.

"Now, Picuti, you go and look on at the cards, and, Elena, come and make some music."

The parish priest, Zirisela, and the others whispered together for a minute, while Elena shook her head, and looked at Cortis with mute entreaty in her eyes.

"I beg your pardon, Doctor Daniele," said Zirisela, "but you have not resigned your seat?"

"No, not yet; but I mean to do it as soon as I am strong enough to think about it; I shall write what I intended to say."

All protested except the priest and Signorina Zirisela. Why? Wherefore? You are wrong! You must always represent us! Even the priest-hater Zirisela said, alluding to the parish priest's silence, that he had his own ideas, but that when certain people were silent, he felt that he must cry, "Long live Doctor Daniele, by Jove! Long live our deputy!"

"I am not silent because I have nothing to say!" exclaimed Doctor Bartolo; but, I say, countess, do you wish us to drink this toast? I don't know if I make my meaning clear."

"Quite clear!" yelled Lao, from the billiard-room.

"Well done, count! You understand more from a nod than most people do from a word. Capital! Just one little glass!"

The others were all taken aback by the priest's indiscretion.

"Look at them!" he exclaimed, raising his voice so as to be heard above the noise. "They are all pleased at my suggestion, countess. And yet they abuse me."

Lao appeared at the door, cue in hand.

"Is this the sort of music we are to have to-night?" he asked.

"Come, come, baroness!" said Clenezzi.

Elena made a gesture of entreaty, but without avail. The senator insisted. As she passed Cortis she whispered,—

"Save me; I cannot play."

Cortis called to Lao, who was still at the door,—

"You begin."

"I? Likely!" and he turned on his heels.

Cortis then tried Signorina Zirisela, but she begged to be excused; she knew so little, and was so out of practice. Fortunately Papa Zirisela intervened, with his loud voice of command.

While the signorina was undergoing her torture, Cortis turned to Elena and asked why she could not play.

"I am tired," she said, "and besides, before all these people! If we two were alone, perhaps I would play; but perhaps not even in that case," she added, after a pause.

"Why not even then?"

"Do not ask me. Perhaps I will tell you, but not now. But you must ask me no questions, do you see?"

She furtively seized one of his hands and pressed it convulsively, as though she were frightened. Countess Tarquinia, hearing her whispering, looked at them both. Then they were silent, pretending to listen to the energetic fingers of Signorina Zirisela.

They both felt how rapidly their bonds were tightening as their plot thickened; and they thought of the future, Elena with terror, Cortis with sinister presentiments. Elena's behaviour, too, changed from that time. She did not seem to care much to hide her feelings, or at any rate, she succeeded but badly, and that sufficed to inflame Cortis's passion. But where was it to end? Would not the moment soon arrive in which they could remain neither divided nor united?

They were the only people who did not applaud when the signorina concluded her performance by some crashing chords on the piano. Elena noticed her omission too late to rectify it, and crossed over to thank her. The senator, coming up quietly behind her, renewed his attack.

"It is your turn now, senator," said Cortis, in a loud voice. "You have told me that you used to sing. Let us have that little bit of Pergolese that Donna Laura sang that evening in Rome."

"Are you mad?" asked the senator. "It is you, baroness, who should sing that. You know those charming little verses which were sent to you at Cefalù, '*Should they seek to discover.*'"

But Elena could not sing; she had never had any voice. Lao, who had entered during Signorina Zirisela's piece, sat down at the piano without speaking, and began to pick out Pergolese's melody, interrogating Clenezzi with his eyes.

"Bravo!" exclaimed the latter. "Bravo! That's it!" And in his worn-out, quavering old voice, he began to sing,—

"Should they seek to discover."

When he came to the lines—

"Ah no! do not give her
Such sorrow for me,"

he put forth such unexpected power that Don Bartolo, who was still playing cards, called out, "Good dog!" and made every one laugh, while Clenezzi continued imperturbably—

> "He wept when he left me,
> Your answer shall be."

Elena alone did not laugh. She asked whose words they were. Clenezzi broke into a panegyric of Metastasio, praising to the skies these verses, full of feeling, full of music, even without Pergolese's divine melody.

"Yes, yes," said Lao, getting up, "these few old verses are worth all the modern stuff; that is fit, I won't say for pigs, for I esteem them too highly, but for donkeys. But even these are false, you know, false to the very marrow. Beetroot sugar! One can distinguish that too in the music. Pretty, yes, but—but—rather effeminate, I think. It seems impossible that those lines should have been written by a priest. But of course Metastasio was only a burlesque priest. A priest ought to feel passion more deeply than that!"

"What will he say next?" exclaimed Countess Tarquinia.

"Is not that true, Don Bartolo?" asked Lao.

"What, count?"

"That when a priest falls in love he gets frantic."

"Three aces!" answered the chaplain, continuing his game. "You're too bad, count. Three aces—three aces!"

Lao turned to Elena.

"Tell me, my child, if a man who loves, and who is really loved in return, would ever leave his mistress for the sake of any other sentiment whatever—for an imaginary duty—like this fellow? What is such love as that worth? If love be true, not even the Code can stand against it!"

"Oh!" said Cortis, and he would have continued, but Lao cut him short.

"Don't preach theories to me," he said. "I am an old man, and know the world. What were you going to say? I don't believe in your heroisms. Rubbish! They are all so clumsy! Out of three persons, two might be comfortable. Not a bit of it! Your hero, the fool, must needs sacrifice himself, and make them all three wretched; for. I ask you, whether the lover won't be wretched, whether the wife won't be wretched, and whether the husband won't be wretched into the bargain? These heroisms are against nature, and can never succeed. The devil!"

Then Elena, in a hard voice, very unlike her usual tone, said,—

"Before doing one's duty, ought one then to look and see what will result from it—who will be pleased, and who displeased?"

"Certainly, in affairs of this kind one ought," answered Lao.

"You have a good leaven of the scamp in your composition!" said Cortis, laughing.

"And do you think," asked Elena, "that Metastasio's personage was right in telling his mistress that he must go away for ever?"

"No," answered Cortis; "not if he thought it his duty, because, having told her, it would be much more difficult for him to do it."

At this moment the game of cards came to an end.

Countess Tarquinia had previously ordered some wine to be brought.

"I drink to our representative!" exclaimed Don Bartolo. And so said all the others.

"Thank you," answered Cortis; "but I cannot accept the toast."

"Oh, yes, yes!" exclaimed Elena. "From me you will," she added, in a low voice.

He dared not say her nay at that moment, and was silent.

"I drank some of that just now," said the senator. "There's no mistake about that wine."

"Priest's wine, signor," observed the chaplain; "poor priest's wine! You can recognise it wherever you meet it, signor."

The conversation suddenly flagged. Every one began to say good-night. Before the room was empty, even, Lao began to complain of the stuffiness.

"Open all the windows for ten minutes," he said to his sister-in-law.

The servants came, carried away the lights, and opened the windows. Cortis remained alone in the room enjoying the dark light of the stars, and the freshness and noise of the wind. He had perhaps hoped that Elena would stay with him, but she had gone out with her uncle, and had followed him to the farthest of the four sofas in the hall, while Clenezzi, slowly making for the nearest, had sat down beside Countess Tarquinia, saying with a sigh,—

"Ah, countess, Pergolese is a good thing, but that *casonsèi!*"

"Well," began Lao, in a low voice, "everything has been arranged as was wished. The only piece of news I have is that he is not going to America."

Elena seized his arm, fixing her eyes on his face.

"Have you not some friends at Yokohama?" he asked.

Elena let go of his arm, and made no reply, although she knew perfectly well that some English relations of her husband's had a house of business out there.

"Didn't you know about them?" continued Lao. "It appears that there are some. At any rate he told the lawyer so. I don't know how it all came about, but I believe some of these people are over in Rome now, and have made some proposals to him. Perhaps they will find him a place. So you will be glad too, won't you?"

"Oh, yes!" she said.

In the large hall there was no light save such as fell

from the lamps upon the green cloth of the billiard-table, on the nine-pins, and on the white shining balls. All the rest was in shadow, and Elena felt more courage as she put this insincere question,—

"Has he started yet?"

"No. At least I do not think so; but I left Rome five days ago, and have just come from Bergamo. You see I wanted money, and I could get it at Bergamo. No, certainly he has not started yet. But he must start ere long, because the lawyer has arranged with all the creditors, but he will not actually pay them until he has gone. It appears that, so far, he has no idea on whose behalf the lawyer is acting. He does not suspect us, but the government, it seems. Perhaps Boglietti has not discouraged that idea! Do you want to know, now, how much it has cost me?"

"No, uncle, please not," answered Elena, getting up.

"Where are you going to now?" asked Lao.

"I am hot," she said.

She went out into the garden through a door which stood near.

Away to the west the great planets were flaming over the black mountains, as they were on the night that she travelled to Rome, on her way to Sicily, and saw them out of the railway carriage window; ominous lights glittered among their fixed splendour, above the darkness, full of the noise of wind and rushing water. Elena stopped to watch them, leaning against the doorpost. Then she turned away, and walked rapidly to the left, turned the corner of the house, and stopped in front of the windows of the music-room. Cortis appeared immediately.

"You are to go to Rome," she said; "back to the Chamber."

He made no answer.

"For my sake," whispered Elena, without looking at

him. "If we were united," she added, "you would go. I should wish it."

"You would only wish what is good," he answered, smiling. "And if it did not seem good to me, I would not listen to you."

"Certainly; but this is good."

"I am not sure. At any rate, I must wait for the general election. I do not know if I should like to return to the Chamber now."

He thought for a minute, and then continued, in a lower voice,—

"All the same, you are right; if we were united, it would be easier for me to return. Another man would dream of living here on intellect and love. Not so I. I should live on love and fighting; I should like you to witness my victories, and to comfort me in my defeats. I should throw myself blindfold into the struggle alone, like Don Quixote. Oh, what a life that would be!—what a life, Elena! Wait."

He jumped on to the window-sill, and thence down to where she was standing, and dragged her off towards the meadows.

"I feel myself bubbling over with strength to-night," he said; "like the days of convalescence in my first youth. I would certainly return to Rome and active politics if I had any hope that we should live there side by side, as we do here. Not otherwise. If you return to Cefalù, I fear that I shall stay at Villascura."

"And what if I stopped here with mamma and Uncle Lao?"

"I think I should go, because you would still be near me, more or less. That will be so, will it not? You will stay with them?"

She pressed his arm, almost laying her head on his shoulder, as she whispered,—

"Should you be glad if I did?"

Cortis turned her face towards his own, and looked into her eyes. She closed them immediately, and walked on blindly, her mouth half-closed, her heart beating, when, suddenly hearing a voice at the windows of the room they had just left, she quickly raised her head, dreading lest any human eye should see her in this attitude of self-abandonment in the darkness. There was a light again now in the music-room.

"Shall we go in?" she asked, stopping in her walk.

She returned alone, while Cortis made a long round to the left, so as to reach the fir-trees without passing the door.

Elena felt ill when she left him—more ill than she had ever felt before. She did not recognise herself; she seemed now to be floating upon her own desires, which would soon become a mighty current, and would carry her away altogether. Her conscience spoke to her and said: "These are the supreme moments; save yourself," but an indistinct flame of love, of alarm, of remorse, seemed to show her that she had already taken the first step down the incline, if only in thought, and that henceforward she must go on, powerless to stop herself. She burst into the hall, fleeing from her misery. There was no one there. Lao, Clenezzi, and the countess had returned to the music-room, where the former was playing the air from the "Olimpiad" with juvenile vigour, while the senator was pitiably sobbing out the words:—

"Should they seek to discover
Where now is your friend,
Your unhappy lover,
Say, 'Death was his end.'

"Ah, no! do not give her
Such sorrow for me;
'He wept when he left me,'
Your answer shall be."

CHAPTER XXI.

THE POEM OF SHADOW AND OF LIFE.

Next day, at luncheon, it was settled to take Senator Clenezzi to Cortis's gardens, returning to Villa Carrè by way of Caodemuro. At one o'clock Elena was sitting in her room near the open window, involuntarily listening to every step that passed in the garden beneath. As she thought, a hope very, very slowly, made its way into her heart. She dared not entertain it, and chased it away at once; but, calling it back again, she rested upon it for an instant, just long enough to feel how soft and refreshing such rest was. What if her husband did not really know what to do with her, if he only wanted to test her? No, no; she would not allow herself to think of that as yet; it was too early. But supposing the letter did not come to-day? Supposing it did not come to-morrow? According to Lao, her husband's departure could not be long delayed. In prudence, she ought to wait some days before allowing herself to hope; but supposing the letter did not even come the day after to-morrow? Then, indeed, might she hope it would not come at all.

The post was late that day. Clenezzi and Cortis were walking up and down the garden in front of the Villa. Cortis often looked up at Elena's window, listening but carelessly to his companion's chatter. Elena did not appear. Towards half-past one Lao appeared instead, dressed, as usual, in his great coat.

"Look here," he said, "are you going or not? If you don't start at once, I shall stay at home."

Elena was called, but she would have liked to wait a little longer. Her uncle completely lost his temper; Countess Tarquinia cried from her window, "What are you about that you don't start?" and poor Clenezzi, not knowing what to do, began to accuse himself of having caused all this trouble, and protested that he would willingly stay at home, and that he had never seen a more beautiful place. Cortis asked Elena if she were still so anxious about the post. She withdrew from the window, near which she had been standing, and from inside her room answered,—

"I am coming."

They started, Lao leading the way, alone, with his head down, and grumbling; then Clenezzi beside Elena, and, last of all, Cortis. There was no cloud in the limpid blue sky, the April breeze scarcely sufficed to stir the grass which just bowed its head, as though tired with too much life. Cortis and Clenezzi were laughing at the funeral aspect of their leader.

"There's a cloud!" cried Cortis.

Lao turned round.

"Of course there is!" he said. "Fancy bringing me out in this abominable weather! Can't you see that it will rain in a moment? A politician, though, can see nothing!"

Cortis laughed aloud. Elena, still silent, looked at him in such a manner as to make him think she was displeased at his merriment, and he replied with another look, very serious, almost melancholy. She guessed what was passing through his mind, and slily smiled at him, while the other two began a conversation about politicians.

"I can stand that one and no other," said Lao to Clenezzi, pointing at Cortis. "Even he is tiresome at times, but not so bad as the others, who look at one as if they were dragging the world, and as if they, the draught-horses, were more honourable than we who let ourselves be dragged. We are pulling you to pieces now!" he cried, turning to Daniele; "we are abusing you, we are turning you out of Italy with our hands and feet, there, out of your own place; your fine words are all very well in the Chamber! Learn political economy from practice, there; it's much better than what you get from books! And if you suffer from the misfortune of socialism, or of Christian democracy, test your theories upon men, and don't go up in a balloon to test them upon the clouds! There, there!"

Every time he said "there," he struck his stick violently against the ground.

"There's the postman!" exclaimed Cortis.

Elena stopped, and a slight shiver betrayed her emotion. The postman also stopped, and fumbled in his bag.

"A letter for you, Signor Count," he said.

"Keep it!" answered Lao, raising his stick; "letters and stones are one and the same to me."

The man laughed, and dodged him as he handed him a letter, and another to Cortis, who looked at the handwriting, and stood surprised and frowning. At last he turned to Elena, and again searched his bag.

"One for me?" she said. And she suddenly felt a a sensation, as of an electric shock, a spasm which seemed to deprive her of life. She took the letter offered to her, looked at it; it was the one she expected; her first and only thought, how not to betray herself!

She tried to say, "Thank you," but could not; and, turning her back upon the others, she gazed at the mountains.

"Beautiful view!" said the senator, coming up to her.

She turned suddenly round. Cortis, who was reading his letter, raised his eyes to her, looked at her for a moment, and walked rapidly towards her. She turned her face away, and said to the senator,—

"Let us go on."

Clenezzi immediately started beside her, and did not leave her until they reached the lawn at Cortis's house, where Lao called him away to the north terrace.

"Elena," said Cortis, stopping.

It was not a voice of command or entreaty; it was his tranquil, resolute voice, which she could not choose but obey at once, in whatsoever place, or at whatsoever time. She had already taken a step in pursuit of Clenezzi; she stopped short now.

"What is the matter with you?" he asked.

"Nothing."

"Do you feel ill?"

"No, oh, no!"

Cortis looked at her in silence.

"Some misfortune?" he said quickly.

"Oh, no!"

This last "no" was said so softly! Elena raised her eyes, as if against her will, to Daniele's face, with a sweet, sad expression, a timid, mute request in them. Was he angry with her for answering so drily, as if she had no confidence in him? He was not angry, but very grave and sad.

"Let us go over the house, shall we?" cried Lao.

Cortis had to give orders to have the house opened and shown to Clenezzi. They all went into the hall, and descended into the French garden, where they loitered about the fountain. Cortis thought that was enough, but Lao exclaimed,—

"We must see everything, everything."

Elena stopped in the hall.

"I will wait for you here," she said.

She remained alone, motionless, listening to the voices dying away among the empty rooms. When she knew they were a long way off, she hastily pulled out the letter, opened it, looked hurriedly at the last few lines, and replaced it in her pocket. The distant voices were not returning. Then she took it out again very slowly, read all through the four closely-written pages, raising her head frequently to listen. When she had finished reading, she folded her hands on her breast.

"Oh, my God!" she said.

She heard steps and voices approaching, and rushed from the hall, seating herself upon the stairs leading to the garden, behind the door, so as to be out of sight. She seated herself there in front of the lilies and roses, now all in flower, the green slope of the hill, the fountain, which seemed to her, as did the flowers and the verdure, to be the real pure joy of earth. Oh, God! how her heart beat, how furiously it kept repeating, no! no! no! Meanwhile the others entered the hall. Cortis was saying, "Well! perhaps I shall be that madman!"

Elena jumped to her feet and joined them.

"What madman?" she asked.

"A madman who will return to Rome," answered Lao in a fury; "who will throw himself headlong into politics again. I hope he'll leave his skin there; it will serve him right."

"Oh!" said Elena.

Cortis smiled.

"I shall often come here," he said, "very often, to renew my courage, my hope, and my life."

His eyes met those of Elena. She understood perfectly what he meant, and gave herself up to the thought of not going, of living near him for ever; and in so doing she experienced a delicious repose, a sweetness that penetrated her, renewing every nerve of her body, filling her with intense delight in all that she saw and heard; the verdure, the flowers, the fountain, even in the air she breathed.

"Have you had a letter?" asked Cortis, opening for her the wooden gate that leads into the garden from a courtyard.

"I?" answered Elena, taken by surprise; and her heart ached again.

"He told me you had," replied her cousin, pointing to Clenezzi, who was walking with Lao.

"Yes," she said, trembling.

She did not look at Cortis, but she felt the shock he had received. Her brief intoxication left her as soon as she heard him mention the letter. In its place she had only now the imperious reality, the picture of her miserable position, of her duty.

"I said the weather was going to change," said Lao. "What do you all think?"

White clouds were coming up behind the peak of Passo Grande, over the branches of the fir trees, which grew thickly in front and to the left of the gate; and the sun shone less brightly on the small open space, on the little path that winds and loses itself in the mysteries of the wood, in the poem of shadow and of life. Lao stopped at the gate to look at the clouds; Elena, meanwhile, walked on slowly towards the wood, hoping that the others would turn back without her. She would have liked to lose herself there for hours and hours, before coming to any decision, thinking how she could defend herself against him who wanted to know all about her trouble! He had said the previous evening: "If that person thought it his duty to go away for ever, he would have been right in not telling his intention to his mistress; because then, his duty would have become too hard!" And now, how could she not tell him? It would have been possible, nay easy, during their walk; but later on!

Her uncle, who had stopped to discuss the weather with Cortis, cried after her: "Elena! To the column!" Could they not leave her alone? They caught her up on the path that rises to the left, under the great chestnuts and the delicate acacias, and which thence winds round the hillock, amongst the bare trunks of the firs and pine trees. Cortis still questioned her with his eyes, but he could not speak. Only once, when Lao and Clenezzi were admiring the highest of the pine trees, could he whisper,—

"You must tell me all, you know."

She looked at him with that dark fire in her eyes, that was always there when she knew that she could look at him unobserved, and answered,—

"If I do not tell you, you must never think—"

Her voice failed her.

"What?" he asked; but he could not wait for her answer, as Lao called him.

The devil! Signor Daniele might really do the honours of his own park! Clenezzi was enthusiastic over it. The damp, soft, smell of spring, the silence, the fresh green, and even the constant shadowing and reappearing of the sun, delighted his still youthful heart. "A canto of Ariosto!" he said. That hollow down there to the left, surrounded with woods, between the hill and that big mountain, and that dark valley over there, close by the hollow, were they in the park? Yes. And what was that village in the sunlight, right away over there—they could just see it through the trees, with its white church? Caodemuro. And what was that noise of running water? The Posena. And the lake? Wasn't there a lake in the park? Yes, but they could not see it from there; it was some distance off in the woods.

"And the strawberries," said Lao; "don't you see the strawberry flowers over there?"

Clenezzi stooped and picked a little wild strawberry. But where was Donna Elena?

"We have lost Angelica," said he.

"'She flees through sad and darksome woods,
Through deserts, and through savage haunts.'"

But Elena had not fled. She had walked on ahead, and was waiting for the others under the old chestnut tree, close by the open space in which stands the column.

"Alas!" said the gallant senator, offering her the strawberry he had picked; "this is too bitter as yet, and I am too ripe!"

Lao complained jokingly of ladies who made their knights pant, then he signed to her to let the others pass, and to wait for him.

"What a face!" he said.

"Can I be gay, uncle?"

"Why not?"

She said that if she seemed ill at ease and silent, it was perhaps the effect of spring and the country, which caused her great but silent pleasure. Then she rejoined Cortis and Clenezzi on the path that winds round to the top of the hill. Cortis had turned round towards her, in order to point out to Clenezzi, through the thick firs and pine trees, the reddish rocks of Corno Ducale.

"Beautiful—beautiful!" exclaimed the senator.

But, according to Lao, that view was nothing compared with the view over to the east, under the boughs of the chestnut, towards Villascura. As the senator was looking at the villa and the French garden at his feet, the ruin-covered rock whereon the church is built, and the green valley stretching far away to the distant country, Elena whispered to Daniele, completing her broken-off sentence,—

"You must not think that I love you less."

He knew it; but every time her sweet lips said it to him, it gave him a fresh joy, a tingling of his blood in every fibre. He fumed because he had to control himself, because he could not at least take her hand, beg her to tell him the contents of that mysterious letter, to share all her troubles with him, to trust him, even to hope in him, because he felt himself strong enough to help her with advice or assistance in all her difficulties. His eyes said all this, and she understood their language; her determination of secrecy left her; she thought that, had they been alone, she would have laid her head on his breast, and have told him all. Never had he or she suffered from not being alone as much as at that moment.

"Did you hear," he said, "that perhaps I am going back to Rome?"

Then his lips formed these words, without, however, uttering them,—

"For your sake."

And when he showed Clenezzi the ancient column, brought thither from the Baths of Caracalla, and read in a voice full of emotion the Latin inscription, Elena understood that he was reading it to her, that he was saying to her: "In winter, and in summer, from near and from far, as long I live, and beyond that again. *Usque dum vivam et ultra.*" Mysterious words, full of meaning.

Clenezzi wanted the history of the inscription. Cortis either did not know or would not say.

How worthy of envy were those two hands so firmly joined together, without a hostile world ever being able to discover either the name or countenance of those who loved each other so dearly!

"Come along!" said Lao; "we got hot with walking, and now we shall catch cold up here. Those two hands joined there always disgust me. I always hope, whenever I come here, that I shall find one of them alone. It's going to rain in a moment. That will never do!"

It did not seem as if it would really rain immediately, but the sky had clouded over when the party descended into the green valley between the hill and the mountain, towards the big lime-tree that Elena loved so much, though now she could not trust herself to look at it. Cortis had suggested that they should go down as far as the path leading through the horn-beams to the lake.

The path, broken away here and there, was not very easy. Elena and Cortis started, but Lao, after grumbling a good deal, and putting out and drawing back first one foot and then the other, and trying the ground with his stick, finished by declaring that Clenezzi and he would not come, but that they would turn off to the right, meeting the others further along the horn-beam path. Elena was seized with a sudden fit of trembling; she felt herself growing dizzy, and her thoughts getting confused.

"At last!" whispered Cortis, turning to her with glittering eyes; he was silenced by the expression that he saw in the fixed, distressed look that met his, and by the whole exhausted appearance of his companion. He passed an arm round her, and Elena leaned against him, silent and trembling, and still gazing at him with stony glance. He anxiously implored her to speak, to trust him, but she could not as yet. She placed one hand on his shoulder, bent her despairing eyes downwards, and, hiding her face, said slowly,—

"I must go away."

"Oh!" he said, "but only for a short time?" He realised fully that it was not only to be for a short time; but nevertheless he was not prepared for her next two terrible words.

"For ever!"

He made no reply, pressing her convulsively to his breast.

"But perhaps I shall not be able to," she said.

He still made no answer, throwing his other arm around her.

Elena raised her face, her eyes looked happier.

"Perhaps I shall not be able to," she repeated, "perhaps I shall stay here." Her mute, timid passion made her speak thus, trembling as she was. She was less deadly pale, and a vague smile flickered in her eyes. She seemed as though she feared to have pained him too much.

"Certainly," he said, without relaxing his grasp, "of course you must stay; how could you have thought of going away for ever! how could you say such a thing? how could you think I should ever allow you to go?"

A slight movement that she made to free herself was obeyed at once. Then she laid her head on his shoulder.

"I ought not to have mentioned it," she said. "You yourself had advised it."

"I?"

"Yes; yesterday evening, when I asked you whether that person who meant to go away had done well to mention it, and you, you answered me—that he had done wrong."

Elena's voice was broken by sobs, her whole body was shaken, and she left her head closely pressed against his shoulder. She could hardly pronounce the last words.

"*Perhaps*, I said. He would not have done right if—He did not finish his sentence, he did not say: if he thought it his duty to go. He remained silent, seeming struck by some new thought."

"Do you see?" said Elena. Cortis protested violently. He had answered badly, the previous evening, if indeed he had answered thus. Was she going to be led by a word thrown out at haphazard, without reflection, without his having any means of guessing that she was going to take it to herself as a piece of advice?

"Tell me everything," he said.

She gazed a moment at the grassy slope near her.

Cortis offered to help her to sit down. She answered, with a shake of the head, that she had rather not, and remained standing, her hands within his, and her eyes cast down. She opened her lips two or three times as though longing to speak, but her voice died away. Meanwhile, he waited anxiously.

Nothing was audible save the gurgling of the stream below them among the black rocks and the water-lilies, and the pattering of small rain-drops upon the leaves of the acacias. A few drops made their way through to where they were standing, but neither of them took any notice.

At last she shook her head and said,—

"I cannot now."

Cortis sighed.

"The letter was from your husband?" he asked. "Is it he who wishes to take you away from here?"

Elena nodded.

"But for ever? What does that mean?"

"Yes," she said; "you cannot understand it now; I will explain it to you."

They were both silent. After the lapse of a few minutes, Elena remarked that they ought to go on, so as not to keep the others waiting. They started without another word, she in front, he behind. Elena soon stopped, and, turning to him, said in a choked voice,—

"You are not angry?"

He seized her icy hands, and pressed his lips upon them.

After another stop Elena turned again, and, looking at him with glistening eyes, without speaking, tried to smile.

They found nobody in the horn-beam path; no doubt the others had gone on. They turned to the left, towards the lake. When they came to the end of the dark walk, and found themselves in the bright daylight, standing by the shining mirror of the lake, they stopped. Silence and loneliness; not a creature to be seen, not a voice to be heard. Seeing that the grass was wet, Elena noticed, for the first time, that it had been raining. It had stopped now; the water lay hushed and motionless. Certainly Uncle Lao must have gone home.

Elena seated herself upon the trunk of the tree whereon she had sat the previous day, and did not observe that it was damp. She was so tired! Leaning her right elbow on her knee, and her chin on the palm of her hand, she gazed at the water. The cloud-capped mountain, the horn-beams, the grasses growing on the bank, and she herself, a dumb, despairing figure, all seemed to bow before the mystery of the deep water, and to interrogate its silence.

"Will you speak now?" asked Cortis gently. She shook her head. Cortis seated himself near her.

"I love you too much," she said in a tired voice, keeping her gaze fixed upon the water; "I am too weak. No, no!" she immediately added, fearing, from an exclamation of Cortis, that she had been misunderstood. "I do not mean in that sense; I am not afraid of that. I know that you are so noble, so strong; I do not fear to to be too weak in that sense. I mean that I have not strength to speak because, I do not know, but I think that, if I do, all will be finished; I shall go away and not see you any more."

She suddenly grasped both his hands, and gasping, half stifled with passion, called him,—

"Daniele! Daniele!"

He gently forced himself from her embrace, and took a few steps along the path to see if there was nobody coming. Nobody. Then he returned to her with outstretched hands.

"Let us go," he said.

She rose obediently, trying to read what was written on his resolute face. Cortis took her arm, and drew her away towards a side path.

"You must be strong," he said. "You must tell me everything, absolutely everything, and at once."

She trembled, and made no answer.

He repeated: "At once!"

"Must I really?" she asked; "must I really?"

"Yes," answered Cortis. "What has your husband written?"

She obeyed, fascinated as usual by that voice, and forced herself to begin her miserable story. She had to stop several times in order to recover strength to go on with her narrative, because her trembling seemed to choke her. She could not tell her story connectedly; she lost the thread, and forgot first one thing and then another. They walked very slowly, she with her head bent, her hands clasping and unclasping themselves with a nervous movement of her arms; he, somewhat bent but cold, looking straight in front of him, interrupting her now and again with some brief question. At the last turn in the path, as Elena was relating her nocturnal interview with her husband in the Via delle Muratte, the solemn promise she had then given, and the scene with the revolver, he stopped short, and listened to her in silence, until she told him of the last letter written by her to the baron before she left Rome.

"And the answer came to-day?" he asked.

"Yes."

"Give it me."

Cortis took the letter and placed it in his pocket without reading it.

"Now I have got it," he said, answering Elena's questioning glance. "I will read it later on, when I am alone, and quiet."

He continued his walk without adding a single word upon the subject of what he had just heard. A few steps from the gate of the house they met a labourer coming in search of them. Count Lao and another gentleman were in the house, waiting for the carriage from the Villa Carrè. Cortis wished that Elena should wait and let them see her, and made her sit down.

"I too had a letter from Rome," he said, after a pause. "My friends want a distinct answer, yes or no, about the editorship of the newspaper."

She said nothing, and he stopped speaking. Just then

the sun shone out briliantly, as it often does when it has been raining, and means to rain again.

"There is too much sun for you here," he said. "Shall we go?"

He almost lifted her from the ground. Elena walked with great difficulty, leaning heavily upon the arm of her cousin, who said to her, as they reached the gate,—

"Trust in me."

She pressed that dear arm in answer, and walked better, seeming to have regained her courage. As they entered the courtyard on one side, the closed landau from Villa Carrè drove in at the other, and Count Lao and his companion appeared from the hall upon the steps. He looked gloomy too. Clenezzi greeted Elena with as much warmth as though she had escaped from the deluge, but Lao scarcely looked at her, and did not ask where they had been. Cortis announced his intention of remaining at Villascura till dinner time. Elena started, but did not speak, partly because her uncle, muttering, "Quick, quick!" seized her arm and pushed her into the carriage, after which he pushed in Clenezzi, finally jumping in himself, and crying to the coachman to drive on.

Cortis did not move until the carriage was hidden from sight by a corner of the house. Perchance his eyes might meet Elena's. Then he entered the house, gave orders that he was on no account to be disturbed, and went into his study.

As soon as he was alone, he pulled out the baron's letter, and threw it, with a mute gesture of indignation, upon the floor. Then he raised his eyes to his father's portrait, which hung over the sofa, facing the writing-table, and with beating heart he studied it. It was the picture of a fine, honest, calm, severe face.

"Thou wert stronger than I am," said the son aloud; "I am giving way now, but I will be worthy of thee always!"

After which he picked up the letter, and, having spread it out on the writing-table, and smoothed it with his hand, he set to work upon it, planting an elbow on either side, and supporting his head between his hands. He read as follows :—

"ROME, 14*th April* 1882.

"DEAR WIFE,

You who read novels, or at any rate who used to read them, for I haven't the least idea of what you do now, will think that all that has happened to me during this past month perfectly natural; but I can't make it all out a bit.

"To begin with, the Government is paying my debts. Why, I can't say, and I don't know, but it is the Government; I gathered that from the words dropped by the lawyer. But that is not the strangest part of the business, because the Government owes a great deal to your husband; a great deal! The second strange thing is this, that a few days ago, Spurway, that English cousin of mine, of the firm of Spurway & Company, at Yokohama, came to see me. I spoke to him about that cursed America, and asked him where else I could banish myself to, and he invited me to Yokohama, where there is quite an Italian colony, offering me a place in the firm, if I would go out with my wife, an arrangement which would suit us both. The lawyer immediately changed America into Yokohama. So this is settled, and it all seems to me a dream. The third strange thing has not yet come to pass, but it seems most likely to happen, and that is, that you, of your own free will, should consent to come out to Japan with me.

"I may tell you now that, had I gone to America, as I thought I should, I would most probably have released you from your promise, and have gone out alone to make the best of the few years of my ruined life that may remain to me. But now I hold to your coming with me. I wish to prove to you, in that 'refugium peccatorum,' Yokohama, that there is some good in me, and that I am fonder of you than you think; and that when all my virtues have been squeezed out of my skin, I may at last go down to the grave in a state of favour with you.

"This new arrangement prevents me from giving you all the time you wished for, as I must start with Spurway on the 19th."

Cortis stopped to calculate what day would be the 19th. It was now Sunday, the 16th, therefore it would be Wednesday next! The letter continued:—

"There is this one compensation, we start from Venice as you desired. We shall go by the P. and O. steamer 'Bokhara,' where we shall be most comfortable. You must be in Venice, at the latest, on the evening of the 18th. Telegraph on the morning of the 18th to T. Spurway, Hôtel Britannia, and I will wait for you at the station. If you have not time to make many preparations, never mind: Spurway tells me that one can get everything out there; and we shall have money. Besides, you can always have things sent out to you if necessary.

"I don't know how you will escape from the clutches of the most illustrious countess, your mother, and the most noble count, your uncle, and from your most reverend adorer, blessed Daniele. That must be your business.

"We shall meet at Venice on the 18th. You are doing it from duty, but, to do you justice, you are renouncing a pleasant life, and, by God, I honour you for it.—Your faithful husband,

"CARMINE."

Cortis pushed the letter away from him in disgust. The idea passed through his head to write and say to him: "Your debts are paid, are they? There is one owing to my father, and you shall pay it to me!" And he imagined himself facing him, sword in hand. He seized the letter, and hastily crumpled it into his pocket, then, sitting down at the writing-table, he crossed his arms upon it, and buried his head in them. He raised it immediately, and shook his clenched fists in the air. Then he rose, walked up and down his study, abandoning himself to the thought that now Elena loved him so dearly as to have no other will but his. Everything was in his own power now; he could say to her, "I take your soul and your body; I wish you to stay here." He seized the letter again so as to see whether the baron made any allusion to Elena's promise, to the possibility of her failing him after all.

By mistake he pulled out the letter he had received from his friends in Rome. Heavens! how could he think of Rome now? He tore it across, and, finding the other, read it again. There was no mention of the promise.

Now he must go to the Villa Carrè and see her; he must not leave her alone at such a time.

As he opened the door of his study, he saw revealed to him, in a flash, Elena's departure, and his own loneliness after she was gone. He stood grasping the handle. At last, hearing voices and steps outside, he went out.

They were caused by Picuti and some other neighbours who had come to make their excuses for having signed the famous protest, which they had not even read, in order to please other people.

The deputation announced at the same time that a counter-protest was in preparation. They begged him not to be in too great a hurry, and not to resign. Cortis thanked them warmly, and said that as to his resignation he could promise nothing; he felt so utterly worn out in body and mind. In any case, his decision depended upon other circumstances which were still unsettled.

Having dismissed them, he walked rapidly towards Villa Carrè. When he reached the gate, a doubt seized him. Had he the letter? Or had he left it in his study at Villascura? His brain was in a whirl. The letter had not been left behind. As his hand touched it, a painful thrill passed through him. He bit his lips, he would have crushed his heart if he could. It was he who must lead her; he must be calm and strong.

CHAPTER XXII.

AS THE STARS AND THE PALM-TREES.

CORTIS and Elena found that it was impossible to spend even a minute together before dinner. Elena went into the garden, thinking that Cortis would have joined her there; but he fancied that he detected a suspicion, an unusual attention, in the eyes of Lao, who was still cross, and did not go to her. He explained his reasons to her with his eyes when she re-entered, disappointed and trembling, as if she feared that he had abandoned her. He suffered no less; but he was master of himself. Elena, on the contrary, lost her self-control, and betrayed herself momentarily. At dinner she ate nothing, alleging a severe headache. She scarcely spoke, and never to Cortis; but she looked at him too often with eyes full of melancholy.

Coffee was brought to the verandah. Countess Tarquinia proposed a drive in the Val di Rovese. She declared it would do Elena good. Clenezzi inquired whether it would be possible to reach the Austrian frontier? No; that was too far for an after-dinner drive. They might go to the frontier on Monday or Tuesday, if they made an early start. With trembling hands, Elena put down her cup.

"I am sorry," she said, "but perhaps I may be obliged to go into town on Tuesday. If I go, I would beg you to let me have the horses."

Her uncle and her mother could not conceive why she should want to go on Tuesday particularly. Elena, in her answer, omitted the word "perhaps," declaring that it was absolutely necessary, but giving no reason whatever. She anxiously waited for a word from Cortis, a suggestion that she should put it off. It did not come; Cortis had turned away to look at the meadows.

"Well," said the countess, after a moment's reflection, "we might go on Wednesday."

But Elena could not be sure of returning from town before Wednesday evening. She wished that her family should remain in complete ignorance until she was at sea. Lao lost his temper.

"What business can you have?" he asked.

The countess interposed quickly, observing that they might go on Thursday. Then Clenezzi, with many regrets, explained that he must leave Passo di Rovese on Tuesday. Every one exclaimed. At this moment the carriage, grinding over the gravel, drew up in front of the verandah, and cut short the conversation.

They wanted Count Lao to drive with Elena, Clenezzi, and Cortis, but the count answered that he had made quite expeditions enough for one day. Did they want to send him into the next world at once?

"Listen," he said to Elena. He drew her away with him, and whispered that, on her return, she was to go up to his room, as he wanted to speak to her.

Countess Tarquinia went in the carriage instead of her brother-in-law. Elena and Cortis sat on the back seat. At first the countess made vigorous attempts to keep up a conversation, but with scanty results. She threw uneasy glances towards Elena and Cortis. They never spoke. What was the matter with them? At last she relapsed into silence too.

The carriage rolled along one of the lofty wooded banks, through which flows the Rovese. How many times had Elena and Cortis walked along that road! A few days before, they had gone down to the river by a little path, and then she had made up her mind to trust him with all her secret. As they drove past it their eyes met, and they silently remembered the happy moments that were gone. They looked at each other now openly, and with but little prudence. That silent drive in the darkness, between huge mountains, towards distant places, made them dream, forgetful of all save their passion. They did not even notice Clenezzi when he asked for the name of two wretched little ruined towers, planted above the Rovese, and looking down upon its white gravelly bed. Countess Tarquinia answered instead.

On the way back, the countess stopped the carriage near the Della Pria Bridge: They must get out and show Clenezzi, from the bridge, the cluster of cottages perched upon the grey rock against the picturesque background of the gully; and below, the narrow fissure through which the green water noisily rushes, pouring itself out towards the fields beyond in a cloud of spray. Elena leaned against the parapet, watching the dark, tragic rocks. Cortis came and stood near her.

"If we cannot get a word together this evening," he whispered, "be in the verandah at six to-morrow morning."

And he rejoined Clenezzi on the other side of the bridge.

How tiresome it was, thought Elena, not even to be able to speak to him freely, or to see him openly! Must she really wait till to-morrow?

Immediately on returning home she went up to her Uncle Lao. On the staircase, that other evening recurred to her memory, on which she had gone up to her uncle after hearing from Daniele those mysterious words, "A grave matter." And now!

Count Lao was still in a very bad temper. Leaning

back in his arm-chair, his knees were wrapped in an ominous-looking rug. He scarcely noticed his niece as she came in.

"Here I am, uncle," said she.

"And here am I, too, and I should have done better if I had never moved. The cold and damp of to-day have brought back all my sufferings. But I deserve them. I wanted to play the hero, and find I am only a very poor creature after all. But that does not signify. I have another cause of trouble."

"What is it, uncle?"

It was very difficult for Elena to keep her attention fixed upon, and to take interest in, what he was saying.

"I have had a letter from Rome to-day," he said. "A note from that Cortis woman, enclosing me this paper. It will interest you; read it."

Elena took the paper, and went to the window to read it. It was a letter from the parish priest to Signora Cortis, wherein much was said as to the frequent meetings between herself and Cortis, and as to the comments made thereupon by the neighbourhood. The priest did not wish to judge rashly, but he deplored the scandal, and the indifference displayed in avoiding it. He would have liked to mention it to some of the family, but did not dare to; he preferred to tell her of it, as she might have some means of doing something. In her note the signora asked Count Lao whether he were now convinced of the truth of what she had said to him in Rome.

"That mischief-making donkey shall never set foot in this house again," said Lao, "but—"

Elena, who was still reading, holding the letter in both hands, dropped them suddenly in front of herself, and drew herself up proudly.

"But what?" she said.

"Gently, my child!" said Lao, "gently!"

"Gently, indeed! What do you mean?"

"What do I mean?"

He watched her silently, and then put out his hand.

"Listen, Elena," he said.

She neither moved nor spoke. He then signed to her to come nearer, repeating tenderly,—

"Listen."

She approached slowly, reluctantly. She required another silent invitation before taking his outstretched hand.

"Well," said her uncle, after a moment's hesitation, "until this morning I was blind, but my eyes are opened now."

Elena did not blush, nor did she lower her eyes.

"And what have you seen?" she asked, trembling. "Have you seen my heart? The heart is free. Have you thought bad things?"

"I have thought that, with your temperament, you will suffer and torment yourself, God knows how much; and I have also thought that Daniele is doing very wrong in attaching himself to you. Devilish wrong!"

"You must not say that, uncle; you must not say that!" burst out Elena breathlessly, leaning over her uncle. "He is so noble, you know; so—"

She could not continue; she felt suffocated.

"Never mind that, my child," said her uncle. "I have not said that he is not noble. I believe he is. I perfectly understand what you mean; but there are things that always begin thus among people like you, and that finish otherwise as they do among people who are not noble by nature. Men are men. He is better than many others, but even he is made of flesh and blood. You know that I have no faith in either angels or saints. If we had divorce in this country! If we had divorce, I should have taken a wife myself! And I would never have exchanged her! And I should have been happy! But we have no divorce, you would marry that other. That was disgusting! But never mind that, we won't talk about it any more. What we have to do now is to think of your honour and that of your family."

"If it is in my hands, it is in good keeping!" said Elena, proudly, pulling herself away from him, and going towards the door. "No, no!" she added, as he called her back. "You have no business to speak thus to me, you!"

She was seized with a convulsive fit of sobbing, unaccompanied by tears, and leaned her head against the door-post. Lao threw off his rug, and got up to go to her; but she motioned to him to keep away, without raising her head.

"It will pass directly. I shall be quite well," she said. "Stay where you are."

But that Lao could not do. He partly reproved himself, then he bewailed himself, and tried to explain away his words. He had not meant that she could dishonour herself.

"If mamma had said this to me," murmured Elena, "I should not have minded; but from you, uncle!"

"I," answered Lao, "only spoke of the world, of your judges, of what people would say."

"The world!"

It would be impossible to imagine greater sorrow or contempt than she threw into her pronunciation of that word.

"My dear child," said Lao, piqued, "I may be a stupid old man, but good and evil report are always things of importance. And if a lady looks as if she misconducted herself, and her family seems to look on calmly, you see what happens."

Elena's eyes flashed.

"I do not look as if I misconducted myself," she said.

"*If*, I said; *if* she has such an appearance."

Elena still looked at him. What did she see in that

dear, grave, mortified old face? Her expression changed rapidly.

"Oh, uncle, uncle!" she cried, throwing herself into his arms; "keep me here with you—always with you! I have nothing to blame myself for, not even a thought!"

She hugged him tightly, speaking in a voice broken by sobs.

"For Heaven's sake," exclaimed Lao, moved and frightened, "what are you thinking of? Who wants to send you away, you silly child!"

He began to laugh nervously.

"Silly child! Don't you know that I have only you in the world? What are you thinking of? Calm yourself, dear! I can't bear to see you so unhappy! You know that, don't you? Of course, I know that you have nothing to blame yourself for! You need not tell me that. But calm yourself: come, calm yourself!"

He pressed her to his breast, smoothing her hair with maternal tenderness.

"Now, go," he said. "Go and make my excuses to the senator. Tell him I will not come down, as I do not feel well, and that I am going to bed very soon. See if he would like to have a turn with you and Daniele. You might go down to the Rovese bridge, which he has not seen."

Now, for the first time, at the sound of his gentle voice, did Elena's tears begin to flow.

"Go, go!" insisted Lao kindly. She did not stir; she seemed not to have heard. Her uncle understood that she did not wish to leave his room in her present state, and that she wanted time to recover her calmness.

"Did Clenezzi enjoy his drive?" he asked. "Where did you go?"

Elena buried her face on his breast.

"And mamma?" she murmured.

"What is it dear?"

"And mamma? Does she know of this letter?"

"No, my child. Of course I have not told her."

They were silent for a moment. Then Lao turned to her and told her that she really ought to go down. She lifted her face, smiled at him, kissed him on the cheek, raising herself on tiptoe in order to reach it, and left his room.

She dragged herself to her own room. She felt so ill, so mortally tired. Falling on her bed, she lay there like one dead, chewing the cud of the bitter thought that her secret was no longer her own.

The fresh breeze of the evening, the scent of the roses and wisteria, and the sad rushing voice of the river entered through her open windows. A warm light seemed to come from the trembling rose leaves; the room was almost dark. Nothing stirred save the shadow of the leaves upon the floor; nothing was audible save the rapid ticking of an invisible little clock. Elena dreamed with her eyes open. She was ill, and could not move from bed; he came to keep her company, and to read to her. Months passed thus, and lengthened into years, and she said to herself: "Do you see how wicked you are? You did not believe that God cared for you, and now see how good He has been to you." There was Daniele sitting beside her bed, reading to her in his beautiful deep voice, looking at her now and then, smiling at her, or very softly laying his lips on her hair; ah! she opened her arms and called him gently: "Daniele! Daniele!"

The roaring of the river, sounding like the complaint of neglected nature, was her only answer.

Meanwhile the darkness was increasing; a star peeped through the roses.

As soon as Elena saw it, she jumped up and sat on her bed. What time was it? How long had she been lying there? She did not know any more than if she had just awoke from a sound sleep. Perhaps it was late, and she would not see Daniele any more that evening. Her head ached and burned; but what did that matter? She hastily fastened up her hair, anyhow, as she had no light, and went downstairs. On the way she met her mother coming to look for her, thinking she was still with her uncle.

"And your headache?" she asked.

Elena answered that she still had it, and that she thought she would soon go to bed. As she went down, her knees trembled beneath her; she had no power in them. She had to grasp at the silken cord that ran down along the wall. Meanwhile, she tried to recall the conversation she had had with her uncle; her head was so confused! It came back to her with a flash, and with the recollection came also her disdain, and with her disdain her strength.

There was no one in the drawing-room. Cortis and Clenezzi were sitting in the garden near the cypress. Countess Tarquinia could not think how they could face the wind. It was blowing a good deal now, and moaning in the fir-trees. But Elena wanted air, and went out just as Clenezzi came in. He tried to detain her, but failing, wanted to go out with her again, when Countess Tarquinia said, "Let them go, the geese," and kept him with her.

Elena and Cortis stood waiting breathlessly to see if Clenezzi were coming out again, or if the countess were going to call them in. They heard her laugh dying away as she passed out of the drawing-room into the hall. Then Elena seized Cortis by the hand.

"Did you see?" she said.

It was quite dark now; they could not be seen from the drawing-room. Cortis, for answer, drew his hand out of hers, placed his arm around her, and pulled her towards him.

"I am not going away, you know," Elena whispered in a weak voice; "I am not going, I cannot. I shall stay here with you, for ever with you!"

He loosened his grasp, not uttering a word, without a symptom of joy or affection.

"Oh, Heavens!" exclaimed Elena despairingly, raising erself; "speak to me, Daniele; tell me what I am to do. I will do anything you wish. I cannot even think now."

"Do you want to make yourselves really ill out there?" cried the countess, opening the drawing-room window.

"We are coming immediately, aunt," answered Cortis.

At that moment the usual set of card-players entered the drawing-room by the opposite door. The countess turned away.

"Well?" said Elena.

Cortis silently pressed her hands.

"Not now," he said, "we cannot talk now; to-morrow morning, at six, on the verandah."

She made no reply, trembling from head to foot.

"I should like to say one thing to you, though," said Cortis. And he added, in a low voice: "There is One whose advice you should seek before mine."

His voice too trembled a little. Elena silently nodded her head. He placed his lips upon her forehead, and said, very gently, as he raised them,—

"Pray."

She covered her face with her hands.

"You know," she murmured, "that I have never been able to pray like you."

"Pray now," answered Cortis.

Elena said nothing, then, suddenly, throwing her arms round his neck, she laid her head upon his breast.

"And you," she said, with beating heart, "do you really believe all that you would have me believe?"

"Yes," he replied quietly; "I believe it firmly."

"And if I believe too, for your sake," continued Elena, "shall I deserve that God should accept such a faith?"

"Yes, yes!"

Elena removed her arms from his neck, raised her face, and said softly,—

"I will pray. Are you satisfied?"

A solemn silence followed. Elena smilingly looked at Daniele, who could not speak for emotion. They were silent, and trembled, feeling that their Father was close by, in the burning within them of their hearts, and above them in the glory of the stars.

"We must go in now," said Elena. "To-morrow at six. Good-bye."

She hastily crossed the hall, and disappeared up the staircase, while Cortis went to show himself in the music-room, where they were playing cards, chattering, and joking. He remained there a short time, and then went out to the fir-trees. There, leaning against one of the old trunks, he greedily recalled her words,—"I will pray. Are you satisfied?" bathed himself in them with a feverish pleasure, exciting himself with the thought of the sublime love which was his, at the thought that God had taken Elena and him for ever, that they were now nearer one to the other, that their union would henceforth contain the elements of holiness and eternity, which neither sorrow or death could remove. He meditated thus, intoxicated with his happiness, which was lofty and untainted by anything earthly, blindly convinced that God said to him,—"Her mind is already yours; she shall be yours in the next world. I intend this to be the result of the love wherewith I have inspired you. Now that she is going, do you go forth also, tempered by sadness; go forth, fight, suffer, be amongst men, a noble instrument of truth and justice; the stars, the mountains, the grave old fir-trees, all bore witness to his answer, and heard him say,—'Yes, it shall be so!'"

He returned very slowly towards the house—towards the light which he could see far away burning in the hall, and shining through the door like an eye directed upon him through a telescope. Elena, perhaps, was upstairs in her room praying. He went and seated himself under the cypress, and remained there till midnight, when she put out her light.

Next morning Cortis came very gently out of his room at a quarter to six. A servant, who was dusting the hall, said,—

"You are early this morning, Signor Daniele."

The fresh, invigorating air came in at every open door; tom-tits were twittering in the cypress.

"Is no one else down?" asked Cortis.

"No one."

He paused for a moment to listen to the birds, and to notice, on the tree, the pale-green and beautiful blue bunches of the wisteria waving in the morning breeze; and up there, raising its head towards heaven, the rocks of Corno Ducale were bathed in sunshine. Even the grey teeth of Rumano, and the long ridge of Passo Piccolo, which faced the verandah, were in the sun. Cortis seated himself in a wooden arm-chair near the door, and waited.

Six o'clock was striking on the clock at Villascura when Elena came out of her room, entirely wrapped in a black cloak. Cortis rose. They shook hands gravely, without any other greeting. She was pale, but her eyes were more peaceful, less restless, than they had been the preceding evening. Cortis said, in French, that they could not stay there, as the servants were passing to and fro constantly. They walked towards the porch. An old woman, near the stables, greeted them; even by the fir-trees they could see people about. Once out of the gates, they turned to the left, following the road leading to Passo di Rovese. There was no soul there. Now Elena trembled; she did not even dare to look at Daniele, who now began to speak. They walked more slowly.

"Shall we cross the Rovese?" he asked gently, answering, as it seemed, an unexpressed thought of hers. "We shall be freer over there."

She nodded assent, pressed his arm without speaking, leaned upon it, setting her lips, and looking straight in front of her.

"Good-bye!" murmured Cortis.

She pressed his arm still tighter.

"I was just thinking the same thing," she said.

"What, dear?"

Elena walked on a step or two without answering, and then she said,—

"As you."

It was not a voice, it was the slightest breath; the soul and not the lips had uttered these words.

And again she pressed his arm, with greater passion than before.

"Oh, Daniele!" she murmured.

"Be strong," said he, deeply grieved. "It is our duty."

"Yes, yes; it was only momentary; forgive me. I am so much more at peace than I was yesterday. I have given myself wholly to God now."

They had reached the first houses; they spoke no more till they reached the deserted river-bank.

"I have made the sacrifice," she said. "Now I feel comforted. I have a spasm of pain sometimes still, but it soon passes. Yesterday I would have gladly died so as to avoid going away; but not so now. Do you know why?"

Without waiting for his answer she hurriedly added, in a low voice, hiding her face,—

"Because I have been wicked, you know, unbelieving, proud, for years past. I have need of suffering. Then God will pardon me, will He not? What I dread now is that I may not believe as you do, and that I only believe because you do. If such were the case, Daniele, what would happen to me in the next world? Shall I be able to go whither you do? Oh, God, you will have such a high place!"

He would not hear of this, denying it with genuine, heartfelt earnestness, and with burning eyes.

"You are humble," he said, "you are holy."

"I am humble before God and before you," she answered; "but not before men. I fear I may never be."

"And I?" exclaimed Cortis.

Neither was he humble before men, he, with his proud contempt for all vulgar arrogance, the proud soldier prepared to do battle for his ideas.

Elena was silent.

"And the sacrifice you are making?" he continued.

"That we must both make," she replied. "Had it not been you I should have been vile. I should have stayed here."

They had crossed the wooden bridge over the Rovese, and were following the little path that turns to the left between a limpid stream and the crumbling sides of the bare mountain. Elena stopped, gently withdrawing her arm from his.

"I have something else on my mind," she said. "I thought I ought not to tell you. I don't know, even now, if I am doing right, but I cannot keep silence; it would be disloyal to you, at this moment."

Cortis, in surprise, asked how she could ever have thought of keeping anything back from him. She fancied there was a shade of disappointment in his voice, and suddenly taking his arm again, she went close up to him, and whispered tenderly,—

"It does not concern me, at all. You know I should keep nothing from you that concerned myself."

She would not say any more till Cortis had told her he believed her.

"It is something terrible, you see. Perhaps when you know it you will not advise me to go away. That is why I feel I ought to tell you."

"Something terrible?"

Elena took the little path which runs by the side of the river, and which had been banked up by large stones to make it safe, and, having gone a few steps along it, she seated herself on the grass.

"It concerns your mother," she said.

"What has happened?" asked Cortis.

"Nothing lately; but many years ago—oh, Daniele, I repent now of ever having tried to tell you."

She was silent, and buried her face in her knees. Cortis, sitting near her, bent down and whispered,—

"Don't say it."

"And what if I do wrong by not saying it?" she answered.

He repeated in a louder tone, almost of supplication,—

"Don't say it!"

"I would that God would inspire me," murmured Elena.

Once more Cortis bent down towards her, and whispered,—

"Alessandria; 1855?"

Elena turned and looked at him in mute astonishment. He looked at her, very pale, with a finger on his lips.

"You knew it?" she asked.

No answer.

A serious look came into her face, and, placing her arm round his neck, she drew his head down, and lightly touched his lips with her own.

There was silence for a space. She took one of his

hands, and, laying it on her lap, caressed it with one of her own, looking at him the while, and trying to catch his eye. But he sat gazing straight in front of him, blankly, at the shadowy stream that ran past them. They remained thus for some time. At length Elena murmured, very humbly,—"Will you forgive me?" He placed his hand on her head for an instant. Immediately afterwards he rose, and proposed that they should go round the grey stone pillars that supported the road above the river. They went and sat by the water that rushed through the opening, curving over the stones, from the edge of the pillars, and rushing away into the sunlight, foaming and chattering. In front of them was spread the light of the sky and green fields away to the horizon.

"The last time!" said Elena.

Cortis inquired at what o'clock she would start. Certainly in good time, as she would have employment for several hours in town before going on to Venice. She would have liked to catch the 12.30 train. This practical side of the question, these arrangements of times and hours, cut them to the heart.

Elena's eyes closed. She struggled anxiously, but vainly, and two tears twinkled on her eyelashes.

"Daniele," she said, "shall we ever meet again?"

"God is merciful," he replied gravely.

The two tears dropped noiselessly. Some minutes passed ere she could timidly ask a question,—

"And write to each other?"

Cortis hesitated a moment.

"I see no reason why we should not," he said at length; "but I think it would be better to complete the sacrifice, and write only as friends."

"Yes, yes," said Elena, with ice in her voice and in her heart; "certainly, only as friends."

It seemed so hard to her, but he had said it; that was

enough for her. She then begged him to write down for her the Latin inscription on the column. He promised to do so, adding that he would write down some othe Latin words for her; those of a saint. He took her hand, and whispered,—

"They are wedded not with flesh, but with heart. Thus also are wedded the stars and the planets, not with their body, but with their light; thus also the palm-trees, not with their roots, but with their summits."

They were sublime words. He repeated them aloud to the sky, to the mountains, to the rushing river,—

"INNUPTI SUNT CONJUGES NON CARNE SED CORDE, SIC CONJUNGUNTUR ASTRA ET PLANETÆ, NON CORPORE SED LUMINE, SIC NUBENT PALMÆ, NON RADICE SED VERTICE."

His face and heart were on fire. His powerful voice seemed still more powerful, mingled with the noise of the water, dominating fate and time.

Elena then asked him how she should behave towards her mother and her uncle. It was most painful to her to leave them without any farewell, deceiving them indeed; but it was impossible to do otherwise. She must leave a letter behind, a greeting, and she had not strength to write; she had so much to say! She then told him of the last conversation she had had with her uncle. She only wished to let him know how much he had been deceived in his sceptical view of Cortis's character. The latter did not dissuade her from this; but he told her that she had better make no allusion to him, or let her uncle believe that his words or suspicions had ultimately decided her to go. For the present, it would be enough to send a few lines from Venice, and to reserve herself for a long letter from Yokohama.

Elena bowed her head.

"I will do so," she said. "And you?" she added, after a pause.

"I start to-morrow night. I am going to Rome."

She rejoiced to think that he was returning to his post in the battlefield; but, nevertheless, she felt that the wrench of leaving her own home, her own people, would be increased by the knowledge that he was going away as well.

"You will write," she said, "and tell me all about your struggles and victories?"

Cortis answered that, as yet, there could be no victories for his ideas; nor, indeed, battles. The only thing they could do was to raise the standard of rebellion against people who were determined to let themselves be crushed.

Another question rose to Elena's lips,—

"And in Rome—"

She dared not proceed.

"I will see," he answered, guessing her meaning; "but we cannot live together; I have tried that."

It was time to go home. So this hour of confidence, this hour of their last day, was over, and life would probably not contain such another for them.

They walked back, slowly and in silence, along the broken path by the stream. Near the bridge at which the Posena and the Rovese mingle their waters, she recalled a remark that he had made some time before about two rivers, which, from afar, are conscious of each other's presence, though invisible one to the other, which rush towards each other, drawn by passionate love, which, when they meet at length, fling themselves into each other's arms, uniting with stormy delight, and then quietly flow on down the valley together at rest.

"That was on the bridge," she said, "on the 12th of June, between nine and ten o'clock in the morning."

"And you said nothing. You looked in another direction. You appeared not even to have heard."

Elena stopped on the bridge, looking back upon the path by the stream.

"I am going away ignorant of so much about you," she said bitterly.

Cortis took her hand, helping her across a plank, which had been thrown over a hole between the bridge and the path.

"The things I wish to know," whispered Elena, "are two."

He made her sit down upon a fallen poplar, near the green margin, and waited till she spoke.

"I should like to know," she said, in a trembling voice, "if you ever loved before—"

"I loved you when I was a boy," answered Cortis. "Then for some years I thought no more about it. During that time I imagined myself in love eight or ten times. I never was really. What next?"

"Next—I should like to know—when—"

She dropped her head upon her breast, and did not continue.

"When I began to love you? I do not know myself. I thought so often that I did love, and then it seemed that it could not be true. It was in October of last year, when you went away, that I saw I could not forget you. You returned in May. Then—"

His heart beat with such violence as to prevent him from continuing.

She knew now.

She rose, taking his arm and drinking in with her eyes, with her soul, every shape and colour of that dear place; the white gravel, the swift, green water with its swirling currents, the meadow on the other side, the great foaming torrent which falls near the houses of the village, built high up on the right and gleaming white in the sun, humble and dark on the left behind the mulberry trees; and above the roofs of these last, the grassy slopes and the fir-trees of Villa Carrè and Passo Grande.

"Daniele, Daniele!" she exclaimed, in a broken voice, "let us go away!"

CHAPTER XXIII.

HYEME ET ÆSTATE.

NEXT morning it was raining. Elena went down into the hall at half-past six. The coachman, who had received orders to bring round the carriage at half-past seven, came out of the kitchen just as Elena was going on to the verandah. He asked her whether she would start at the hour named, even if it were still raining. Elena nodded, and he went away. At the same moment a servant came to inquire of the "little countess" whether he should take the senator's coffee to him or not. Would they start if it rained? Elena stared at him. For the moment she had forgotten that the senator was to go with her. Yes, she would certainly start. Perhaps a little later? No, because Clenezzi had to catch the eleven o'clock express for Milan.

"The rain certainly will not last long," said the servant after studying the weather.

Just then the sun came out. Romano and Passo Grande were quite black under a weighty pile of clouds; Villascura and the meadows were touched by the sun. The rain looked like glittering dust. The porch formed a sort of telescope, and away beyond the fir-trees the sky showed a pale greenish hue, while it was turquoise over the plain.

Elena went out without any umbrella, walking up to the old fir-tree with drooping branches, which has now disappeared, having yielded, after centuries, to a storm, as if to verify the sad dream of its young mistress whom it never saw again. Elena laid her hand for a moment on its huge, faithful trunk, and turned away. The silvery cloud had broken here and there over Corno Ducale, displaying in the sunlight some greenish rock which looked as though it hung in mid-air. Was it an omen? A nightingale was singing in the fields. "Yes, yes, yes," it seemed to say, but Elena would not believe it, and with a sigh continued her farewell visits. She went into the little sitting-room, and, tired out, seated herself on the sofa, watching the bunches of roses, the tendrils of the vines, the magnolias, and the grass in the meadow swaying in the wind. The red and white draperies fluttered, and so did the curtains, while the windows shook with a slight, continuous rattle. The volume of Châteaubriand lay open on the table. The faded flowers were still there. Elena took up the book, and once more read the words, "jamais ternie." Good God! she felt that she could die. She hastily closed and laid down the book; then she took it up again, meaning to carry it away with her. Before leaving the room, she opened the drawer of the table, and gazed vacantly at the words and dates therein written. The last was "29th June 1881?" She remembered that by the note of interrogation she had meant to imply, "Shall I ever come back?" She hesitated a little, then, taking up a pen, wrote in a hand that trembled like a leaf, "18th April 1882?" The words and figures looked as though they had been written by a child.

When she came outside again, she found that the rain was nearly over. Through the clouds over Passo Grande a patch of pale blue sky, looking like smoke, was visible. Cortis's window was open. Elena knew that he started at dawn for Villascura.

It had been settled between them that he should do so. She feared to betray herself, to break down if Cortis was present at her departure, or even if she saw him shortly before she started. She knew that he would come and greet her at a corner, where the road that she would follow is joined by one leading straight from Villascura.

Countess Tarquinia, in a dressing-gown, was at her window. She called Elena, giving her a string of commissions to do in town, and begging her not to be late for dinner next day. Nothing irritated her uncle more than that! Elena made no answer, and went up to her own room. On the verandah she met Pitantoi.

"If it is true," said he, "that they are going to send all the present deputies to the right-about, and that then they will give us fishermen votes, we will plump for Signor Daniele."

Elena answered "Bravo!" in a low voice, and offered him her hand.

"Gesummaria, little countess!" ejaculated Pitantoi, surprised and confused. "Well, well!" he added, as she insisted, "we will do this too!" and he scarcely touched the little hand that squeezed his in its gratitude.

As she passed the door of her uncle's room, Elena blew a kiss to it. Lao had protested, the previous evening, against such an early start. He was not going to get up at that hour either for God or man! Elena felt glad, now, that she would not see him. She placed the volume of Châteaubriand in her travelling-bag, as well as a branch cut off a rose tree, with its buds, leaves, and thorns. She kneeled down for a moment by her window, and then hastily went downstairs. On the verandah she found her mother and Clenezzi exchanging their last farewells. Bags, umbrellas, and cloaks were piled upon the wicker table near them.

"How pale you are, Elena!" said the countess. Senator Clenezzi thought her looking pale too; but more beautiful in consequence, if that were possible. The countess was furious with Cortis, who was out, nobody knew where.

What an extraordinary creature he was, to be sure! The senator made excuses for him; Elena said nothing. The countess went into the drawing-room, beckoning her to follow.

"What is the matter?" she said kindly. "Bettina tells me she is sure something is wrong."

"No, no, nothing," answered Elena, and, running away from her, she returned to the verandah, and asked if the carriage ought not to have come.

It still wanted ten minutes to half-past seven.

"By-the-bye," exclaimed Countess Tarquinia, "I noticed that you were taking a trunk with you."

"Yes," answered Elena; "I am taking a good many things into town that I don't want here."

Five minutes later the carriage creaked over the gravel, and thundered into the porch. It was closed, because it was still drizzling.

"Well, dear countess—" began the senator.

Elena feared for her self-control; she hastily got into the carriage without a word to her mother, and shrunk back in a corner.

"The baroness is in a hurry," said the senator, as he followed her.

He had scarcely taken his seat when a maid came down with a message from Lao, begging the senator to go and say good-bye to him. Not the contessina; he did not want to see her.

"God help me!" thought Elena.

Countess Tarquinia stood by the carriage door chattering until Clenezzi returned.

"Here I am!" he said, hurrying along. "The count wished me to tell Donna Elena that he is angry with her for starting to-day, and so early. And he also said that if she did not come back for dinner to-morrow, he would not care."

"How is he?" asked the countess.

"He says he is very bad; but I think he looks better than he did yesterday."

During this time the senator had been settling himself down beside Elena; bags, umbrellas, and rugs were already put in.

"Countess," said Clenezzi, "will you say good-bye to Don Bartolo for me?

> **Should he seek to discover**
> **Where now is his friend,**
> **His unhappy lover,**

tell him he is gone!"

"*Dead!*" corrected the countess thoughtlessly. "Drive on!"

"They are one and the same thing, countess, when one is leaving your house!" returned the senator, leaning out of the window as the carriage started.

Neither of them had remarked Elena's pallor, or the misery depicted on her face. Indeed, God was helping her!

She unconsciously closed her eyes. Clenezzi immediately began to talk of the delightful visit he had had, of the beautiful things he had seen, of the kindness shown him.

"Do you not feel well?" he suddenly asked. "Does your head ache?"

Elena opened her eyes, and said wearily,—

"Yes, yes, my head aches."

Clenezzi wanted to tell the coachman to turn back, but she stopped him, seizing his arm, and saying,—

"No! pray don't!"

She closed her eyes again, wishing to think of him in silence. In a few minutes she would bid him a last farewell. How fast the horses were going! She opened her eyes again. God, how fast! She wished that that mile of road might be as long as eternity.

At the foot of a hill the coachman let his horses walk. Presently he turned round, and said,—

"Here is Signor Daniele," at the same time stopping his horses.

"There he is!" exclaimed the senator. "I am glad of the opportunity of saying good-bye to him."

Cortis came round to the right-hand window. He looked pale and weary. Neither he nor Elena spoke a syllable.

"My dear Cortis," said the senator, and he stretched out his hand. Cortis shook it without speaking.

"Are you coming into town too?" continued the senator. "I thought perhaps you were thinking of it. Come along!"

Elena made him an imperceptible sign that he should refuse. That would be too great a trial! They had decided, the previous evening, not to face it. It would be much easier to part thus, never to meet again, without even the final good-bye!

Clenezzi thought Cortis was hesitating.

"Come along!" he repeated.

"I cannot," answered Cortis.

Elena opened her bag, took out of it the Châteaubriand, showed it to Cortis, and replaced it, after having taken from it a letter, which she handed to him.

"For you," she said.

Cortis took the letter and her hand in both his own, made a sign that he had something to whisper to her, murmured "good-bye" into her ear, whereon he also placed a light kiss which she received with closed eyes, gasping for air with parted lips.

Cortis stepped back suddenly, and waved his hand. The horses started forward. At the same moment she put her head out of the window. Cortis hurried towards her, thinking she meant to throw herself out, but her face was gone, and he could see nothing but her little bare hand hanging limply out of the window as though it were dead.

The carriage had been out of sight for some time, and he was still looking after it.

He walked homewards tired out, unconscious of everything save of a dull pain at his heart. He did not enter the house, but followed the path that winds up to the top of the gardens. He leaped the hedge near the great lime-tree, and went on towards the column. There, among the chestnuts which keep watch over the valley, he threw himself down on the grass, still wet with rain.

It was all over now; he was alone.

What had he done! The sun was darkened, the world dead, his heart frozen. He called: Elena! Elena! Plants and leaves maintained their mournful silence. He lay there motionless, without thought, watching the white clouds floating above him, their shapes constantly changing, as though they were governed by some invisible spirit.

He never knew how much time had elapsed. He sat up at last. He was in pain, bodily and mental. That letter, that last treasure that remained to him from Elena, should he read it at once? At first he had intended to keep it for the evening, for a still more disconsolate hour.

He looked at it. It had been in her hands. Henceforward it was sacred. He placed it to his lips. He gazed at it again, kissing it, and, as he did so, he threw his mind and soul away over the meadows and valleys after her.

He opened the envelope, and found only these words,—

"In winter and in summer, from near and from far, as long as I live, and beyond that again.—18th April 1882."

Cortis gazed at the solemn words as though turned to stone. His breast heaved, his breathing became difficult, a tempest of grief burst from him. He bit his lips and beat his brow; a few drops fell from his eyes on the sheet of paper lying on his knees.

When the paroxysm passed, he felt relieved. A voice whispered to him: "What if she returned some day, even after long years?" He pictured to himself her dear face spoiled by time and sorrow, thenceforward beautiful only to him, sweeter than in her youth; he pictured to himself her hand still youthful and graceful, her voice still sweet, her eyes, tired and restful, which still repeated, but timidly, "As long as I live, and beyond that again."

And what if something should even now happen to prevent her departure!

He drove away this thought. The sacrifice had been freely made, for a good purpose; and he had given way enough to weak nature. He would not do so any more. He rose with determination, and as he walked on he thought of Rome, his newspaper, the feverish work which he felt he required.

As he walked down among the firs and the pine-trees, a vision of his future rose before him. Battles with pen, with tongue, in the press, in the Chamber, at meetings, for the sake of his ideas about government, and against public indifference; his first victories; the falling away of his friends, the sarcasms of so-called liberals, the abuse of so-called Catholics; indomitable perseverance, the help of God in his labours; times of terrible crisis, days of anguish, unexpected difficulties; then fortune, days of power, a great road opened to social regeneration in a Christian and democratic sense, and on this road, in front of everything else, Italy.

God required him wholly for this work. God took from him family, love, youth, and called him with fiery breath to do His will.

Before entering the house he went to free Saturn, who for months past had been chained up. The huge dog rushed wildly over the meadow, dashed into the hall bounding round his master, who, seizing him by the fore-paws, raised him up, and gazed into his shining eyes.

"Saturn!" he said, "poor Saturn!"

She had been fond of Saturn.

Cortis let him fall again on all fours, and went into his study, whither the dog followed him, keeping close to him, watching him narrowly, and wagging his tail violently every time that his eyes met those of his master. The said master was writing this telegram,—

"*To Senator P., Rome.*

"I start at once to put myself wholly at orders of friends. CORTIS."

He rang the bell.

"Send this at once," he said to the servant; "then go to Villa Carrè and fetch my things; let the coachman be here at two to drive me into town. Saturn will come with me."

"As far as the town, sir?"

"As far as Rome. If they ask any questions at Villa Carrè, say I am coming there directly."

The servant bowed and left the room.

Cortis, finding himself alone, rose to his feet. He folded his arms, looked fixedly into the eyes of his father's portrait, and said aloud,—

"There!"

THE END.

www.ingramcontent.com/pod-product-compliance
Lightning Source LLC
Chambersburg PA
CBHW030903270326
41929CB00008B/551
* 9 7 8 3 3 3 7 0 2 9 7 7 7 *